About the
Border
Terrier

Verité Reily Collins

KINGDOM

Kingdom Books is an imprint of T.F.H. Publications.

Published by Kingdom Books
PO Box 15
Waterlooville PO7 6BQ
England

Designed by Add Graphics
PO Box 15
Waterlooville PO7 6BQ
England

Contents

Acknowledgements

I should like to thank all the many people who have helped me with my research for this book, especially the following:

Mrs Madelene Aspinwall for invaluable advice, help with reading part of the manuscript and giving so much of her time and knowledge.

Mrs Frances Wagstaff and the Southern Border Terrier Club for invaluable help and the loan of Miss Garnett Orme's books. This club is mentioned much more often than the other clubs simply because I have been a member since the early 1980s.

Joy and Ted Maker for walking and looking after Wyvern and Widget.

Mrs Elaine Camroux-McLean of The Kennel Club for her invaluable help and assistance and for finding the impossible whenever I needed an answer.

Sissel Bagge Blindbæk from Denmark, Dr Jeremy Cherfas, Lisa Connelly from the USA, Mr H Deighton, Mrs Trak Fryer, Lorna Jones of the Cumbria Tourist Board, Sue Holleron, Brenda Sandham and Sue Wheeler with their PAT dogs, Mrs Ruth Jordan, Jack Price, John V Roberts, Mrs van der Horst-Siraal and Mrs E Jabroer-ter Lüün of the Netherlands, Mrs Diana Tillner of Germany, and everyone else who has been so kind in answering my numerous queries.

Betty Rumsam, who edits the marvellous *Southern Border Terrier Club Year Book*.

Mrs Jena Tuck for so much sensible advice, help when I needed it and useful information.

Steve Dean for the chapter on Breeding.

And last - because I still don't know how to thank her properly - Johanna Farrer.

Introduction

History of the Border Terrier:
The little working dog with a courageous heart.

My mother's family have owned Borders for over 100 years. She lived in the country and loved hunting. My father entered the Royal Navy when he was 13, met Mother when he was serving in Egypt, married her there, and eventually they arrived back in England.

The hunting fraternity wanted to see what Mother had married, and held a dinner in honour of my parents. Seated next to the most formidable dowager in the county, Father was on his best behaviour, until she boomed at him, 'D'you hunt?'

'If you mean women, yes!' was his reply.

But my parents were united on one thing: they both liked Borders. I can remember as a child watching Daddy going off down the garden, spade over his shoulder, to dig our Borders, yet again, out of an earth.

It was Widger who shared my trials and troubles, lent a sympathetic ear when I had been naughty, and lay still under the bed-clothes whilst I was tucked up.

Now I have two Borders, and they turn a flat into a home. Being adaptable dogs, they are happy in London and are fascinated by all the smells on lamp posts. Riding around with the two sitting in the back of my tricycle (bought for their benefit so they could travel round in the basket) it is great fun watching tourists do a double-take, then frantically focus their cameras on my two - sitting as if butter wouldn't melt in their mouths.

However, people often stop me to say that they have been thinking of getting a puppy, and mine look so sweet they would love one - where can they buy one?

In a few short sentences I try to ask if they really know what owning a Border entails? I love the breed and would hate to see a Border in an unsuitable home.

So this book is written for those people who are thinking of owning a Border, to help you decide if it is the right dog for you, and for 'new' owners who know the breed is special - but why?

Incidentally, as with so many past events, when researching for this book I found some dates and places conflicted. I have therefore tried to take a mean average, or else made a stab at working out which is the most sensible solution. My apologies for errors, but please let me know so that I can correct them in future.

A basic history

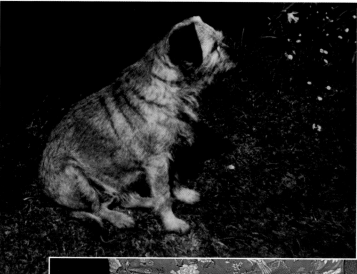

Chapter One

Top: Weenie, c 1940. An early family dog.

Above: Let sleeping dogs lie!

Watching a typical Border curled in front of the fire, with its nose almost touching the logs, or laying claim to the softest cushion on a chair, you would find it difficult to believe that these terriers belong to one of the toughest working dog breeds. But see them out doing the job for which they were bred, loping for miles across country and gamely ready to tackle anything asked of them, and their courageous working side comes out.

Research proves that dogs were the first animals to be domesticated, share our ancestors' caves and help them catch their food. The first ones

A familiar view of a Border Terrier: the early Borders were bred for digging.
Aphrodite of the Windy Spot.   Photo: Theo van der Horst

were probably wolves or similar animals but, eventually, domesticated dogs were bred for their abilities, and the terrier type, able to root out vermin and chase food such as rabbits for the pot, have been around for many centuries.

The name 'Border Terrier' is derived as follows: 'Border' from the Border Hunt which works on the borders of England and Scotland, and 'Terrier' from the French word *terre*, meaning ground or soil. Fourteenth century texts and drawings describe two sorts of terrier; one with crooked legs and a short coat and the other with longer legs and a shaggy coat.

Originally bred as a working dog by the Border folk living between England and Scotland, Border Terriers worked hard for their masters, tackling fox, badger, otter, wild cat, rabbit, and anything else that could be added to the pot.

Today this country gentleman has become so popular that in 1994 the Kennel Club recorded 2766 registrations, putting Borders into the 'Top Twenty' for the first time ever.

In the middle of the 18th century a painting of 75-year-old Arthur Wentworth, earth stopper to William Tufnell Joliffe amongst others, shows him with two distinctive Border-type terriers: long legs, undocked tails and V-shaped ears. According to Janet Melly, writing in *The Southern Border Terrier Club Year Book*, Mr Joliffe kennelled his hounds at Nun Monkton Priory, about 10 miles north west of York; the country hunted was at the border between present-day Middleton and York and Ainstey.

Recently Ward Lock reprinted *A General History of Quadrupeds*, first published in 1790. It states that the terrier has a most acute sense of smell, is generally an attendant on every pack of hounds, and is expert in forcing foxes or other game out of their coverts. It goes on to say the terrier is the determined enemy of all vermin: weasels, foumarts, badgers, rats, mice, and others. It is fierce, keen and hardy; and in its work 'sometimes meets with very severe treatment, which it sustains with great courage and fortitude'.

Around 1800, Thomas Bewick, a Northumbrian famous for his woodcuts, produced an engraving of a terrier that looks similar to a Border Terrier. His home, Cherryburn, at Mickley, Northumberland, is owned by the National Trust and they have a copy of his book *1,800 Woodcuts by Thomas Bewick and his School*, with copies of engravings. It is interesting to see how dogs have changed in the last 200 years.

In the Rev W B Daniel's *Rural Sports*, published in 1807, there is a print showing a huntsman and two terriers that look like Borders. Then in 1818 a report appearing in *Sporting Magazine* told of a pack of hounds with terriers which hunted a fox for eight hours, covering about 50 miles.

During the last century hunting men wanted a dog able to follow a horse and still be game after a hard run and realised these brave little dogs were ideal to take out for a day's sport; so the Border's fame spread amongst sportsmen. However, they are not always popular with the sporting types. A Border's motto could well be *Festina lente* - make haste slowly. Borders come slowly to maturity, and the only time they will rush into danger without thinking is when they see their prey across a crowded road. They can spot a cat taking a walk halfway down a long street and then, whoosh - they're off! But when working they assess the situation first, and will move slowly until sure of what is at the end of an earth. Once they've found out, there is nothing stopping this fearless little terrier.

For over 100 years my mother's Northumbrian family, the Forsters, owned these little dogs and, ever since I can remember, there has been a Border to share my life. Smuggled into bed, they gave comfort during thunder storms, shared all our adventures and never complained when dressed up as a courtier one day and a pirate the next. When something went wrong they were always there to sympathise. And a walk without a Border zig-zagging around one's feet isn't worth contemplating.

Coquetdale

Experts suggest that Borders, Bedlingtons and Dandie Dinmonts descend from terriers bred in the border region of Northumberland, the Border coming from Coquetdale between Rothbury and Otterburn. My grandfather, Charles Langstaffe Forster, bred these dogs and was one of those who were keen to see them established as a recognised and particular breed, sharing a kennels at Otterburn where he kept these terriers for hunting.

Eyewitnesses say there is evidence of dogs similar to the Border Terrier in the 18th Century; looking at old tapestries and paintings you can sometimes see what must have been Border ancestors. The canine historian 'Stonehenge' talks about a 'pepper and mustard' terrier, bearing a resemblance to the long-legged Bedlington, and often crossed with the Dandie Dinmont, and refers to them 'in these times' (that is, around 1790). A portrait of 'Pepper' dated 1805 hangs in Dove Cottage, Grasmere, and has been identified as a Border who lived until he was 15.

Taipan's companion

In 1820, William Jardine, co-founder of the famous merchant company Jardine, Matheson, appears in a full-length portrait. Lying at his feet in this most impressive painting by George Chinnery is a terrier. An authority on Borders who has seen it hanging in a descendant's home in Dumfriesshire says this definitely is one. Now Jardine, working in China, clearly knew the importance of appearances and, however beloved the terrier, it is obviously there as a statement.

Jardine, co-founder of the important and impressive Jardine, Matheson empire, was a fascinating person. Leaving his home near Lochmaben in 1802 to take up an appointment as surgeon's mate in an East Indiaman, he was captured and made a prisoner of war, but exchanged in South Africa. In 1817 he left the East India Company and became a 'Free Merchant', looking towards China for business, and eventually becoming a partner with James Matheson. In the days when traders accepted 'joint and several' liability, you had to trust your partner, and Jardine and Matheson chose each other well.

Legends surrounded the two. One anecdote tells of when Jardine was clubbed hard on the head from behind in Canton. He didn't even turn round, which so impressed the Chinese they nick-named him 'iron-headed old rat'. One wonders if he took Borders with him on his eight-month-long voyages to China.

Hunt Terriers

Jacob Robson, member of a famous Border family, kept hounds at East Kielder until 1857 when he moved to Reedwater, amalgamated the pack with that of Mr Dodd of Catcleugh, and hunted it as the Reedwater Hounds.

In 1869 Robson's son, John, took over the mastership, and the name of the pack was changed to the Border Foxhounds. As the fame of the Border Foxhounds began to spread so did that of the terriers on which they relied for digging, and it was not long before the breed became known as Border Terriers. They were expected to run for as many as 20 miles in a day behind hounds and, when a fox had been found, to go underground and harass it so that it bolted from its earth.

When he married in 1879, John handed over the mastership to his brother Jacob who, with E L Dodd and Simon Dodd as successive joint masters, held the position until 1933: a record period of 54 years. During the latter part of his tenure he became the oldest and longest serving huntsman in the country. In 1933 he handed over the mastership to his son, another Jacob, who eventually handed over to Ian Hedley in 1954. Today Michael Hedley is master. When Jacob Robson died in 1985 he was 97. Border folk, like their dogs, seem to live to a great age.

The North Tyne Hunt and its predecessors and the Liddesdale Foxhounds, formed about 1800, also had influence over the breed's development.

Today many of the Border hunts use Jack Russells and other terriers. They follow the hunt on quad bikes, so there is no need to utilise the Borders' gameness and hardiness to follow hounds. However, shepherds and farmers (and poachers too!) appreciated the hard-working qualities of the little Border who, once the day's work was done, fitted into the home, happily taking his ease in front of the cottage fire. And that is where he is often to be found today; the countryman appreciates this 'little demon' oblivious to hard, cold weather and able to fit in anywhere.

Industrial Revolution

The recognition of different dog breeds stems mainly from the time of the Industrial Revolution, when families took their local breed of dog with them into the towns when they moved to find work. Competitions for dogs were held in pubs and other places where working men gathered after their hard day, which provided recognition for different types. It would not have taken long for the sporting gentry to adopt and try to improve the different breeds.

Although Borders were hunting terriers, the Victorian desire to idolise and categorise dogs meant that all breeds were being analysed and 'types' were being

The Terrier from *A General History of Quadrupeds* by T Bewick.

noted. Although Borders have now won their way into the show ring to take top prizes, most Border owners fell in love with these dogs because of their working characteristics which were in-bred in a true Border and prized by the gentry and the working man. Long may it remain so!

Matches

Probably because their dogs provided a link with their homes in the countryside, working men started to have matches to show off their dogs, and The Kennel Club records that the first organised dog show was held in the Town Hall, Newcastle-upon-Tyne on 28-29 June 1859. The show was organised by Messrs Shorthose and Pape at the suggestion of a Mr R Brailford, and there were 60 entries of Pointers and Setters. Strange to relate, in this, the home of the Border Terrier, not one was entered, and it was another 60 years before they were recognised as a breed.

For the next 10 years the shows were held twice a year, until by 1870 it was obvious that a controlling body was necessary to legislate in canine matters, and from these beginnings in Newcastle The Kennel Club developed. There is a record of a Border called Bacchus being exhibited in 1870, but then nothing for some years. Border owners seem to have been more concerned with their dogs' working abilities than with showing them off.

Incidentally, asking a friend who had high hopes of his dog why he hadn't shown her at a recent Crufts, he looked at me in amazement. 'But it was a huntin' day,' was his quite reasonable excuse.

Raby Castle

A famous painting in Raby Castle, near Durham, shows the first Duke of Cleveland with his favourite Terrier, a typical Border. This picture was painted around 1830. There is also a Turner print of the castle, showing the Earl of Darlington (as the Duke then was) in the foreground, mounted and accompanied by his hounds and what I am sure is a Border Terrier. According to Elizabeth Steele, the Curator, the little dog was obviously a great favourite with the Earl and also appears in a picture by Henry Chalon (animal painter to William IV) painted in 1820.

Hutchinsons' *Dog Encyclopaedia* states that, as far as it is known, the first mention of a Border Terrier was in a short note published in a journal in 1882, saying these terriers were to be found in Westmoreland and Northumberland. They were described as small and very active, kept entirely for digging out foxes in the rough country, and exceptionally brave.

The Dogs of Scotland

In *The Dogs of Scotland* published in 1891 D J Thomson Gray wrote:

> The Border is by no means a rare animal, although confined to a limited area, and to one part of the country, and as regards antiquity may claim to be the original terrier of the hills, from which the Dandie and Bedlington sprung. Unlike the Dandie and Bedlington, which are a compound of two or more breeds, the Border Terrier still retains all its pristine purity. Bred for work and not for show, fancy points are not valued in proportion to working qualities, still the breed has many distinctive features which are carefully preserved... Their intelligent eyes, hard coat and general activity stamp them as an intelligent breed which has not yet been contaminated and 'improved' by the fanciers.

Miss Hester Garnett Orme, a stalwart of The Southern Border Terrier Club, copied out an article by Juteopolis, and wrote on it 'Written in 1909 the oldest article we have'. This quotes from a letter written by Jacob Robson saying that these terriers have been kept in the Borders for a very long time, but the name is of a recent date. Robson goes on to say, 'My father had some very class representatives of the breed - about the years 1840-1850.'

Curiously he goes on to say that from what his father told him 'the Dandie of 50 or more years ago resembled the Border terrier in many respects - more so at any rate than they do now'. His brother owned a painting of a local character, 'Yeddie' Jackson, executed about 1825, with 'the very type of terrier we have still'.

Once a Border devotee, you and your descendants become fans. Our faded sepia family photographs from the 1890s usually show a Border Terrier edging into the picture somewhere, very scruffy in comparison with today's stripped dogs.

Early Border Terriers

Newminster

Famous Border family names such as Robson, Redesdale, Irving and Percy are to be seen in all Border papers, and the Renwicks with the Newminster affix are probably unique in that four human generations have bred Borders.

The founder of the Newminster dynasty was Sir George Renwick, the first Baronet (1850-1931). He was a shipowner and Conservative MP and he owned Newminster Abbey near Morpeth. On his 81st birthday he was photographed with a Border. His eldest son, John (1877-1946) was an Master of Foxhounds (MFH) and carried on the family's line, breeding many Challenge Certificate (CC) winners. His Grakle won nine CCs in the 1930s, but he was far more concerned that his dogs were capable of working.

Today, Lionel Hamilton-Renwick is a well-known equine portrait painter, and one of his famous subjects was The Queen's horse, Aureole. He is a hard-worked and well-known judge at Crufts and other dog shows, and proud of his family's long association with Borders. The present-day Newminster Borders belong to Mrs Julia Percy, sister of Sir Richard Renwick.

1897

In the *Encyclopaedia of Sport* of 1897, edited by the Earl of Suffolk, Rawdon B Lee, writing on terriers, says:

> Perhaps the most interesting are the Border Terriers, which are met with in Northumberland and other of the Northern Counties and for which is claimed an earlier existence than the Dandie Dinmont or Bedlington Terriers, which also hailed from the same locality... They obtain their name of Border Terriers from the fact that they were frequently used and bred in the Country hunted by the Border Fox hounds. The favourite colour for them is red or black and tan. The Services of these Terriers which follow hounds regularly are often called into use, and they are sent into most dangerous places amongst rocks and peat moss drains from which they sometimes do not return, so determined are they in pursuit of their quarry.

A Forster family photograph including Borders.

Miss Hester Garnett-Orme wrote a wonderful book called *Border Tales*, and old copies can sometimes be found on bookstalls at dog shows or in Charing Cross Road. The Southern Border Terrier Club has some of her papers, and reading these gives a fascinating insight into breeders and the breeding of Borders. In her papers is an extract from J Maxtee's book *English and Welsh Terriers*, published in 1908, which says:

> ... the Border Terrier is as yet comparatively unknown, the breed, which for a generation has been bred for work, has never deteriorated and today is as game as it was in the days of Ned Dunn, of Whitles, Reedwater, and Teddie Jackson, both of whom were renowned for possessing a strain of these game terriers.

The terrier is, of course, best known to followers of the Border Foxhounds, while there are families like the Dodds, the Robsons, the Elliots and the Hedleys with which it has been identified for generations. No terrier with a poor nose, a poor coat, or deficient in courage would be of any use, any more than would one deficient in stamina.

Standard

It is interesting reading this report, written at the beginning of the century, to see that much of what it says about the Border still holds true today:

> In weight this Terrier would scale from 14 to 18 lbs, while an average shoulder height would be 14 inches. The coat varies considerably from the Red of an Irish Terrier, grey-brindled, dark blue and tan, with tan legs, or black and tan. The nature of the coat also differs, for whereas some are smooth, others are broken-haired, the former being more in request. The head partakes of the Fox Terrier but is neither so strong or so long, while the ears, instead of being carried close to the head are half pricked. Unlike the majority of the Terriers the one under notice is not docked.

And thank heavens for that! Borders' long tails are ideal for pulling them out from whatever hole they want to get stuck into, and the extra few centimetres of tail to grab as it dashed past has often saved me from having to wait whilst a Border takes off on its own business.

According to J W H Beynon of *Dog World*, this terrier is 'ancient... for there is little doubt that the Border Terrier as he is now known is one of the very oldest breeds of Terriers in Great Britain'. Beynon says the dog was well known in the Cheviots and wild country either side of the border between Scotland and England, and 'for centuries past many old Border families have jealously guarded their particular strain of terriers and fiercely combated any attempt to have them exploited as a commercial proposition, or as they contemptuously expressed it, "make a fancy dog of him"'.

Flint

One very famous early Border was Flint (whelped in 1894) owned by Mr Dodd. According to his owner, Flint was a marvellous working terrier. He had a splendid nose and was never beaten to find his fox. Though not often asked to go to ground during the last year or two of his life, he was always ready if wanted. One occasion after drawing a blank, Flint was missed, and 'it was thought that he would have gone back to a hole. We hurried back, but met him on the way, and at once his face showed that he had been at a fox... Later a shepherd's wife living close by came running to us, and said that Flint had bolted another fox from the hole after we had left, ran him down to the burn, and caught and worried him in a deep pool, and that she had the fox in the house'.

Dodd records that Flint won more prizes than any Border Terrier 'ever has done' and he was a capital dog with the gun and a splendid companion.

Royalty

As Prince of Wales, Edward VII was a staunch supporter of the movement to prevent the cropping of dogs' ears and from 9 April 1898 dogs with cropped ears were ineligible for any show held under Kennel Club rules.

Looking at Victorian pictures of dogs, you often come across a typical Border face, but with pricked ears. One wonders if some people who followed fashion might have cropped their Borders' ears. It certainly makes it difficult to identify a dog portrait as a Border or some other terrier. However, Iona Joseph, the animal painting dealer, recently sold a picture, *Border Terrier in a Landscape* by W J Stevenson, which is dated 1879 and definitely shows the V-shaped Border ears.

When King Edward commissioned the master craftsman Carl Fabergé to copy the animals at Sandringham, two Borders, a red and a blue, were sculpted. The red one is in agate with rose diamond eyes, and the blue in blue and white chalcedony, again with rose diamond eyes. However, Pamela Clark of the Royal Archives in Windsor Castle, who made a special search of the records for us, regrets, 'I can find no mention of any Royal Border Terriers,' so one assumes they belonged to workers on the Sandringham Estate.

In a typical Border pose, crouching and ready to attack, these exquisite animals are obviously barking at something and, at the recent fabulous exhibition of Fabergé at The Queen's Gallery, someone with a sense of humour and understanding of Borders had positioned the dogs barking at a cat, obviously just about to give battle.

A Border Terrier in a landscape, signed and dated W J Stevenson, October 1879.

At the time Edward VII had a beloved and pampered white Fox Terrier called Caesar. After lunch on Sunday 8 December 1907 he accompanied his master and the house guests to the dairy at Sandringham to view the animals modelled in wax by Fabergé's sculptors before they were sent off to St Petersburgh to be finished. Today these sculptures are in The Queen's private collection.

Mongrels

Because of their rarity, people often didn't know what these dogs were and called them mongrels - and still do! Mr Lionel Hamilton-Renwick tells the story of a relative coming to London and exercising his Ch Grackle in Hyde Park. As happens with Borders, Grackle decided there were more interesting smells across the park and was lost. Eventually he was picked up and taken to Battersea Dogs Home, where the champion was registered as a 'mongrel'.

Clubs

During the First World War Borders continued working, and breed lovers, who had been working hard for recognition, 'were rewarded by a splendidly attended meeting at Hawick Show on July 24, 1920', according to Beynon. At the meeting Provost J C Dagleish outlined the advantages of forming a club to promote a greater interest in the breed. Many famous breeders were in the audience, including John Dodds, John and Jacob Robson, W Barton, T Lawrence, Strothers of Wooler, and T Hamilton Adams.

Eventually, after a long discussion, everyone voted to give a club a trial, and it became the Northumberland Border Terriers Club. The Dodds and the Robsons were appointed to draw up a standard of type. To keep it all in the family, my brother's Godmother was Audrey Robson, née Dick.

Shortly after, at a meeting of the Kennel Club on 1 September 1920, approval was given for the formation of another club, which became The Border Terrier Club. Since then this club 'has progressed quietly from small beginnings' to the happy and successful club that it is today, celebrating its 75th Anniversary in 1995.

The club did an enormous amount of work to establish the Breed Standard, both in the 1920s, and again in 1980s when attempts were made at standardisation of all breed standards. (See Chapter 14 for more on the Border Terrier Club.)

Weight

Even in those times there was a dispute over the optimum weight for a Border, and today Mr Hamilton-Renwick says as a judge he still has Borders presented whom he considers much too big to do the job for which they were bred. *Plus ça change ...*

V L Wood wrote to *Our Dogs*, 'I am so glad to read in your columns that prominent Border people (whose opinions are of real value) are becoming alarmed at the size to which the Border Terrier is now attaining' and went on to regret the benching of the breed:

> ... as I have always feared that the great show-bench fetish of 'bone' would gradually get the breed too big, as in so many other breeds of sporting Terriers.
>
> It is a thousand pities to see Borders of 17 and 18 lbs on the show bench, but it is nothing short of a national calamity when it comes to the matter of work. What use is a big Terrier with wide shoulders to go down our narrow drains?

According to W Sibbald Robertson he remembered seeing a large class of Borders at Jedburgh Show in 1898. Writing in *The Field* he recounts: 'the Judge hesitated between two for first and second place, and finally, having measured them round the chest with his handkerchief, he gave the first prize to the smaller.' In another letter to *Our Dogs* Adam Forster put it succinctly:

> As a breeder of the Border Terriers of the small type... I quite agree that there are many dogs shown that are much too big for working purposes... under a real Border Terrier Judge, those big Terriers are generally put in the proper place - ie outside.

That's telling them!

Recognition

Probably the first registration was in 1913 when Moss Trooper, born 2 February 1912, a blue-and-tan dog, was registered with The Kennel Club under Any Breed or Variety of British, Colonial or Foreign Dog - Not Classified. He belonged to Miss M Rew, and was by Sly (unregistered) ex Mr J Robson's Chip. A further 41 Borders were registered in this section up until 1919, although an application for a separate breed register had been made in 1914 - and rejected.

1920 was an important year, as the breed received the recognition of The Kennel Club, and on 30 September the first Challenge Certificates (CCs) were awarded at Carlisle by Mr S Dodd to Tinker, a 15-month-old dog owned by Miss Bell Irving, and to Liddesdale Bess, who won the bitch's CC.

Writing in *Our Dogs*, F W Morris said:

> ... after many years the Kennel Club has 'recognised' the Border Terrier. It must not be forgotten that *Our Dogs* has played an important part to achieve this distinction, and I feel now that a great victory has been won... We now know where we are, for a standard has been drawn up, a club formed, and it only remains for fanciers to join up and add 'grist to the mill'.

Mr Morris must have known my grandfather and his family, as 20 years later he wrote a very sympathetic obituary when my grandmother died. She was a Holford, and bred Alsatians with the affix Tonevale.

1920s

Controversy raged in the columns of dog magazines whilst devotees of different breeds extolled the virtues of their favourites, claiming that other Terriers were no use for working. The Orme records produce a wonderful report describing a day with the Percy Hunt when Peter, son of the famous dog Titlington Tatler, went to earth. After some time it was found that Peter was busy with a badger. Time passed and the decision to dig had just been taken when Peter was found pulling the badger by the throat. Luckily for the animal it was dead, as it had been pulled about seven yards by Peter, who incidentally weighed 6.8kg (15lb) to the badger's 11.8kg (26lb).

This story is quite believable; when my current pair were small Widget would pull Wyvern around by the neck for fun, Wyvern weighing half a kilogramme or so more. One day I found deep puncture marks around Wyvern's throat; he had never complained but would allow Widget to dig in his teeth to pull him across the resistant carpet.

Entries to Crufts

It is interesting to see how Border entries to Crufts have increased in the past 50 years:

1936	57
1948	94
1965	119
1971	92
1990	122 (most popular terrier)

In comparison, in 1920 there were 45 Golden Retriever entries and, in 1990, 321.

Walter Baxendale welcomed the breed, and said that 'a word, and that a good one, must be spared for the game little Border Terriers, the most recent addition of all to the Kennel Club registry... though exception has been taken to the "capture" of the breed by the southern camp' (the Vice Presidents were all Masters from Southern Hunts such as the Beaufort, Dulverton and Old Berkely). He berated northerners, saying that it must be admitted that it was 'their own dilatoriness at a period in history when it was a case of "now or never" that Mr Hamilton Adams and his friends came, saw, and conquered .... There now exists the perfectly ridiculous position of a Border country breed, pure and simple, being owned by and catered for by southerners'.

The Field in 1930 contained an article on Border Terriers by A Croxton Smith entitled *Little Warrior Dogs* in which he said they are 'gentle and affectionate in the home, they delight in waging war on foxes, badgers or any sort of vermin that are the hereditary foes of all the terrier tribe'.

Second World War

During the Second World War the Border was still making news. According to an article in the dog press in 1940, few breeds exhibited in this country had a longer show-life; a dog which in most breeds would be considered past his prime would be capable of winning the Veteran class and the Challenge Certificate at the same show.

The Government appealed to dog owners to offer their dogs for service with the troops: a Border would certainly have made a good morale booster. Some 5500 dog owners responded, amongst them Border Terrier owners, and they were asked to write to the War Office, endorsing envelopes and post cards with the words 'War Dog'.

At one time it is said that food was so scarce there were only enough rations for two weeks; food convoys were unable to get through with vital supplies. Foxes were killing off lambs destined to feed the population, so Fell huntsmen were recalled from their units to help put down this menace.

Mrs Twist

Mrs Twist was a noted Border breeder with the affix Hallbourne, and President of the Southern Border Terrier Club. One of Mrs Twist's most famous dogs, Ch Fox Lair, born 1934, had the distinction of winning three CCs in succession at Crufts. Luckily for those wanting to search out Border pedigrees many of her letters to other breeders, asking for details of dogs' pedigrees, have been preserved in Miss Orme's papers.

Reprinted from the DOG WORLD ANNUAL, 1958.

HALLBOURNE
Border Terriers

**CHAMPION
DINGER**

**CHAMPION
BARB WIRE**

**CHAMPION
ALDHAM
JOKER**

**CHAMPION
HALLBOURNE
BADGER**
Junior Warrant and
M.F.H. Certificate.
Stud fee four gui-
neas, plus carriage.

HALLBOURNE BLUE VINNY, one C.C.

**HALLBOURNE
BRANDY BALL**
2 C.C.s

**Ch. HALLBOURNE
BLUE VAL**
Stud fees 4 gns. plus carriage

**Ch. HALLBOURNE
BRICK**

Direct male line of CHAMPIONS for five generations

All particulars from—**MRS. E. TWIST,**
Old Hall, Littlebourne, Canterbury, Kent.   **Tel.: 222**

Mrs Twist was a noted Border breeder with the affix Hallbourne.
She kindly gave permission to print this page.

In 1943 Miss Orme quotes from a letter Lord Lonsdale had sent to Mrs K Twist :

> I have Terriers now who are descended directly from the original Border Terriers, and we have the pedigrees since 1784... the Border Terriers are a cross-breed and the origin is that the Duchess of Northumberland had a very nice brown bitch which was crossed with one of our Terriers - who very often were brown. Several of mine were brown colour and they were always called Lowther Terriers. She crossed them with some others, and the farmer next door started a breed called Border Terriers. But before that they were always called Lowther Terriers.
>
> Then there was a Lady who started a breed of Terriers at Howtown, near Ullswater, and we suddenly heard they were called Lakeland Terriers. I went to look at them, but they were no more like the original terriers than I am, and the whole breed have got mixed up, and the Ullswater Terriers and Border Terriers have got so mixed up that they are practically the same thing and I have no details of any of them and I have not kept any for the past few years. I am afraid I cannot be of much use to you except to say that Border Terriers are a cross between one of our Lowther Terriers and a brown Northumberland Terrier, bred in Northumberland.
>
> (signed) Lonsdale

Hmm.

Mrs Twist corresponded with a wide variety of Border owners, and anyone wanting to research breed lines must be indebted to her for her painstaking work searching out old pedigrees. This fascinating correspondence can borrowed from the Southern Border Terrier Club; there is a deposit of £20 (refundable) and non-members have to pay a hiring fee of £20.

Although the War interfered with her breeding programme (her home was within range of bombers and V2 rockets), in April 1942 she received a letter from Rev Roland Allgood who wrote:

> Many years ago now, when this gallant little breed began to be recognised outside its own Country, all our old supporters of the breed sensed a great danger (most of them shepherds on the hills and hunting men of all classes). They were terrified that once the breed got into the hands of the Show Bench People, that the old breed would be ruined as so many of our other sporting breeds like the Sealyhams have been ruined, as far as their sporting pro-clivities go, by these show bench people, and that in a few years we should be shown some of the absurdities which you see now in other breeds. So much so that a great number of them refused to register their dogs at all.

[At last, when registration became more or less a necessity:]

> ... a meeting was fortunately held up here to standardise and safeguard the breed, if possible, from this unfortunate fate. I remember it very well as I attended that meeting which took place at Alnwick, but even then many of the old breeders even after this precaution had been taken, refused to register at all. The meeting took place about 1913-1915. And that is the reason why you find yourself up against the difficulty that you are realising today. And I very much doubt if you will have much luck in your research beyond a certain date...

I remember at the meeting I mentioned above, how some show bench person had managed to squeeze his way into the meeting (though we tried to keep them all out) addressed the meeting thus: 'Mr Chairman, I have often noticed when judging Border Terriers that most of the best ones seem to have a little moustache, and I submit that this point should be mentioned in the Standardisation'!! There was an awkward pause - and then an old man from the Hills let forth: 'Aye, he said, and do you know what will happen? In less than three years time you will have something like the bloody German Emperor back in your blasted Show Rings'!

During the War Border breeders were still offering puppies for sale, and advertisements in the 1940s offer 'dogs for four guineas, bitches three guineas'. Prices hadn't gone up much (inflation was an unknown word) since an advertisement from *Dog World* in 1924 offered the son of Ch Titlington Tatler for a stud fee of four guineas, and Tweedside Red Topper puppies bred by Mrs David Black for two guineas each.

In the 1930s there was a vogue amongst fashionable women in London for unusual breeds, and sadly Borders were included amongst these. Mincing along Mayfair pavements, a dog on a lead was considered an accessory to set off your new costume and hat. Luckily this didn't last long, and by the 1940s Borders were back where they belonged: as a working dog and companion.

Now we know

People have often said that Sir Walter Scott owned Borders, but in December 1942 Mr M H Horn wrote:

> It is surprising how often the Border is quoted as being the result of the energies of some character from one of Scott's famous novels. Admittedly many of his books are set in the border country, but didn't mention the Coquet Valley. It is within memory of older breeders that the Border was called the Coquetdale Terrier, but to connect its origin with any of the Scott characters, actual or fiction, is as useful as crediting the immortal Pickwick, or even Mr Jorrocks with such an honour.

And Miss Orme has written beside this letter 'Well! Now we know!!'

There was much confusion, but in a letter from Mrs Salisbury of Liphook to Mrs Twist she says the Dandie was an acknowledged breed in Scott's day, and could trace their pedigrees back 30 generations to Sir Walter's own terriers. A famous character, Piper Allen, was supposed to have owned Borders, but again Mrs Salisbury knocks this on the head: 'I know of no evidence showing that he kept terriers of the Border type.'

Mr James Dodd was reputed to have in his possession a letter dated 1800 and written to his grandfather by James Davidson of Hyndlee (believed to have been the original of Dandie Dinmont in Guy Mannering). According to A Croxton Smith: 'He is supposed to have terriers of two sorts...', and in his letter Davidson tells of having bought 'twa reel devils o' Terriers, that had hard wiry coats, and would worry any damned thing that creepit'.

And if that isn't a description of a Border... !

Apparently it was Davidson who called his terriers Mustard or Pepper, according to colour, and how many Peppers have there been since? Including Queen Beatrix of the Netherland's Pepper.

John Renton, writing in *Dog World,* was indignant that a correspondent had stated that 'in his opinion the average pedigree Border is not a worker', and replies:

> ... in my opinion, Borders have never done as much work as they have done during the war years. There has been very little work with hounds; most gamekeepers have been in the Services, and the work of getting rid of foxes has been in the hands of farmers and their shepherds. I have seen more foxes during the war years than I saw for almost 20 years before the war, and have seen 15 adult foxes killed with guns and terriers in one day.

Size

The War was coming to an end, and John Pawson, Hon Secretary of the Southern Counties Border Terrier Club had time to write to the dog press saying:

> Without fear of contradiction, I say I have worked more Borders, and over a continuous longer period, than anyone else, and I have found that the ideal size is the medium, and I am glad to say that it is this size which is so popular today...
>
> I would point out that we have the original Border Terrier Club,.... in view of the more favourable turn of the war, the subscription has again been asked for, and with breeding increasing, and the demand for Borders astonishing, we can look forward to large entries at the first Victory Show.

He does not indicate what a 'medium' Border should weigh, however.

Enthusiasts were asking that Borders have their own classes at shows, rather than having to share with other breeds. But some people still had to re-start their kennels, and there were reasons why this wasn't going to happen very quickly: Mr R Ogle writes that he didn't breed from Durridge Imp, as 'I intend going to Holland with Mrs Ogle to see our dear boy's grave'.

Adam Forster

One person whose name is synonymous with Borders and their breeding is Adam Forster. Sadly I don't think he is a relation, so I can say what a tremendous influence he had on the breed.

In 1949 Forster wrote to Miss Orme telling her about his famous Borders. Apparently when the Northern Border Terrier Club was formed, there was a cup for Best Dog and Best Bitch which, once it had been won three times, became the property of the winner's owner. Forster's Vic won that cup three years in succession, and was the first Border to win it outright. 'The last time she won it she had the torn face but one of our rules there was "if any part of the terriers' face was missing through legitimate work, that part was deemed perfect"'.

One of his favourites, Reward, lost both eyes working, but still insisted in following. One day Forster and his friends were busy working, when Reward

> ... hunted round trying to find a hole. She had only her nose to go by and as soon as she found it in she went and tackled the fox. We were glad when we got her out. She bred some good dogs but Ch Ranter was the best. Many people say he was the best Border ever shown in the North, he won where ever he went.
>
> A few of the outstanding dogs I have bred (all from the old Vic line) Coquetdale Vic, Coquetdale Reward, Miss Tut, Ch Ranter, Fighting Fit,

Rival, and Fearsome Fellow, whom I still have, 11 years old and my opinion the best of the lot. I have had Borders for about 50 years or more and I still think they are the grandest little dogs alive.

Forster's Furious Fighter was aptly named. 'He went simply mad if a fox was in a hole.'

Council

In 1951 The Kennel Club acknowledged that Borders were an important breed worthy of representation on their Council, and Mr J J Pawson was elected.

By now Borders had been a Kennel Club recognised breed for 40 years. Jane Buckland in *The Field* noted that 'one hundred and thirty-four Border terriers owned by the members of the Southern Border Terrier Club have gained working certificates with 44 different hunts since 1945', and asks how this has been achieved?

Credit must be given to the Border Terrier breed clubs whose members saw what was happening to other working breeds, stressed the importance of retaining the working qualities of the Borders and resolutely opposed any alterations to the standard as drawn up by their breed's founders.

Present day

There was a *frisson* of alarm recently when Ch Brannigan of Brumberhill won the Terrier class at Crufts, and was to be paraded in the ring to compete for Best in Show (BIS). Breed lovers were torn between pride in a Border Terrier coming up for the supreme championship and worries that, if Brannigan won, unscrupulous breeders would cash in on his and the breed's new popularity and probably ruin the breed.

Brannigan looked a picture as he paraded around, and probably the best solution came about when he was made Reserve. He had beaten all the others and had his moment of glory, but one could sigh with relief that the snobby 'trophy' dog owners wouldn't be clamouring for a Border. (Even so, breed enquiries multiplied.) But there was sympathy for his handler, Ted Hutchinson, who had done more than anyone else to show that Borders are the best dogs, in both the field and the show ring.

Borders are happy in town and country provided they have their home comforts and plenty of exercise.

City life

Another Industrial Revolution has taken place recently, with country people having to live in cities. Of course their dogs go with them, but concerned owners often wonder if their dogs will adapt.

Terriers seem to take anything in their stride. We came to live in London, as we had sold our house in the country. However, we kept a field so that Digger could return to his old haunts. Our first weekend we decided to take a picnic back there to give Digger a treat.

Treat be blowed! As soon as we parked in the field Digger sniffed around, then sat by the car and wouldn't move. He loved the smells of London, and wasn't going to be left in the country. After that we sold the field.

Let any Border Terriers sniff a fox, and they are off: even London Borders. There are foxes in most London parks, and they are a menace to town life. Barnes has had to issue very expensive dustbins to residents, with heavy locking lids; otherwise foxes tip them over and scavenge inside. Visiting a friend living there I commiserated with her about all the dreadful people who were littering the road, as there were piles of rubbish strewn all over the pavements. 'That's caused by the foxes,' she explained.

Borders are a happy creatures anywhere as long as they have affection, proper meals and something to keep them occupied, anything from bones to worry to passers-by to bark at and warn off. They make very good anti-burglar devices, too; but that is another story...

Exports

Most of our favourite breeds in the UK, such as German Shepherds, Poodles and Labradors, have been imported,

but the Border Terrier is probably one of our few native dogs. Although 'terrier' comes from the French *terre*, it should be noted that Norman French became the Court language in this country after the Norman Conquest. Henry III would therefore have used this language and, when he granted John Fitz-Robert permission to keep dogs of his own to hunt foxes in Northumbria, it is almost certain that Fitz-Robert would have adapted local dogs to his needs rather than importing dogs from across the Channel, many miles away.

Since before the War the Border has been exported and become almost as popular overseas, particularly in countries with a similar or colder climate. In the Netherlands Queen Beatrix has Borders and so do many of her subjects. Borders are gaining in popularity in America and Canada, New Zealand, the Scandinavian countries, Germany, Switzerland and many more. Club year books regularly contain reports from clubs all over the world, and as they write to their Secretaries they can be seen to be uniformly proud that their best stock is descended from imports from Britain.

Eastcoast of the Windy Spot proves that it is not only her head that is like an otter's!
Photo: Marian ud Horst-Siraal

The breed standard:
some famous kennels

Two magnificent Dutch Borders: Int Ch Ins Cygna of the Whiskered Gentry with daughter Beachcomber of the Windy Spot. Owner: Marian van der Horst. Photo: Theo van der Horst.

Breed to type and judge to type, and all will be well.   Adam Forster

This book has been written in the hope that the reader will not want to popularise the breed but to know more about Borders. I also aim to show anyone who is thinking of buying a Border and has never owned one just what they are taking on, and perhaps make them think twice. Also, if people are told how to contact reputable breeders, they are in a better position to avoid Border 'puppy farms', should any come into being.

Breed Standard
The Border Terrier was originally bred as a working terrier to follow its quarry underground, cornering it, and either dispatching it or harassing it so much that it bolted from the earth.

Anne Roslin-Williams writes in her book *The Border Terrier*:

Although the standard has been criticised for leaving too much to the imagination, I maintain that if one knows the job of a working terrier, and has taken the trouble to find out from a good source the basic anatomy of the dog, the Standard puts the finishing stitches to the tapestry of the Border.

In this chapter we will go into the various elements of the standard and, if you carry a copy of this with you when looking at Borders, you won't go far wrong.

The Kennel Club Breed Standard

General Appearance: Essentially a working terrier.

Characteristics: Capable of following a horse, combining activity with gameness.

Temperament: Active and game as previously stated.

Head and Skull: Head like that of an otter but moderately broad in skull, with short strong muzzle. Black nose preferable, but liver- or flesh-coloured one not a serious fault.

Eyes: Dark with a keen expression.

Ears: Small, V-shaped; of moderate thickness, and dropping forward close to the cheek.

Mouth: Scissor bite, ie upper teeth closely overlapping lower teeth and set square to the jaws. Level bite acceptable. Undershot or overshot a major fault and highly undesirable.

Neck: Of moderate length.

Forequarters: Forelegs straight, not too heavy in bone.

Body: Deep, narrow, fairly long. Ribs carried well back, but not oversprung, as a terrier should be capable of being spanned by both hands behind the shoulder. Loins strong.

Hindquarters: Racy.

Feet: Small with thick pads.

Gait/Movement: Has the soundness to follow a horse.

Coat: Harsh and dense; with close undercoat. Skin must be thick.

Colour: Red, wheaten, grizzle and tan, or blue and tan.

Size: Weight: *Dogs:* 5.9-7.1kg (13-15^{1}/2lb); *Bitches:* 5.1-6.4kg (11^{1}/2-14lb).

Faults: Any departure from the foregoing points should be considered a fault and the seriousness with which the fault should be regarded should be in exact proportion to its degree and its effect on the terrier's ability to work.

Note: Male animals should have two apparently normal testicles fully descended into the scrotum.

© The Kennel Club

My interpretation of the Breed Standard

One famous Border judge says she always re-reads her copy of the Breed Standard every night before judging an important event.

General Appearance: Recently there have been some Border Terriers that look like Jack Russell crosses; some have legs that are too short, others would be much too big to work underground. If a Border doesn't look right, keep a mental picture of a good Border in your mind, look at the Breed Standard, and together these should tell you what is wrong.

Characteristics: Border Terriers are bred to 'run' with the hunt. This does not mean slavishly to follow each twist and turn of the horses or hounds, but instead to take an intelligent line across country, and keep up with those who might be mounted on a heavy hunter or a small pony. So a Border must look capable of carrying out this function, and therefore have long legs.

Temperament: Happy and friendly but courageous.

Head and Skull: Anne Roslin-Williams says 'it was gratifying to hear a young boy... who was going around the benches at a show, say, after staring long and hard at one of my dogs, "I could breed otters from that one"'.

Am Ch Bever Lee Molly Malone CD DG CGC TD, owned by Lisa Connelly of North Carolina.

Eyes: These dogs have eloquent dark pools, useful for conning the public that they are starved of food and affection (either will do).

Ears: These often provide the clue to the breed in old pictures of dogs, as the drooping V-shape is so distinctive.

Mouth: It is essential that the Border is not undershot, as it will be unable to do its work if the bite is incorrect.

Neck: If our athletics coaches could harness the strength of the muscles in a Border's neck, we would win more gold medals.

Forequarters: They are strong but slim and straight.

Body: 'Being able to be spanned by hands' refers to men's, not women's, hands.

Hindquarters: Look as if the dog could run a long way.

Feet: They really are very neat and cat-like. One Border was named 'Tippy Toes' which is a good description of the way they walk. Their pads are very sensitive, especially when they walk through stinging nettles.

Tail: Look for the ring of hairs near the base. Useful for identifying your Border in a sea of other dogs; the wagging tail sticking out of a forest. The tail usually looks like a straight thick carrot, and is never docked. Dogs of all colours tend to have a ring of contrasting colour (usually silver) a little way down the tail.

Gait: They seem to 'bounce' along, especially when young.

Coat and Hide: The coat is the hair; the pelt or hide is the skin. The Border must have enough loose pelt for you to be able to grasp a handful of skin. The thickness protects from scratches and bites. Coats are often very thick, and stripping a Border is like painting the Forth Bridge: finish at one end and it's time to start at the other.

Colour: The Border's coat has very distinctive colours, which is part of the charm of the breed. Very often puppies change colour as they grow up. Points (ears and muzzle) are generally dark, but sometimes self-coloured.

> *Red* - Colour varies from light sandy red to the rich colour of a fox.
>
> *Grizzle* - This colour is popular as it often goes with a short, close coat, hence less to strip. The base colour is red with lots of blue/black hairs giving the 'grizzle' appearance.
>
> *Blue* - Called blue, although it may look black, because if your dog has to be shaved for veterinary treatment you will see that the skin underneath is definitely a blue colour. The colour goes right down to the roots, with tan legs and part-coloured head. With age the coat is broken, with grey, red and fawn hairs growing through to give the correct speckled appearance.
>
> *Wheaten* - Most people think this pale creamy fawn colour has disappeared, but you sometimes see very light coloured Borders. Trying to find a true Wheaten colour for this book was impossible; owners say this just doesn't exist any longer. Does anyone know of any true Wheatens?

The ears and nose are usually black or very dark; although liver colour is acceptable.

In the matter of colour breeding, it must be remembered that the sire predominates; therefore, if the sire is darker than the dam, it may safely be assumed that the majority of the puppies born will be darker in colour than the bitch and, if she is already too dark, a lighter dog would do much to change this.

Size: Much is made in the Breed Standard of size, and this is important because a Border has to enter drains or holes inhabited by the fox who, although he weighs more, is long and lean, and so slimmer. Borders often get in by turning on their sides and scratching their way in, using their long claws. Once when a Border Terrier was taken to have these clipped the grooming parlour refused to cut them, saying that it was criminal to take away its advantages.

Size has always been a bone of contention. *Border Barks* of 1949, written by William Lilico, mentions a letter from a very successful exhibitor who remarks on the variations in type and incidentally the size of exhibits, and advocates more detailed standards on lines of the American one. Wisely, Lilico muses: 'since Border Terriers have played a large part in my life for many years, I am too conservative in my views anent this but I still have the idea that as regards type the interpretation of the present standard is at the discretion and knowledge of the judges.'

However, if they are too big, Jack Price of Oxcroft says: 'you want a spade to put them in not to dig them out'.

Wyvern (blue) and Widget (red) enjoying themselves on the beach.

Faults: A few white hairs on the chest are allowed, but it is a fault if any of the feet are white, as this is thought to come from a throwback to cross-breeding in the past. One authority says:

> We know that somewhere in the early history of the Border a white-haired breed was used, and though the fault is by no means as common as it used to be, a small percentage of Borders have white feet, or a white blaze down the chest, surely the outcome of some breed used in its formation. This defect is not confined to the Border solely; other breeds also meet with the same trouble.
>
> It is all right to have a small amount of white on the chest, and there is one picture of a recent champion showing a clearly marked large white diamond on his front. However, white feet are not acceptable. This fault has almost been eradicated, and you should not breed if either parent has any white feet.

Borders are working dogs. 'Min', belonging to Mr and Mrs Wright.

Breeding

Anyone who wants to breed from their Borders should first of all go back to the breeder who supplied their original Borders for advice. By far the majority of Border breeders are honourable and want the best for the breed, not their pocket.

The Breeder will be able to look at the blood lines, and suggest potential mates, or give advice on whom to approach. So far Borders are relatively free from inherited problems and this is because for the last hundred years owners have gone carefully into the breed lines before mating their dogs. Anyone who owns Borders loves them and should want nothing but the best for their dogs.

Mr H Deighton of Brockhole Borders says it all:

There's a lot to be said, for a dog well bred.
        One that shines and oozes quality.
But even the best stud, can appear a dud,
        With a bitch with the wrong pedigree.
So if you have a lass, you think has class,
        Look for a stud that will suit her line.
He may be past his best, but he'll still beat the rest,
        With your bitch and the points you seek to refine.
In lots of minds, dogs the variety of Heinz,
        Still produce a 'sport' I do not deny,
But as they proceed and it's their turn to breed,
        Good litters are rare however hard they try.
To hear people boast, is sad, 'how many' their stud's had,
        And the results seen in the ring make them curse.
They're just driven by greed with no thought for the breed,
        And the repute of their stud gets worse.
For a job well done which can be lots of fun,
        There are some excellent books to be read.
Just breed with care, and you will get there,
        The perfect Border has yet to be bred!

Stud dogs

If your breeder can't recommend a suitable stud dog then a look in the Club year books will show members' advertisements with 'We occasionally breed from...' or 'At stud to approved bitches'. Jean Dawson goes one further: under a picture of her Ch Fairfax Bumble Bee is the caption 'Bumble is happily at stud to approved bitches'. I bet he is!

If there is one thing Border dogs are generally good at it is their efforts to increase the Border population. My Grandfather's Borders roamed far and wide playing Casanova to the county's bitches. But more of that later!

There was a lovely story in one of the Southern Border Terrier Club's Year Books telling of a Border owner who had invited a friend plus bitch for the day. Her friend's bitch had come in season, so the hostess shut her dog in an upstairs bedroom. When her friend arrived, being told the coast was clear she let her bitch out for a run.

Hearing a noise they looked up to see an eager Border launch itself from the upstairs bedroom window and come flying down onto *terra firma*. Once he had landed safely, he and bitch quickly disappeared into the bushes.

Moral: never underestimate a Border's abilities.

Avoiding problems

Don't think you are causing problems by going back to ask the breeder's advice. Sensible breeders want to ensure that only good breeding stock is used so that Borders keep their healthy lines. There are some problems which crop up occasionally, such as a bad bite, caused by an undershot jaw, and no-one should breed from an animal that has this problem or any other inherited faults. Your breeder will probably know if this is a possibility, although no-one can be 100 per cent certain what might happen.

In some lines there is a tendency to throw dogs with Monorchidism and Cryptorchidism (failure of one or both testicles to descend to their normal position in the scrotum). As far back as 1955 a sub-committee of The Kennel Club met representatives of The British Veterinary Association (BVA) to discuss the subject. The BVA had received reports that the incidence of Cryptorchidism in dogs was increasing, and was being observed sufficiently regularly in a considerable number of breeds to give rise to concern.

One of my dogs suffers from this; when we saw him as a young puppy everything seemed all right, although I did query the lack of equipment. The breeder assured me this was normal, and by the time we found out it wasn't, we were told 'bring him back and I will give you your money back'. The breeder must have known that this would be totally unacceptable. So care should be taken when breeding if this has happened in any near relation.

Pedigrees

Today most dogs' pedigrees are accurate, but Miss R J Fair, writing to Mrs Twist in 1948, said 'I'll be goggle eyed yet over these pedigrees.' Anyone who has been confused when researching dogs from the 'old days' will sympathise with her observation. Some of the old pedigrees were just written on scraps of paper and seemed to be a 'conglomeration of Flints, Wasps, Nettles and Tibbies. And Vics'. I am no expert, but I love to listen to the real enthusiasts who spend hours poring over a pedigree working out possible combinations, and then produce a real champion.

If you don't know whom to contact, just go to the next Border show, look at the dogs and choose the ones you like the look of best, and then start asking questions.

In pedigree breeding, tracing descent in the male line is much simpler in Borders than in other breeds, 'because of the persistency with which breeders used the same sires... Champions such as Revenge, Rival and Whitrope Don appear time and time again'.

Revenge, from whom 10 full champions descend, only appeared by accident. Often asked by a friend to provide him with a puppy for fox hunting, Adam Forster eventually gave the friend the choice from a litter; rejecting a bitch he chose Revenge. Later the friend returned and, seeing the bitch had developed well, exchanged animals. Months later Revenge won his two classes at the Newcastle Show, and the friend returned wanting another exchange - which was refused.

Adam Forster appears so many times with superb dogs; Coquetdale Vic (see Chapter 11) was the first outright winner of the club's Challenge Cup and was almost unbeaten in the ring. She never appeared at a championship show, a win at a small Border show being regarded as of greater merit than one at the larger events of the year. She was not only a show dog, but one of the gamest workers in the country. She had the misfortune to have the whole of her underjaw torn away by a fox, but it did not affect her working ability.

A dignified breed

Dignified little dogs; I have never known a Border that wasn't a character. They know their place and are utterly devoted to owners.

Walking around Crufts the other day, I was struck by the noise other breeds were making, whereas the Borders Terriers paraded with great dignity, and sat quietly whilst waiting their turn. The Border ring was a haven of quiet: pity other dogs don't copy them.

Housedogs

Border Terriers make excellent housedogs. They will come in soaked and dirty from a wet winters' walk, and within half an hour have licked themselves and each other clean. Looking at my two whilst they are mopping up after a visit to the Common, they look just like cats (but for heavens' sake don't tell them so) as they lick every bit of mud off their coats and feet.

Watchdogs

Although not bred for the purpose, most Border Terriers are excellent watchdogs. When the Crime Prevention Officer came to inspect my new flat and tell me what burglar deterrents to put in, he looked approvingly at the dogs and said: 'thieves don't like dogs.' A pity the anti-dog brigade don't think of this.

Just the idea that a dog is in the house can be enough to deter a burglar. On my ansaphone the message says that as I am out 'please leave a message with the dogs'. Friends have copied this as a deterrent to potential burglars casing the joint.

Widget was only about six months old when he woke most of the street at 4.00 am one morning. Growling and barking, he didn't stop for what seemed like hours, but it was probably only a minute or two. The next morning I started out to placate the neighbours and met Robert on the doorstep. Before I could embark upon my apology he told me that, thanks to the noise made by my dog, he had woken up to find a burglar in his bedroom. Of course after that Widget was the hero of the street, and now barks at any unexplained noise. The dogs made so much noise last night that they scared off someone who had crept down my area steps.

Socialising

Apart from barking at strangers, Borders are usually quiet except when playing with each other. When Borders visit, the best thing is to throw them all into part of the garden where they can work off their excitement and exuberance before allowing them back into the house. If you don't have a garden, leave them in the hall or a soundproof room until they have worked off their joy at seeing their friends: an hour will usually suffice.

Generally they are very friendly with other dogs, and will happily play with dogs five times their size, as long as they are introduced carefully. My grandfather had Borders, my grandmother Alsatians, and there were always Labradors, whippets and others - and guess who ruled the roost?

Singing

There is one other noise that no-one can explain. Generally for no apparent reason Borders will suddenly start to howl. Some people call this singing. Playing together, they suddenly stop and give voice. People say this may be because they have often been kept in kennels alongside hounds, and they are imitating their baying.

Wimsey had a habit of 'singing' at precisely 9.00 pm. No sooner did the clocks start up, and the announcer say 'This is the nine o'clock news,' than he would give voice. My Grandfather would reach over and wallop him with his long stick and Wimsey would stop - only to start again precisely 24 hours later. We also had to shut him out of the drawing room if we wanted to play the piano, as he was convinced he had a good voice and would love to join in.

Fitzroy enjoying a wrestling match with a Queensland Blue Heeler.

Kennels

There are many famous Border breeders, and I would love to mention all their kennels, but there isn't enough space. So I have made an arbitrary (defined in the dictionary as 'despotic') decision to include those kennels who have helped with anecdotes and advice, here and elsewhere in the book:

Dandyhow

One of the most famous lines is Mrs Sullivan's Dandyhow. Most of today's champions are descended from her famous Brussel Sprout and his son, Shady Knight.

The name came from the single 'dandy' rail line behind them, and Howgate was the name of their road. Mrs Sullivan said her father had Borders and she grew up in a house with them.

Almost every breeder has Dandyhow in their lines, yet Mrs Sullivan says producing this line was a matter of 'looking at the Pedigree, looking at the dogs - and a lot of luck'.

Ch Dandyhow Cleopatra was the top CC winner in 1994 and the Border world was looking forward to seeing her at Crufts 1995. But sadly this was not to be; Mrs Sullivan's son-in-law was elected to the Committee of the Kennel Club, and this barred her from exhibiting Cleopatra at Crufts. As a slight compensation, she did win at the 75th Anniversary Border Terrier Club Show at Carlisle shortly afterwards, and as we go to press Cleopatra has just notched up her 11th CC.

Farmway

Mrs Aspinwall says she has a small, long-established kennel that prides itself on temperament and quality. Wherever you go in the Border world, there are Farmways, named after birds. They grow up in a wonderful world, at the end of a farm lane with views from the house over the Thames Valley. Her calm good sense (echoed in her

Borders' temperaments) is much appreciated, and she represents Borders as Liaison Officer to The Kennel Club.

Hollybridge

Susan Williams' Hollybridge house-reared puppies bred for type and temperament are occasionally available to approved homes, and she undertakes to take back or help to re-home 'any Border I have bred at any point in its life should circumstances warrant'.

For anyone who is interested in tracing their Border's pedigree, Susan offers to help trace this if you send a stamped, self-addressed envelope to 187, Bamford Road, Heywood, Lancs OL10 4AG (tel: 01706-623660). She has copies of all The Kennel Club stud books and breed supplements from 1919 to the present time and will gladly help anyone who contacts her.

Mrs Aspinwall with some Farmway Border Terriers.

Maxton

In real Border Country, Jean and Walter Gardner have the Maxton Kennels. Son and grandson of veterinary surgeons (it's extraordinary how many vets own Borders Terriers: they know a good thing when they see it), Walter is a noted judge and has bred Borders for many years, although today he doesn't have many to pass on.

The real reason why I have included the Gardners is that they have written a delightful book *About the Border Terrier*, to which I have constantly referred when writing this book. Any time I have been at all doubtful about something someone has said, I have looked it up in Walter's book, and there is the answer. He is a typical Border owner, and when I asked him about something happening in Dumfriesshire his immediate reaction was, 'Would you like me to go and see them for you?' Incidentally, his book has a most informative interpretation of the Breed Standard which clears up any misunderstandings one might have. In his job with the Department of Agriculture he had plenty of opportunity to see Borders at work and at play, and he has written a chapter on the geneticist's view of breeding.

Oxcroft

Jack Price of Oxcroft is a great character, well known as a breeder. He is firm about the size of his Borders, and it was interesting to find out from Diana Tillner of Malepartus in Germany that 'to maintain our Border at the size we prefer, we are continuing to breed from our Oxcroft line'. Oxcroft Rocker, who went to Malepartus, was a grandparent of one of my Borders.

Thoraldby

When researching for the section on Borders overseas, I kept coming across this kennel's affix, and Peter Thompson says they have sent Borders abroad for many years. Like many breeders, he is concerned that only good Border stock should be used for breeding, and is worried that when people ask a vet what will make a good pet, 'not too big and easy to look after', Borders Terriers are often recommended. With so many puppies being bred from any stock he thinks the system wants changing to something like that current in Germany, where dogs are graded, and only those graded 'Excellent' are bred from.

His Borders are great characters: there is one who will pick up an egg from the farmyard and walk outside with it held carefully in its mouth, hidden from its mates, and then eat it when away from them. Unbeknown to humans, another learnt how to slide open the car windows, and dived out when driving past something it saw of interest in the road.

Professor Milton sent a Border Terrier down to Thoraldby to get a Working Certificate, although when tracing the pedigree back seven generations it was found that not one ancestor had been worked. This didn't matter: the Border knew instinctively exactly what to do.

Peter is very proud of Ch Loriston Amber, his top brood bitch, and Ch Thoraldby Glenfiddich, top stud dog.

Oxcroft Rogue and Oxcroft Bluebell.

Top dogs

Recently *The Kennel Gazette* invited top judges to select the all time greatest Border Terrier. This table shows their choices:

Judge	Dog	Reserve Selection
J Baxter	Ch Dandyhow Shady Knight	Ch Nettleby Mullein
E Hutchinson	Ch Dandyhow Shady Knight	Ch Full Toss
J Short	Ch Dandyhow Shady Knight	Ch Full Toss
Mrs P Grayson	Ch Portholme Manly Boy	Ch Thoralby Glenfiddich
Mrs M Aspinwall	Ch Dandyhow Shady Knight	Ch Dandyhow Burnished Silver
		Ch Dandyhow Duttonlea Steel Blue
P Thompson	Am Ch Traveller of Foxley	Ch Dandyhow Duttonlea Steel Blue
Miss A Roslin-Williams	Ch Dandyhow Shady Knight	
	Ch Step Ahead	
	Ch Brannigan of Brumberhill	
R Williams	Ch Step Ahead	Ch Dandyhow Shady Knight
H Wright	Ch Step Ahead	Ch Dandyhow Shady Knight

Others mentioned as Reserve Choices: Ch Vanda Daredevil; Ch Hawkesburn Nutmeg; Ch Deerstone Douglas; Ch Duttonlea Suntan of Dandyhow; Ch Brannigan of Brumberhill (three times).

A lovely Border collection from the Wilderscot kennel.

Do you really
want to own a Border?

Owning a Border is a commitment.
Johanna Farrer

Before you become the proud owner of a dog of any breed, are you prepared to join the 'unwanted' majority? Are you capable of handling the fact that at times it will feel as if the whole of Britain is against dogs and their owners? More and more local bye-laws are being brought in, banning dogs from public places such as beaches. This is happening on a great many beaches in the South, although in Northumberland I am glad to say that Borders and other dogs are still welcome. However, some people do come up to owners walking their dogs and make comments about dirty animals. Most frustrating, but Borders treat these sort of people with silent contempt; probably the best way.

So, you have decided that you do want a dog, and feel you can handle disapproval (sometimes very vocal!) from the anti-dog lobby. But are you sure that the Border Terrier is the right breed for you? Would you buy a car if you didn't know how to drive? Buying a Border Terrier without knowing anything about the breed is a similar exercise.

However much you believe that a Border Terrier is the right type of dog for you, learn as much as you can about the breed before approaching a breeder. It is best to join a breed club first. There you can meet other owners and also breeders who may be thinking of breeding and to whom you can put in your request for a puppy when their bitch whelps. The best breeders usually say, 'I always have enough people wanting a puppy before I consider mating', so it is worthwhile making an effort to find just the Border for you.

Club secretaries are unsung heroes and heroines who give up an enormous amount of time to run the clubs, and you couldn't choose better people to give you impartial and helpful advice if you are interested in purchasing a dog.

Ruth Jordan of Rubicon Kennels gave helpful advice when a purchaser phoned her about purchasing a Border, telling him there was a kennels very near him that had a litter. However, the potential purchaser soon turned up on her doorstep with the indignant comment: 'The other breeder didn't ask a single question.'

Breeders must ask questions; Mrs Jordan says 'people have to go through a catechism' before she will let them even think about purchasing one of her puppies, and that is how it should be.

Beware of kennels that say they always have puppies for sale; concerned breeders only breed:

- when they know they have someone waiting for all, or almost all, of the litter.
- when they need another show dog.
- very occasionally, if they want to carry on the line.

Look at the Club year books, and you will see advertisements saying 'puppies occasionally available to good homes', or 'visitors are always welcome to see our small family of Border Terriers' (translation: we want to see how our dogs get on with you before we will even let you think of buying one of ours). On a less cynical note, this type of invitation is the ideal way of absorbing Border lore, and having an informed chat with knowledgeable people who will help you find the ideal Border for your needs.

As Sue Pickerin of the Hobhill affix says: 'Puppies very occasionally for sale.' Note the 'very'.

Independent, thinking dogs

Remember that a Border Terrier is bred to work underground, away from Master's commands. It is therefore expected to think for itself, unlike most working dogs, which react to instructions from their human master. It can be frustrating when you go to call a Border to find it is using some of its working equipment

Borders need plenty of exercise: Pip and Briar enjoying a friendly fight on their daily walk.
Photo: C Ricks

(nose or digging skills, for example) and considers that it should not give up its investigation until it has worked out everything to its own satisfaction. It therefore has no intention of returning to you until its investigations are completed.

Since it is a thinking dog, you **must** do everything you can to think ahead, so that your dog won't go walkabout. Look everywhere for potential holes and block escape routes. Try 'thinking Border'. Even so, Houdini must have been in their ancestry; they do go walkabout. Can you handle this?

Five miles a day?

People often admire my pair of Borders, and say they are thinking of buying a dog, and this type seems ideal. Trying to dissuade them, because you should never buy any dog on a whim, I stress they will have to walk their dog for at least five miles each day. This seems to put them off.

The Border is a working dog, happiest when it gets good exercise and plenty to interest it. It can be quite content living with an elderly couple who will give it lots of attention, loves being part of a family, and is happiest when it has a full and energetic life.

There isn't too much opportunity for Borders to work in London, although there are foxes in the Cemetery over the garden wall which my two are longing to get at, and rumour has it there used to be a Border at the Mansion House that had the time of its life ratting when the streets were empty after everyone had gone home from the office. To compensate, Londoners' dogs get to run around the local parks, chasing anything that moves and socialising with other dogs. Strangely enough there is more space in the parks for them to run off the lead than in many country villages, where fields are often off-bounds.

However, if you can give them interest and exercise, then according to the Barnes vet, Mr Julian Maurice, the Border Terrier is a 'small handy sort of dog' that doesn't have the snappy terrier temperament. 'They are rather a specialist type of dog so you get owners that have looked carefully into buying a dog. Breeders don't mess them about with them' - and they are probably the smallest dog that hasn't been spoilt by breeding for fashion.

If you are about to own your first Border it is vitally important you:

- take advice from someone who knows Borders.
- buy from a reputable breeder.

On its own

A Border is a sociable animal. Its temperament encourages it to go up to anyone, human or other dog, and socialise. It likes bigger dogs such as Dalmatians and Alsatians, and loves a good body-bashing session with a Rottweiller.

However, it will be extremely unhappy if left on its own during the day, and will bark from boredom. Its bark is meant to be heard several feet underground, so it will travel. With anti-noise legislation becoming stronger, if your Border barks and barks from boredom all day you could find yourself in Court.

Houdini

I can't think why more Border Terriers are not called Houdini as they are escapologists *par excellence*. Mrs Lee of the Tythrop kennels says Borders have little idiosyncrasies like climbing up fences, so these have to be made Border-proof. Then they dig under the fence - and that has to be proofed. Finally, thwarted up and down, they take to biting and boring through a fence. Therefore be warned: providing a suitable Border-proof fence will be an expensive priority. It helps if you have an SAS member in the family to advise on suitable containment.

A Border can also dig its way, or climb, out of many kennels. We left Wellington in a hotel kennel one night with his brother. Come the morning he had climbed more than three metres of chicken wire and drowned in the swimming pool, which (contrary to the law) had been left uncovered.

So you still want a Border?

If the above points can be answered satisfactorily from the Border's point of view, and you decide you do want to be owned by a Border, then now is the time to consult fellow members of a breed club. However, you will probably learn from their tales that often the Border either chooses you, or you suddenly realise this is the dog for you.

Major Derrick Ide-Smith is a Past President of the Southern Border Terrier Club, and became a Border enthusiast when his friends' car boot opened at a Hunt meet, with a Border Terrier pup sitting in the back. Ten Otterhound couples came out of the transporter; seeing these the puppy jumped out and faced up to the hounds. 'That's the dog for me.'

Choosing your Border

You have found out from a friend what you should be looking for and, longing to hold your own puppy, you phone the first breeder.

This is when the hard times start, and you have to be patient for your dog's sake. A concerned vendor will ask you all sorts of questions, so it might be as well to think about these now:

- Are there children in the family? This is no barrier, but a good breeder knows that certain lines have a better temperament with children than others.
- What are you going to use the dog for? Working? Showing? A family pet? Again breeders will want to know.
- How old was your last dog when it died? The good breeder will understand if it was run over at an early age, but will want to know why if it died early. Obviously this will give him or her some indication of how well you look after your dogs.
- Who will look after it?
- Can you give it enough exercise, and who will ensure this every day?

The Kennel Club also asks:

- Can you afford to buy the dog you want?
- Can you make a life-time commitment to the dog (on average more than 12 years)?
- Can you afford to feed it and pay the general vet's bills plus annual animal medical insurance? Even a Border that doesn't eat much and is generally very healthy costs something in weekly upkeep.
- Will there be someone at home with the dog? (Dogs get lonely, like humans.)
- Will you find time to train, groom and generally care for the dog?

... and then goes on to suggest that even one 'no' answer means you should think again before contemplating buying a dog.

If these questions are answered satisfactorily, then the breeder may ask you to visit. A litter may be available, but he or she wants to be satisfied that the dogs will go to a good home before committing any of the carefully-reared litter.

Good breeders won't sell a puppy in the run-up to Christmas. Harrods Pet Department stops selling any puppies at the end of October, saying: 'a puppy needs two months to settle in before the upsets of Christmas'. Crackers are a particular hate of young - and not so young - dogs.

Harrods only sell eight breeds of dog: those that they think are easiest to look after. They do not sell Border Terriers, preferring to put enquirers in touch with breeders. However, the manager is very helpful if you have puppy feeding or other problems.

Widget was particularly troublesome when it came to eating his leads. His teeth went through smart leather like a knife cutting through butter, so Harrods suggested an 'indestructible' nylon lead. Widget gave up after hacking his way through half of the lead - the rest has held out for five years! These leads are bright red and, with matching collars, look very smart in London. However, when I take the dogs to Badminton or out in the country, I have to look for an old bit of rope so they look less 'poncified'.

If the breeder doesn't know you and doesn't ask any questions, ask yourself if you really have confidence buying a puppy from this kennel. You could be storing up considerable trouble with an unsound pup who might not have real Border characteristics.

Code of conduct

The Midland Border Terrier Club has a very sensible Code of Conduct, and a hardworking Secretary, Mrs Jena Tuck, who is always ready to help prospective owners. With their permission we repeat their Code here:

1   To maintain the best possible standards of health and quality of life for their dogs.
2   To exercise their dogs in such a way as will not cause offence to others.
3   To ensure all their dogs wear properly tagged collars and are under effective control when away from home.
4   Members will clean up after their dogs in public places, or anywhere their dogs are being exhibited or exercised.
5   All breeding should be aimed at the improvement of the breed.
6   To breed from only Kennel Club registered Border Terriers, of sound stock and of good temperament.
7   Accurate breeding records and registration papers must be kept.
8   Stud services and sale arrangements should be mutually agreed - preferably in writing.
9   It is not in the best interests of the bitch to be mated before her second season, and she should not be bred from more than once a year.
10 No bitch should be required to have an excessive number of litters. It is not necessarily good for a bitch to have a litter, and breeding from her will not cure a tendency to false pregnancies.
11 Both dog and bitch should be fully inoculated and regularly wormed as advised by a veterinary surgeon.
12 No one should breed a litter unless they have the time, facilities and finances to devote proper care and attention to the rearing of puppies and the well-being of the dam.
13 It is the responsibility of the stud dog owner to check these points before agreeing to a mating.
14 To take every possible care as to the placement of puppies, and to advise of the characteristics of the breed. To take back or help re-home any unwanted Border Terrier they have bred.

15 Puppies should not be transferred to their new homes under the age of eight weeks.

16 No Border Terrier should be sold to Pet Shops or Dealers or to homes where they will be left alone all day.

17 The quality of the stock should be honestly evaluated and accurately advertised. No Border Terrier which has obvious physical defects should be sold without the buyer being made fully aware of the faults and Kennel Club registration papers withheld or endorsed.

18 At the time of the sale each new owner should be given all relevant Kennel Club documents, a completed pedigree form, diet sheet and information about training, working and inoculations, also a Code of Conduct.

19 It should be impressed on buyers that they should contact the breeder in the event of any problem concerning their Border. Breeders should make every effort to be of assistance in these circumstances.

20 Members of The Midland Border Terrier Club are expected to abide by this Code of Conduct and any breach of the code may result in refusal of membership.

Jena and Terry Tuck are stalwarts of The Midland Border Terrier Club, and own the Nettleby affix. Anyone wanting to obtain a Border Terrier from them is first introduced to a great many adult Borders, who carry out their own vetting procedures. Sniffing will obviously play a part, and if it is summer women should be ready for the cold wet nose on the leg! Only when the adults have sniffed and approved are prospective owners introduced to the puppies.

First impressions

Jaynie, my adopted sister, and I were looking for a puppy for our parents to replace one that had just died. We had good reports of one breeder, and made an appointment for a preliminary look. It suited her for us to come on a day when we were going to a very smart reception so, as we wanted to leave plenty of time to talk to the breeder, we went dressed up to the nines so that we didn't have to return home.

The breeder opened the door, took one look at us and gave us the impression she didn't want us darkening her doorstep. It took two hours of sweet talking before we overcame the first impression we had given and the senior dogs were allowed in to give us the once-over.

Borders enjoy the company of bigger dogs: For'-c'sle of the Windy Spot with friend. Photo: Theo van der Horst.

Thank heavens the dogs liked us and came and sat on our feet. So don't go looking for Border puppies in high heels and thick make-up; you'll have a hard time convincing a concerned breeder that, yes, you really will be able to give the dog sufficient exercise when you take off your high heels.

Family opposition

You've decided that a Border Terrier is the one for you, but the rest of the family seem hard to convince. Why not follow veterinary surgeon Colin Price's example? He works for the Charity Petsavers, and owns Millie. Before she arrived he borrowed a client's dog to take home and say 'We want one like this'. Needless to say the family saw sense once they had seen a Border.

What to look for

If you can, take a friend who knows Borders with you. If no-one is available, then you will have to check everything over carefully. Usually you will get to see the father and mother and perhaps some older dogs first. You can look to see if these Borders Terriers are what you want, and the breeder will see how you relate to the dogs.

Then ask to see the pups with their dam (mother); watch as they run around and play. Take plenty of time - a good breeder will have made sure they are available for a thorough, and long, appointment.

A good puppy will take part in games, move well with straight limbs and a confident air. Before picking up any puppy ask the breeder to show you the best way to do this. Take its mouth carefully in your hands and roll back the lips to see if the teeth are set correctly. You should be able to grasp the hair and skin and have a good handful. Does it have the right sexual equipment?

You will probably have seen the puppy when it is less than three months old, and too young to have had all its inoculations. If you can keep it away from other dogs, especially when exercising, then it can come to you as soon as it is weaned; otherwise it is usual to leave it with the breeder until all inoculations are administered - for which you will have to pay.

It will need to be vaccinated against distemper, hard pad, hepatitis, parvovirus and leptospirosis. They sound awful, and they are, so make sure your puppy is protected; all of these diseases are very distressing for the dog, which probably won't recover if it catches them.

Housetraining

I have known some breeders that will undertake this but it adds considerably to the cost, and you will miss out on some of your dog's puppyhood. If you haven't owned a puppy before, especially a Border Terrier, keep the first two or three days free to housetrain the pup; Borders learn quickly.

Take the puppy outside as soon as it has eaten or drunk or, if you can catch it, as soon as it wakes up. Very often the puppy will start to sniff around the ground, or scratch the floor. That is the signal to take it outside quickly (holding it well in front of you!). When it performs it is praised, patted and allowed back into the house. Borders pick up the routine quickly, as they react to praise.

At night you have to decide if you are going to keep the puppy in your bedroom in a box or cage lined with newspaper, or if it is going into the kitchen or anywhere with a washable floor. Authorities differ, so it is up to you. I am of the 'poor little thing, keep it by me' school but, if you choose the kitchen, spread large quantities of newspaper (hopefully your pup isn't one that scrabbles everything into one corner) and put the pup into its cardboard box. Then shut the door.

You will be heart-broken by the howls that come out from behind the door, so keep a loud CD and the whisky bottle handy! Suddenly you won't hear anything; the pup has fallen asleep. The next morning you will have to clear up, but this gets to be less and less of a problem, especially if you have spread newspaper everywhere.

Acting

Borders are excellent actors, born with thespian qualifications. As I was saying good-bye to a friend one day, Winston's paw was accidentally trapped in the door. The cries had to be heard to be believed, leaving my friend a shattered wreck. A damaged paw was held up, and I swear tears were coming out of his eyes.

But something made me suspicious, so instead of gathering him up and making a fuss of him, I said 'Dinner?'

A howling puppy was transformed. He shot off on all four paws and stood by his bowl looking up expectantly, tail wagging. My friend was speechless, and said she would never have believed it if she hadn't witnessed the performance with her own eyes.

Walking on the lead

Puppies will need a puppy collar or an adult one made smaller. Make sure it has an identity disc, as you would be surprised how enterprising puppies are; you will never know how many holes there are in your garden fence until you become the proud owner of a Border Terrier. Fit the collar carefully so that you can insert a finger between the collar and the coat, but tight enough so that the puppy can't wiggle out of the collar backwards.

When the puppy is in a happy and docile frame of mind, choose somewhere with no distractions, put on the lead and tug gently. As soon as you do this you find out your puppy has grown suckers on its pads and refuses to budge. Entice it with a tiny piece of its favourite food, encouraging gently. Two minutes of this is adequate the first time, gradually going for longer and longer until the puppy needs no encouragement to start walking with a slight tug from you.

When you get it walking on the lead it will often try to tug you forward. It is useful to have a rolled up newspaper, which you can use to tap the puppy on the nose if it starts to tug in front of you, saying 'No!' at the same time. Eventually the sight of a lead means walks, and Borders will come running.

Incidentally, it is as well to check collar fit on adult Borders, as leather can stretch. As I was watching a polo match one day, the dogs were tied up on the palings at the bottom of the stand. Widget was bored and wanted to talk to me. Suddenly, I heard laughter and realised spectators weren't watching the match; they were watching Widget, who had carefully hooked the bottom of one of the paling sticks through his collar and was levering it off.

As soon as he was free, he shook himself, acknowledged the applause with quiet dignity, and trotted up the stand to sit by my side.

Pedigree

Unless you get a puppy from a terrier man or someone who has a good strain of working dogs but isn't a registered breeder, your puppy will have a pedigree.

There are inverted snobs who say that pedigree dogs are in-bred and not as good as mongrels, but most Border breeders are concerned to keep the character and temperament. In general, they are lovers of the breed, keeping their dogs with them, often in their homes, and more concerned with keeping the Border characteristics in their puppies than with making money. Long may this be so!

Every puppy from a good breeder will come complete with its Pedigree Certificate, which usually goes back five generations. If you have a pedigree pup it is great fun to look up its certificate to see if it is related to a show dog that does well,

Pebbles dressed up ready for Christmas dinner.
Photo: C Ricks

and when you meet other owners you can compare character and characteristics and find out which ancestors are shared between your dogs.

It is possible that a breeder might falsify a pedigree, which is one reason why it is so important to go to a recommended breeder.

Over 50 years ago Mr Hamilton Adams wrote to Mrs Twist, who bred Borders at Canterbury with the Hallbourne affix:

> I came up to London today to talk over your letter with the Chairman. It is not only in Borders that we are constantly having this trouble but in all breeds. We, as the KC (Kennel Club) cannot guarantee any pedigree, we only certify that it is a copy of what is given to us. We have to rely on breeders... The real bottom of the trouble are the dog shops, who care nothing for our disqualification.

Dog or bitch?

Some people are certain which they prefer. If you are unsure, either will do: there is no difference in gameness, companionship and faithfulness between one Border Terrier sex and the other.

A bitch will come into season for several days about twice a year, resulting in spotting of blood and much interest amongst the local Romeos.

A male dog, especially a Border, will try to go walkabout if it catches one whiff of a bitch in season within a wide area.

Otherwise there isn't really much difference, although I know Border owners that prefer one sex or another will disagree!

If your male puppy grows up into a good adult you may be approached and asked if you are interested in mating. Then you go to the Certificate and look to see if this 'marriage' will work.

Year books

If you are still undecided where to start looking for your Border, most Border Terrier clubs have a year book, which you receive free with your club membership (a real bargain). If your club doesn't have one, The Southern Border Terrier Club, The Border Terrier Club and The Midland Border Terrier Club all have excellent year books with information and descriptions (with photos) of the breeders in membership. The advertisements give you some idea of the 'look' of the kennel's progeny, and some idea of their characters (breeders and dogs). Send £5 to the appropriate address in **Useful Addresses**.

If you don't find what you want, then look in the back of the Year Book under Members. Anyone with a name in capital letters (for example: Swithin, Mrs P S

SWITHINDALE, 50 The Close ....) means that Mrs Swithin breeds borders and has the affix 'Swithindale', so is recognised and may well have Border puppies. Even if she hasn't, you will find there is a network of good breeders who, once they have satisfied themselves that you are potentially a good Border owner, will give you the name of other breeders whose bitches have just had litters and who might have puppies available.

So become a member of a Border Terrier Club before choosing your Border, and you will benefit from lots of helpful advice. Average subscription is £7 a year.

Children and puppies mix well when the children are taught to treat the puppies with respect.

Are Borders good with children?

Yes, but.. A Border Terrier is a small dog, so a point to remember is that any child that can walk or crawl will loom over it, which can be threatening for the dog.

A dog is not a toy, and no child should be allowed to poke a dog's eyes, pull its ears or tail, ride on it or misuse it in any other way. Dogs and children get on well provided that the dog is treated with respect, and most owners will tell you that their Border Terriers are devoted to their children. But allow children to tease the dog and it can have, yes... a dog's life. So for the Border's sake don't allow children to play unsupervised. Step in when play becomes too rough, and the child and the Border will grow up inseparable.

Most Borders won't tolerate anyone interfering with their food, but this can be irresistible to a child. It is best to keep children out of the room when you feed the dogs, and then they won't be frightened by a snarl if they come too close to the feeding bowl. However, my brother Edward loved charcoal biscuits, and the long-suffering dogs used to stand by as he picked them out of their bowl, until he was caught one day and a stop put to this. Did the dogs tell on him, I wonder?! But some dogs wouldn't be so generous, and might snap at children that do this, so watch out.

You often see dogs sharing their little owners' food and ice-creams. Before you scream, my very sensible Dr Drouet once said that all his children had eaten their full peck of dirt, and it hadn't hurt them. Watch out for it and stop it if you can, but this 'sharing' nearly always takes place out of your sight.

Widger often slept on my bed, shared bed-time biscuits and was hastily thrust under the bedclothes when the parents came to say goodnight - and he stayed there without moving or making a sound.

Dogs need sleep, and therefore children must be taught to leave them alone when they are tired. And make sure children's toys are kept away; tears come when a puppy chews up a favourite toy, or the dog can swallow small things such as marbles with disastrous consequences.

Incidentally, it helps to forge the bond between you and your puppy if you let it sleep on your lap sometimes and can let the puppy know that you devote as much attention to its needs as to the children's.

Socialising

With other dogs the Border Terrier's first instinct is to go up to them, tail wagging, and introduce themselves. They are sociable animals, and love to play with other dogs, but might ignore anything that smells too much of lap dog.

If the other dog growls the Border will defend itself, and won't stand any nonsense. I never mind when mine are out in the park, but get annoyed with fussy owners who rush up to put their dogs on the lead whenever another one approaches. The worst ones are those that excuse themselves by saying 'he doesn't like other dogs'. If that is the performance that happens each time, no wonder the dog gets annoyed and shows its displeasure.

However, socialising with other animals is fraught with problems. Although Borders will tolerate cats and other animals that share their home, often forming abiding friendships, outside the front door anything on four legs is fair game: the faster it moves, the more fun in the chase. In London people walk their pets in local parks, which is fine when they are dogs or even Vietnamese pot-bellied pigs, but there are several pole-cats and even a fox that are regularly walked, and the owners can't think why dogs won't leave them alone.

Climbers

As well as being good diggers, Borders can climb. Mrs Judge had a wonderful Border called Bugger, and photos to prove she could climb chain fences. On a sadder note, I have already mentioned how Wellington scaled a three metre fence to escape from hotel kennels in the New Forest and subsequently drowned in the swimming pool.

So before you take delivery of your puppy, take a good look round the garden and try to put yourself into a puppy's mind; what can it dig up, climb, wriggle through or enlarge? And ask another owner to check out the battle zone for you, because as soon as your back is turned a Border puppy will try out all four disciplines like an Olympic athlete in training.

A large notice warning visitors to shut gates is essential, and time taken to introduce the puppy to tradesmen can pay dividends.

Pecking order

Borders definitely have a pecking order; people who won several say this means not only that you should not chastise the pack leader in front of the others, giving them a chance to crow, but also that if some of the Borders have been out hunting or visiting they must be introduced gently back into the pack. Even more importantly, if one has been out to be mated or work as a stud dog, the others will sniff the returner, want a piece of the action - and then wallop! So people who own several Borders say they go

Briar 'helping' with the gardening.   Photo: C Ricks

softly, softly, praising and patting the ones that were left behind and making a little fuss of the others to show they are so pleased to see them again. Sounds stupid? Not really. Remember, these dogs have excellent reasoning powers; wouldn't you feel jealous under the same circumstances?

Kennels

Border Terriers will assure you that they are only used to beds, preferably with duvets into which they can snuggle. If you are going to have your Border in the house, draw up rules before the puppy arrives, and make sure everyone sticks to them. If you are going to keep it outside in a kennel, make sure this is well-built, warm and wind-proof, and has a bed raised off the floor. Ask the advice of other Border owners; Mel Freeman keeps his Borders outside in kennels, and they have their own radio hanging from the roof. If he is going out he leaves this on so that the dogs have companionship.

'What, me... spoilt?' Katie in bed.
Photo: E Jabroer-ter Lüün

A word of warning: Borders have such pleading eyes that it is essential to keep to the ground rules, whatever the family says.

Only dogs

If you have a lone Border Terrier think carefully before putting it in an outside kennel; they are hardy little dogs, but they do like companionship and pine if left on their own for too long. By the same token they should not be left alone all day, either in a house or in kennels.

The Battersea Dogs Home book says:

> If you are thinking of confining a puppy to an outside kennel, perhaps the decision to keep a dog should be reviewed. Dogs need companionship. Being left alone in an outside kennel for lengthy periods is unlikely to bring out the best in a dog's character.

Pip and Briar on a walk:
Borders need companionship.
Photo: C Ricks

Dread-nought and Dinghy of the Windy Spot.
Photo: Theo van der Horst

Choosing

Sometimes Border Terrier ownership just creeps up on you. Jim Stewart was working on a construction site when he saw the foreman arrive with a puppy on a string. He was taken with the dog and found out it was a Border. Of course, you know the rest - Jim started out on the 'Border Trail' and now has four. As we talked he had two bookends formed by a 14-year-old and a 12-year-old.

'A dominant bitch keeps everyone in line,' he commented, 'but if a younger one has a litter then jealousies can start.'

They are first and foremost friends and companions and, with a young family, having Borders to take to shows means something the family can do together. (In these days of instant entertainment in theme parks, the good old-fashioned dog show seems to have been swept aside. Perhaps if more children were taken to these to amuse themselves there would be fewer cries of 'I want...')

Jim thinks that you lose out on the fun of ownership if you have too many Border Terriers. His four keep him occupied but are a manageable number. When we spoke he hadn't shown a dog for over two years, but still goes to shows because 'it's more of a social occasion'.

Playtime

Border Terriers, like any other dogs, love playing with you. Old socks (but make sure they aren't nylon), an old slipper or belt (with all buckles and eyes removed) or anything old makes a good lure and encourages the puppy's natural instincts. When they start to grow up it is surprising how strong their muscles become and, fastening their teeth into their plaything, they will happily swing well above the ground trying to get it away during play.

My two love a white toy made by Nylabone and called, rather grandly, the Plaque Attacker Dental Floss Exerciser. This is actually special dental floss for dogs, made of a type of nylon that breaks up in a way that cleans the teeth, rather than breaking up and landing in the stomach: the more they pull on it, the better it cleans the tartar from their teeth.

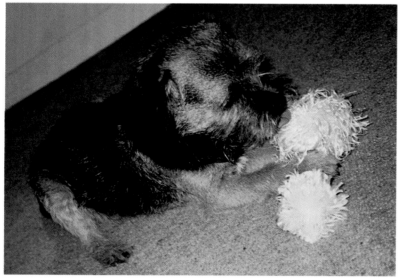

Wyvern with the Nylabone® Plaque Attacker™ dental floss.

The Kennel Club

All puppies should be registered by their breeder with The Kennel Club (your breeder will tell you how to transfer ownership). A puppy is eligible for six weeks' free Kennel Club Healthcare cover, provided it was purchased direct from the breeder, is not more than six months old and that you register the transfer of ownership with The Kennel Club within 10 days of purchase.

The Kennel Club says you should ensure that the breeder provides a signed Pedigree Certificate and signed Kennel Club Registration Certificate. The breeder should sign the reverse of the Registration Certificate to transfer the ownership to you, and you should then countersign it and send it together with the transfer fee (currently £6) to the Kennel Club.

Ian Logan, Registrar at The Kennel Club, says 'achieving a good partnership with your dog will prove to be one of the most rewarding relationships into which you will ever enter. It is important therefore that you take as much time and trouble as necessary and select the right puppy for your personal circumstances'.

The puppy has no choice in the matter. It's your decision. Make sure you make the right one for you both.

Border Terrier Welfare

If you don't want a puppy, or want to give a good home to a Border that has to be re-housed, Border Terrier Welfare (BTW) (see **Useful Addresses**) might be able to help.

This is an independent, self-funding voluntary organisation formed to help place Border Terriers needing new homes, and has a number of representatives throughout the country who help with re-homing.

Mrs Gwen Baldwin is the Co-ordinator, and the Hon Secretary is Miss Sarah Wishart, who say dogs are passed on only as pets, pedigrees and registration papers being retained by the Welfare. As some of their Area Representatives are also breeders, they may be able to give helpful advice. They would far rather you asked what owning a Border entails than buy a puppy which is unsuitable for you and for which they may then be called in to find another home.

Dogs are not bought or sold by the BTW, but donations are requested from new owners to help meet the many expenses incurred, especially vet's fees and car mileage. As Sarah says:

> Only fully inoculated dogs are passed on, and in some cases dogs may need medical treatment.
>
> We usually have a waiting list of people requesting our dogs. Reasons for re-homing may vary; many are due to death, sickness or domestic circumstances. A number of Border Terriers come to us because of 'problems' in the previous home; every possible care is taken to re-home them most suitably. We always suggest that prospective new owners find out as much as they can about the breed before deciding that a Border is the most suitable dog for them.

In one year BTW re-housed about 100 Borders, and the reasons for re-homing were many and various, such as death of owners, broken marriages and straying, but by far the greatest number were due to Borders 'being in the wrong home' or 'surplus to requirements'. Welfare ask, 'Is more care needed in homing puppies, particularly as the breed is becoming more popular?'

Not all BTW stories are unhappy: a link has been forged with Hearing Dogs for the Deaf, and several puppies are now trained and working happily with their owners. Then Gwen Baldwin tells the story of an elderly Border being collected from Sheffield Dog Pound. As she was obviously lost an advertisement was placed in the dog press, to no avail. After several weeks the carer was due to go on holiday, and as a final effort an advertisement was placed in *The Sheffield Star*. This had a very happy result; it was seen by the owner, an elderly widow in Sheffield, and the dog was restored to her.

Border Terrier Welfare always welcome donations, such as proceeds from coffee mornings, and to gather together their friends (and make some money!) every October they hold their AGM, which is also a 'fun' day including a talk on something of interest to Border owners. Contact Sarah Wishart for details.

Training

Border Terriers are thinking dogs, and won't perform tricks to order. People may say that you can't train Borders, but on investigation you find they have wanted them to do circus acts, totally alien to the gentlemanly instincts of Borders. For housetraining, walking on the lead and general sociable behaviour the Border is quicker than most to learn.

Border instinct says anything that runs away is to be chased. This includes unknown cats, rabbits (including pet ones), and also chickens. Broadcaster Phil Drabble has a marvellous way to stop his puppies chasing after livestock, particularly chickens. He keeps a pocket full of corn and watches the puppy carefully. As soon as it starts to chase something it shouldn't, he throws a handful of corn (carefully avoiding the eyes) whilst saying 'No!' in a loud, firm voice. The corn is a nuisance and distracts the puppy, who begins to associate 'No!' with something that will cause a problem if he persists - so he stops.

Ask any expert, and they will probably come up with the following golden rules for training a puppy:

- Start training early before a puppy gets any bad habits.
- Start with teaching to walk to heel, sit down, stay or wait, lie down and come back to you. You can see your Border thinking things out before he obeys.
- Always train the dog on a lead. No lead means the dog can run off and do what he likes. Only train for a few minutes at the beginning.
- Never shout at the dog or get angry. Keep your voice happy. When frustration comes into the tone, that is the time to stop.
- Be consistent. You might think it a good idea to change but your puppy won't understand.
- Keep the same tone of voice for the same commands.
- What you teach must be consistently obeyed. Never be satisfied with 'he gets it right half of the time'.
- Remember to praise. When the puppy gets it right you will be pleased, so let your pup know so that he can share in the delight.
- Borders sometimes have 'off' days, just as we do. When that happens just leave the training until the next day. Training should be fun, so allow time for playing and exercise.
- It is all worth while when friends say, 'Your dog is so well behaved.'

Bones

Winston had the sense to come running to me one day. He was playing in the park, and someone must have left some bones out for the foxes under the bushes. Of course he had found one, started to chew it, and a large sliver had got lodged in his throat. Luckily he came running to me, rubbing his head on the ground and uttering distressed wheezes. He didn't whimper as I put my fingers down and found the bone lodged at the back of his throat. I had to yank it out quickly, probably hurting him in the process but, being a Border, he didn't complain, just licked my hand as a thank you.

Many people say that dogs eat bones in the wild, but how many might die because no-one is there to help? Take your vet's advice about bones that are suitable and keep an eye on well-meaning friends who think chicken and lamb bones are perfectly all right. 'After all, my cat eats them,' said one, forgetting that cats and dogs are built differently.

Fleas

Believe it or not, in the old days people thought that dogs drew fleas away from humans. Today dogs pick up fleas from parks, public areas, other dogs and cats, and where foxes have been. Most just bring them in to the house so everyone can have a good scratch.

I have tried just about everything, but the only product that works on my pair is Program, manufactured by Ciba. A summer course costs nearly £30 per dog, but it is worth it to be free of these horrors. Two summers ago I had to call in the Pest Control Officer from the Town Hall as the carpets were infested with fleas the dogs had picked up from the local foxes. He told me I was about the last person in the street that had had to call him.

'But it must cost the Council a fortune to control them! Why not get rid of the foxes?' was my naïve question. Looking pityingly at me he said:

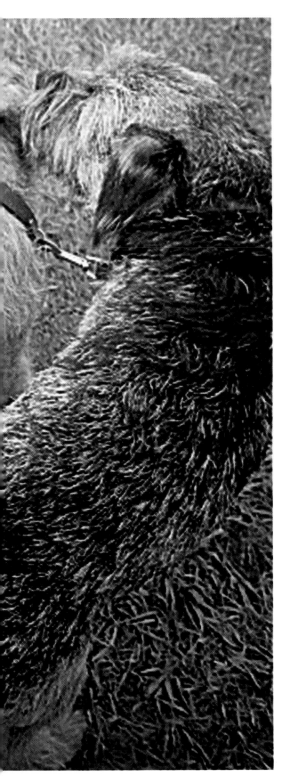

'It's more than my job's worth - the conservationists would be after my skin.'

He's quite right; a neighbour had lost a cat and put up a notice on the cemetery gates, asking if anyone had seen the cat, as they were worried that a fox might have killed it. Underneath someone had scribbled: 'Foxes don't kill cats.'

Faults

'Their only inherent fault is that they run away,' says Mrs Sullivan of the famous Dandyhow kennels. Off they go on their walkabouts, and they will come back when it suits them, provided they haven't got lost. In case this happens, it is essential that you have your dog identified in every way possible and belong to the Fell and Moorland Working Terrier Club in case the worst happens and they are lost down a hole.

... and finally

Do you have a sense of humour? Because without it you just will not get on with a Border, who definitely enjoys life, has his own private jokes, and will try them on you given half a chance.

Widget and Wyvern: inseparable friends.

Chapter Four

Looking after
your Border Terrier

Terriers are born with about four times as much original sin in them as other dogs.
Jerome K Jerome

For all the problems they cause, Border pups are so adorable that you just can't help falling in love with them. If your pup is to survive and grow into happy adulthood, however, you have to watch it carefully, and make sure it has the best care and attention.

There are excellent books that give practical and sensible advice on bringing up a puppy, and some of these are mentioned in the **Bibliography**. So read one or two books, and then use common sense. If you haven't looked after a puppy before, remember that, like children, they love attention and need discipline, regular food, a warm place to sleep and plenty of exercise.

The following hints are gleaned from my own experience and that of other Border owners.

One or two pups?

Most people will be happy with one dog as a pet. However, I find I am happier with two. This is because occasionally I have to go out for the whole day, or go abroad. Although my dogs thoroughly enjoy their stays with Patrick, my brother, or in their favourite kennels, I feel happier leaving the two of them together in these places to keep each other company. When I can take the dogs with me on my travels in this country they enjoy it, but again I feel happier in the knowledge that they will be company for each other as I leave them in a strange hotel bedroom to go down to dinner.

In deciding whether to buy one or two pups, bear in mind that Borders, especially if they are of the same sex, can be jealous of each other. My two males are tremendous pals, but it has been known for Borders to hate even their siblings - it can happen in the best families!

Best friends: Widget and Wyvern on their 'custom-built' tricycle.

Names

Your puppy will have a kennel name under which it is registered with The Kennel Club, and this has to be distinctive and unique, but for its 'normal' name a puppy can be called anything. Do think of the effect if you have to call your dog across a crowded area. Some friends who thought it very funny to christen their pups 'Widdle' and 'Piddle' regretted it all their adulthood.

Everyone has their own system for naming their dogs, and mine is to choose a name that begins with 'W', after my Grandfather's dogs who were all 'Wellisford W__'.

We have run out of the more usual ones such as Wimsy, Wattle and Weeny and have come to more exotic handles. Plushcourt Blue Dragon is called 'Wyvern' from the old Saxon name for a dragon, and Plushcourt Engineer just had to be called 'Widget', after mechanics' demands 'Gimme the thingummy - the widget'. One dog was called Winsome after my parents won 17 guineas at bridge and were able to buy her as a brood bitch.

I sometimes feel a bit silly when the dogs are out in the country, as countrymen usually call their borders Gip, Vic, and other one-syllable names. So mine are also known as Wiv and Widge, and are quite happy to answer to both.

Sometimes a posh name isn't such a bad thing, as long as it is seen to refer to a dog. A recent article in *Dog World* told the story of Billy, a typical Border, who was being exercised on an extending lead. He vanished down a foxhole with his owner hanging on for dear life and trying to wind him in, shouting loudly 'Stop it, Billy, please don't!' A gallant farmer, hearing her cries, came rushing over to rescue her, as he was certain she was being raped.

Collar

By law, every dog must have a collar with some form of identification. Mine proudly carry the National Canine Defence League's disc, which has an inscription stating that vet's fees are guaranteed if they should be injured and the owner can't be found.

The collar should be loose enough to be comfortable but not loose enough to slip off easily. As I found out at the polo match in the incident that I described in the previous chapter, Borders are adept at ridding themselves of loose collars! (See also **Identification**.)

This lively Border Terrier is carrying a Gumabone® Plaque Attacker™ from the Nylabone range. It is sensible to choose toys that will be safe and healthy for your growing pup.   Photo: Karen Taylor

Puppy toys

There are many toys on the market, but do beware of those 'indestructible' toys with a bell inside. Any Border Terrier worth its salt will have the toy broken open and be attempting to eat the bell within a few minutes. They love chewing shoes, so keep old ones as treats for them. Don't let puppies chew string as they have been known to swallow this, with disastrous vet bills as a consequence. Let them worry old socks, the older and smellier the better, but make sure they are made of pure wool or cotton; nylon can damage the teeth.

If you decide to buy special toys for your new puppy, choose those which will help its development. The Nylabone range, which helps to promote healthy, tartar-free teeth in a dog, has already been mentioned. (See also **Toys.**)

Bed

Puppies will chew anything, and bedding has a specially nice flavour. The best puppy basket is a cardboard box lined with torn newspaper. This can be changed when wet, or replaced if chewed to pieces, and costs nothing to renew.

Like most dogs, Borders consider the only place for their sleep to be your bed so, when your dog outgrows the cardboard box, it will need a bed of its own. Today beanbags are very popular. Buy one with a dark cover (a light colour looks dirty after day one) and with a zip so this can be washed frequently.

Like most dogs, Borders will consider the only place for their sleep to be on your bed. Widget would certainly agree!

Experts warn that if the dog sleeps in a wooden dog box lined with straw the straw should be changed every week. Never use wood shavings or sawdust as these can cause breathing problems and be poisonous to a dog. If you are using old clothing take off buttons and trimmings.

Sleep

Sleep is vitally important; in fact a dog can die if it doesn't get enough. Puppies have a habit of dropping off just where they have been playing, often right where you might put your feet.

Having the bad luck to live underneath a restaurateur, who would return at 3.00 am and play his quadraphonic stereo system at full blast, I used to bless the months he went off to Los Angeles and I had peaceful nights. On one occasion, when I was looking after my parents' dog when they were on holiday, I had to take him to the vet as he seemed off colour.

'This dog is sick - he is suffering from lack of sleep,' said Mr Maurice, looking at me accusingly. Then he told me dogs died if they didn't get enough sleep.

Pleas to the restaurateur did nothing; ringing the doorbell produced a bucket of water on my head. So I phoned the police, went

Let sleeping dogs lie - they need their beauty sleep.
Photo: Mick O'Shea

in and soaked myself with water, and the police arrived to find me in floods - of tears. My neighbour was sternly told to keep the peace and the dog and I had undisturbed nights after this.

Training

People say it is difficult to train Borders Terriers, perhaps because what they mean by 'training' is asking them to perform tricks. In that case, they are forgetting that a Border has been bred to think for itself when working alone, and is far too intelligent to be taken in by someone wanting to turn it into a party showpiece.

Tricks? No. Training for work? Yes, although Borders work instinctively.

This was shown when I was moving house and the removal men took down a forgotten fox's mask from the top of a cupboard. My Border puppies had never seen a fox, but launched themselves at the mask. The removal man thought they were after him and fled, hotly pursued by two Furies trying to latch on to the mask he still held in his hand. To this day, if I go anywhere near the cupboard where the mask once sat, my dogs hear and come tearing into the bedroom to try and get at their enemy.

Generally Border Terriers are easy to train, provided they think the training is sensible and not designed to turn them into performing dogs. If your Border does not want to obey your commands, it might be because either it is bored or it thinks you have asked it to do something unnecessary. We can't expect Borders to think for themselves when working deep underground and then to lose all powers of reasoning when above ground.

If your Border realises that you don't like something it has done it will think carefully of the consequences if it wants to repeat the misdemeanour. It is the tone of voice that tells your Border you are cross. Border owner David Brown just had to say to his dog, Nigel, 'Do you want a smack?' and Nigel immediately stopped whatever mayhem he was creating.

That isn't to say that Borders are always well-behaved to our way of thinking. As has been said before, a Border is bred to think for itself when working, and therefore if there is something happening which a Border thinks is of concern, off it will go. It may be instinct. If only we knew instinctively where they had gone and when they would deign to return!

Borders will wait for you - for so long. But catch a sniff of 'work' and they are off, only to return when they think their work is finished, and not understanding in the slightest why you are so angry.

It is no use shouting unnecessarily at your Borders; they won't forgive or forget. Eignwyre Enchantress was a superb Border and one of her progeny, who would wet herself if anyone shouted at her, was fearless when working and suffered terrible wounds without a murmur.

Spend a few minutes each day training your Border to sit, stay, come to heel and walk properly on the lead and you will soon have a well-trained dog. After this, it is fun to join dog training classes. Your vet will have details on his or her notice-board, or your dog's breeder may know of classes in your area.

Jumping

Dogs that jump up at visitors are a menace, so they should be trained at an early age to welcome guests with a tail wag, not to ruin tights or frighten children. Tell them 'Sit!' when you answer the door, with much praise when they do this. It will come!

Excavations

If only one could harness a Border puppy's desire to dig to Australia one would have a ready-made plough at very little cost. One friend has devised a way of stopping her dogs from digging up the whole garden by adapting an idea from Desmond Morris's book. She watches from a window and, when the puppy gets near the prize plants, she throws a glass of warm water or a soft beanbag near it. It associates this annoying occurrence with digging, and often this will stop its efforts.

If you think this is too drastic, another friend gently lifts up the puppy as soon as it starts digging and puts it in a special area where it can dig to its heart's content. However, as digging could be a sign of boredom, it is a good idea to have something to occupy the puppy and take its mind off excavating.

Transition

All too soon, though, your puppy will be an adult dog; although Borders still keep many of their puppy traits and tricks...

The famous 'animal watcher' Desmond Morris says the dog is a fascinating animal, but so familiar that we take it for granted. Watch your Border and see how its behaviour sometimes mimics your own and is sometimes totally dog-like and sometimes exclusive to Borders. Morris is right when he says 'terriers are the small vermin-killers... [with an] unusually stubborn and independent personality, originally linked to the need for them to keep after their prey when isolated and working alone'.

Boredom

Borders, being such active dogs, suffer from this problem more than most. Their wants are simple: something to chase, chew or worry, and frequent walks. Left on their own, Borders get up to mischief, so be warned.

My Grandfather tells the tale of one of his Borders who managed to climb onto the dining room table, launch itself across a 2m gap and land neatly on the sideboard, where it demolished a 2.5kg joint of beef. The puppy was less than a year old.

Then there was the friend who thought she had left a chicken cooling on top of the stove, but couldn't find it. It wasn't until she saw a greasy patch on the floor with a small feather in one corner that she worked out that her dog had climbed onto a chair and taken a flying leap, up half a metre and across 2m, to demolish the chicken, bones and all.

Nigel's owner (see Chapter 11) thought he was going mad; he was sure he remembered food, but when he went to the fridge nothing was there. Then one day he noticed a sausage paper on the floor and worked out that Nigel had gone to the fridge, eaten sausages, bacon or whatever he fancied, and then closed the door so that Master wouldn't know what had happened.

Sulking

Border Terriers are adaptable, living happily wherever their home is, be it in the countryside or town. Noses down, tails wagging, they are a very happy breed, but woe betide you if they think you have scolded them without just cause.

Borders sulk, and owners will tell you that it can be days before your Border thinks you have been ostracised for long enough and deigns to acknowledge you again if it thinks you have been unreasonable in scolding it. Frank Wildman says one of his Borders sulked for two weeks after he scolded him. Frank owns the Ragsdale affix, and I am pleased that his famous Blueberry is grandmother to my Widget, whose father was Ragsdale Why Not. (Now what makes me think that is what Frank says when offered a drink?!)

Some owners say that they give a light gentle smack, but it is difficult to catch the culprit, and these tough little dogs think this is play. If you are going to speak sternly or 'read' a lecture, do it immediately after the puppy has misbehaved. Puppies and dogs live in the present and won't remember that they have misbehaved even a few seconds later. But admonish them when they know they have misbehaved and they get the message - before they bound off with tails wagging.

Waiting

I have been told time and time again that waiting for the return of a Border who has decided to 'go walkabout' is one of the major problems of Border ownership. However carefully they are fenced in at home and watched while they are on walks (even familiar walks), they can still suddenly do a disappearing act. They behave impeccably for months, even years, until they suddenly catch a whiff of a smell that means work or romance. They wait until your back is turned - and they're off.

Everyone knows the dreadful moment when you've called and called your Border and begin to realise that it has probably gone to ground you know not where. One time Winston disappeared into the tents near the Serpentine; we could hear cries and, eventually, a small boy found him trapped by his collar, which was twisted round one of the underground tent supports.

So whether you work your dogs or take them for walks anywhere there just might be a hole, it is worthwhile belonging to the Fell and Moorland Working Terrier Club. This club provides a lifeline of calm support and, if the dog is trapped underground, will hire earth-moving equipment to dig it out.

You get some funny looks in the country. As a travel writer I often visit and write about hotels in areas I don't know. If the dogs are with me I ask the landlord where I can exercise them avoiding badgers and other 'enemies'. I am pointed in one direction, and find that the hillside is littered with sett holes; I have been sent that way as people think I am baiting and expect me to go in the opposite direction from that they point out.

One day these dogs will land me in serious trouble, but I wouldn't have it any other way.

Parks

One advantage of London's parks is that many of them, like Hyde Park and Battersea Park, are fenced in. That doesn't mean that you shouldn't watch your dogs at all times but, if you are near the edge and it hears something interesting, it can look through the railings and watch what is going on.

Once one hardly ever saw another Border in London but, since Brannigan's appearance at Crufts and the Border featured on *All Creatures Great and Small*, their numbers have increased considerably. There were four of them in our small, local West Park in Chelsea the other afternoon. People used to come up and ask me what sort of dog mine was or say, 'What an attractive mongrel!' Now, they come and tell me how much they like Borders.

Dog messes are a nuisance, and thank heavens for plastic bags! One advantage of living in London is that many of the parks have dog loos, where one chats sociably with other owners while dogs are sniffing around. There are also special bins in which to place the mess so that you do not have to carry it home in the plastic bag. However, Urban Fox also lives in London's parks, and he is not so careful about cleaning up his mess. Not only do people then think they see dog dirt and blame our animals, but dogs consider it a most elegant perfume and love to roll in it.

Identification

You will never be able to keep your Border by your side at all times, so how to ensure that if it disappears you can find it again? By law all dogs have to wear a collar carrying a means of identification; usually this is an engraved disc. Some of the more popular methods are:

Discs: The National Canine Defence League (NCDL) has a 'Lucky Dog Club'. Membership gives your dog a strong engraved disc with your address and telephone number on one side; they advise against putting your dog's name on the disc as a thief will know it and it might go against you if the dog is stolen and you have to prove ownership.

On the other side is a message guaranteeing that in the event of an accident the NCDL will pay the vet's fees. You are still liable for the costs, but valuable time could be saved by operating on the dog immediately, even if you can't be contacted.

You also get a small card to carry around, telling people whom to contact if you are injured or die.

Membership currently costs £10 annually, and this includes free insurance cover, free disc and an interesting newsletter.

Register: National Pet Register will place your dog on a central register and give you a small, thick red plastic tag to put on its collar. On the tag is printed your dog's number and a number (0800 581553) for finders to call free of charge.

Chips: You may have taken off the collar, or it can work loose, so it is sensible to have a dog 'chipped'. Indentichip is a newish form of identification to help find lost or strayed dogs. Your vet inserts a microchip into the dog's neck; mine used a local anaesthetic, as she said Borders had much thicker skin than most dogs, and injecting the microchip might cause pain. The chip is inside a syringe and is injected into the back of the neck; once it is in place the dog can be identified if lost.

Each indentichip has its own number which can be scanned on any of over 2000 machines sited in Battersea Dogs Home, other charities that collect stray dogs, dog wardens' offices and RSPCA centres, and it is also recorded on a central computer with your details, plus alternative telephone numbers.

Amongst the first dogs to be 'chipped' were Oxo and Bisto, two Cocker Spaniels belonging to Her Majesty The Queen.

Dogs have to have an identification disc but, if the collar is lost or the disc falls off when you lose it, there is only your description with which to identify your pet. As few people actually know what a Border Terrier is, there are many stories of them being listed as 'mongrels' and possibly never collected. Identichip say that 50 per cent of strays are never reunited with owners since they cannot be identified. Given the way that Borders stray for miles, it seems a sensible idea, and The Kennel Club recommends this system for identification. Vets who offer indentichipping will have scanners of their own so, if your dog is in an accident and needs urgent treatment, the vet can contact you immediately.

Identichip say the chip cannot move or break and there is no discomfort for the pet. Battersea Dogs Home, the RSPCA and SSPCA now identichip every animal they re-home. Let thieves know your dog is 'chipped' as this is a means of identification if it is stolen. Identichip say they cover pets for third party public liability insurance up to £1,000,000.

But don't forget that even if it has been 'chipped' your dog must also carry identification on its collar.

Strays

Recently Battersea Dogs Home and concerned charities have tried to alert the public to the fact that 'a dog is for life' and, happily for concerned dog lovers, this seems to be working. Battersea Dogs Home has declared a fall in admissions, with fewer owners abandoning pets.

Borders are not often seen at Battersea. One year four Borders were recorded, but one was a scamp that used to go walkabout and, when he was bored, turn up at Battersea and wait for his owners to claim him.

Moving

When you sell your home and move, don't forget to alert any agency with which your dog is registered (see **Identification**) about its change of address. A new home is strange for a dog, too, and dogs have been known to try to return to their original homes. New neighbours might not understand dogs, so it is helpful to introduce yourself and your dogs to them.

National Pet Week

This is a registered charity to promote responsible pet ownership and to make people aware of the benefit of pets to people. In an attempt to counteract the anti-dog feeling affecting our lives, this charity runs different events once a year to bring owners together and inform the public of the benefits of owning a pet.

They welcome help with running a function during National Pet Week, such as a talk in a local school, a display at a dog training club, a sponsored dog walk or anything else you can devise. The address and telephone number can be found in **Useful Addresses.**

Feeding

As they are grow up you will notice that your dogs demand food less often - even Borders Terriers! Eventually they will be down to a main meal, usually late afternoon, and perhaps a very small meal or some biscuits at breakfast time, especially if they are going out to work that day.

Dogs are meat eaters, and if you are a vegetarian consider this. Desmond Morris says in one of his books: 'A recent trend to give pet dogs vegetarian diets is even worse than all-meat diets.' The dog is an omnivore, and needs a balanced menu, which should include roughage and vegetables in small quantities.

Some owners think their dogs should fast once a week, believing this replicates conditions in the wild. However, if we followed this to its logical end, you would sling a dead fox, sheep, or whatever animal in the garden and let your dogs gorge on this, then leave them one or several days before slinging in another carcass. (Incidentally, the dogs would get their vitamins from the food inside the gut.)

Bit extreme, isn't it? So vets will tell you to feed every day. After all, we thrive best on regular meals, and there is no reason to differentiate from dogs' needs.

Barking

Dogs reflect their owner's moods, and living in London makes one suspicious of strangers. The dogs have cottoned on and always bark when there is someone at the door or near by, which gets one a reputation amongst a certain type of unwelcome visitor. However, if you don't need a guard dog, you will have to train your dog, gently but firmly, to be quiet, if only for the sake of the neighbours. In a survey by BUPA into noise pollutants, barking dogs topped the list of 48 of the most maddening noises, ahead of pneumatic drills, rush-hour traffic and even Concorde.

Local authorities have a statutory duty to investigate complaints about continual barking, and environmental health officers can take legal proceedings against owners whose dogs offend; if they are found guilty the top fine is £20,000. It would take much time and reams of letters to reach this stage, but your time and money could obviously be better spent.

According to Peter Neville, Hon Secretary of the Association of Pet Behaviour Counsellors, a dog will bark because it is excited, alarmed, defending its territory, suffering from separation anxiety, sick or just bored. The most common incidence of boredom is caused when a dog is left alone all day whilst the owner is out at work.

Sometimes it must be frustrating for dogs when their owners don't take notice of their warnings. Mine were tied up outside Café Gloriette, opposite Harrods, where I was sitting at a table on the pavement. Widget started jumping up and down; I thought he was trying to say he was bored and just told him to be a good boy and lie down. When it was time to pay I discovered that someone must have used a long hook to grab my handbag and Widget had been trying to attract my attention to let me know what was happening. When I went to explain, the management were very unsympathetic, saying 'This often happens', and demanding their money. Asking why they didn't have a tent card on tables warning clients to beware, I was answered with a shrug. I returned to pay, but that is the last time I will ever go there until they alert their clients.

Another time there was a terrific racket and, looking out into the street, I could see two football supporters twisting the dynamo lights off my cycle. I had had over £280 worth of damage done by fans in one season, so I dialled 999. In one of the largest cities in the world, when there is trouble with football louts there aren't enough policemen around to answer these calls. It took 21 minutes for 999 to answer; the operator had five telephones going to try to get through. Complaints to authorities, including MPs, produced the answer that, if you choose to live near a football ground, you have to take the consequences. Yet if a dog chases a cat the owner receives a stern telling off, and recently someone who contravened a bye-law while walking their dog in the local cemetery was fined £100. Meanwhile, football fans who had done thousands of pounds worth of damage were let off with a caution.

Dogs just don't understand humans sometimes.

Sex

Yes, this is often uppermost in a male Border's mind, especially in the spring. Unluckily for him, female dogs will only accept sex at certain times, leaving a potentially frustrated dog. Until the next squirrel hops across its line of vision, that is.

Sometimes the frustration becomes very bad and male Borders have been known to go off their food. One well-known authority has said, 'If your Border is off its food, you must seriously consider it is either in love, or dead.'

In his book *Dogwatching* Desmond Morris says:

> When the long-awaited period of female heat does arrive, the bitch spends the first phase of it living up to her name. In fact there will only be a few days in the early spring, and again in the autumn, when she will accept the male's advances. So, for the lucky male domestic dog, which has not been castrated by his owners, has not been brought forcibly to heel at every sight of a bitch, and has not been kept shut in when a bitch is on heat in the neighbourhood, which has not been attacked and driven off by rival dogs, and has not been rejected by the typically choosy bitch ... there will be only 50 out of 52 weeks of sexual frustration during the year.

I can't think why my male dogs are such happy animals!

As far as the bitch is concerned, if she hasn't been spayed, she frequently has her *amours* reduced to the equivalent of a '"short time" in a red light district'.

However, if we allowed dogs a free rein to indulge their sexual appetites we would have millions of unwanted stray dogs, so there has to be a balance. Just be ready with ideas to distract your dog when he has sex on his mind.

Noise

Dogs, particularly Border Terriers, can sense changes in the atmosphere and, if both of mine come to sit by my side whilst I am working rather than lying at my feet, I know thunder is imminent. Sure enough, a few minutes later the storm will break, and two normally very brave dogs sit trembling under my feet.

This all started one Bonfire Night, when a neighbour set off rockets from upper window-sills and one flew right over the three-storey house and landed in my back garden on top of Widget. Since then, unexplained loud noises worry them.

Other countries ban the sale of fireworks or only allow official firework displays, yet every November we allow millions of pets to have a miserable time. Not to mention the children who are injured and the fire brigades that are called out to 300 per cent more fires than on an average night. Local police and fire stations would like to ban fireworks but say no-one listens to them.

One 6 November I thought all fireworks had finished, but one went off in the street and, tearing his lead out of my hand, Wyvern took off. He was heading towards a major road but, when I reached the corner, I could see nothing. For five hours I searched the roads and under cars looking for a flattened body. Eventually neighbours helping in the search heard whimpers in their basement and found him crouching at the bottom of a 2.5m drop, unable to get out.

Perhaps the best way to stop dogs being frightened by fireworks is to get local councils to ban the sale of fireworks to children and encourage one gigantic party in a local park. Wandsworth does this, and people come from all over London to watch and take part.

Grooming

Borders are usually easy to look after. A few minutes a day with a brush, and the coat is generally kept in good condition, although vet Karen Young, speaking at a Breed Club event, said you should not brush too much as you can take out the undercoat. She also recommends Evening Primrose capsules (one a day) as being good for the coat. However, now I know how much these cost, I give myself a daily dose as well.

Your vet will show you what else needs to be done, except for plucking or stripping. 'Stripping a Border is like painting the Forth Bridge: just when you come to the end you have to start all over again,' sighed a friend.

Border coats can get an 'overblown' look: all hairy and bush-like. This usually means the coat needs stripping. You can either ask friends' advice about the best local professional groomer or try to do the job yourself. Do ask advice before using a local pet parlour; Borders have been known to leave having been shaved rather than plucked.

If you have time, or if you live near your dog's breeder, you can ask their advice and, if possible, get them to show you how it is done. I always knew that when I turned up on Frank Wildman's doorstep he would look at my dog with horror and take him outside to the stripping table. Half an hour later, an impeccably-groomed dog would bounce into the room.

Stripping is removing hair from its follicle while it is in telogen, or the shedding phase of the hair cycle. As you remove this dead hair, a new fresh coat comes up. Many people say this method brings about a truer, richer hair colour and the desired rough texture of the coat.

Frank showed me how to take a small amount of the longer hairs in the fingers and pluck. An old pair of leather gloves can help prevent sore fingers, but most people will say that stripping combs or knives are no use.

Many Border Terrier clubs have teaching sessions when some kind member will tell novices like myself how to do it. If you can bear the shame, turning up to one of these sessions with the scruffiest dog will bring a gleam into the demonstrator's eye, and your dog will be given a superb grooming whilst used for demonstration purposes.

Fleas

These are becoming more and more of a problem. Centrally-heated houses with fitted carpet are a flea's idea of Millionaire's Row housing, and Karen Young reminds owners using flea spray not to forget to spray the carpet cleaner bag as well as the house.

Two years ago my vet recommended Program to counteract this nuisance. This tablet is given once a month throughout the late spring and summer, and it seems to do the trick. It acts like a contraceptive pill for a flea, staying in the dog's blood so that, when the flea bites and sucks, it is rendered sterile. It is especially good if you don't want to spray the house. For the first time since coming to live next to the Brompton Cemetery, which is a haunt of flea-carrying foxes, I have hardly scratched all summer. Previously my skin was a mass of bites, as fleas seem to love my blood, but for the last two summers there has been a bite about once a month - no more.

At a recent Border Terrier Day with The Southern Border Terrier Club, Karen Young said:

If it weren't for fleas, many vets would be out of business. The vast majority of dogs with fleas you don't notice, but dogs can be allergic to fleas. A dog starts scratching in spring, rubbing its face or chewing its feet. (Incidentally most fleas found on dogs are cat fleas, capable of jumping 35cm.) It's the house that has got the problem; spray the house and be careful if you have fish tanks that spray doesn't get into the water. The spray should give protection for up to three months.

Dogs and the law

You are responsible for your dog's behaviour. As has already been said, one of the most common complaints against dog owners is incessant barking, often caused by leaving a dog alone all day.

Dogs that worry livestock are a problem, and farmers that suspect their stock is being worried have no hesitation in shooting on sight. You could be in trouble, because a Border Terrier can look just like a fox. Even if you were subsequently proven to have had your dog under control, and it hadn't done any damage, it would be dead. If you want to know more, read the Dogs (Protection of Livestock) Act 1953. Livestock include cattle, sheep, goats, swine, horses and poultry, and Agricultural Land covers market gardens, allotments, nursery grounds and orchards.

Incidentally it is a defence if the livestock are trespassing on your land and the dog is owned by or in the charge of the owner of the land trespassed upon, provided he does not cause the dog to attack.

Third Party insurance is essential and if you belong to a Breed Club they can usually arrange this for a reasonable sum. The Southern Border Terrier Club arranges this for £5 per member's dog per year, and most other clubs have similar arrangements.

Living in the heart of the country, with a lush lawn that was a magnet to the next-door farmer's cows, my father was constantly waging war against cattle that trespassed on our land. One day the dogs started barking. We looked out and saw the lawns full of cows, so rushed in to wake up the parents.

'I know it's 1 April!' said Father, as he turned over and went back to sleep. Then of course the dogs and we children were blamed when he saw that day's damage.

Country code for dogs

The National Farmers' Union and the Countryside Commission have prepared a code for dogs and their owners:

- Take your dog to training classes.
- Keep your dog on a lead until you are confident that he is under control, and keep the lead on at all times where there are farm animals.
- Never allow your dog to chase anything - it is a habit which is hard to break.
- Never allow your dog out on his/her own - and make sure you know where he/she is at all times.
- Know what to do in the case of an accident happening to your dog in a place where veterinary attention is not immediately available.

Study the Country Code for yourself and train your dog in country awareness. According to the Battersea Dogs' Home book, if a dog is harmed in any way an owner can bring an action for damages in respect of the injury in the same way as he can for himself, his car or any other property.

Tradesmen

Introduce your dog to the postman and milkman at an early age, to avoid accidents. Nowadays postmen don't deliver letters to dog owners whose animals threaten them. (On second thoughts, it does stop one getting bills.)

Choking

However carefully you look after your dog, it will pick up most things in its mouth, as a way of identifying what it is. This could have dire consequences and sometimes you might have to be cruel to be kind.

If your dog seems to have swallowed a foreign body that is lodged in its throat, one vet says:

> ... grasp its tongue and pull it forward, and then attempt to pull out the foreign body with your fingers, or failing that tweezers or cooking tongs. The dog will be fighting for breath, and might even try to bite you - you just have to realise that you must act quickly if the dog has any chance of recovering.

And if it is bitten by a wasp or bee it is straight to the vet's for an anti-histamine injection.

Summer

Borders are bred for the cold northern climate and our hot summers are not their favourite season. Don't forget to change your dog's water frequently and check that it hasn't drunk the bowl dry. Don't worry if not all the food is eaten. Just remove it, as it will go off very quickly. One of my Borders won't eat until about 9.00 pm, and although vets say they should be fed with enough time to digest their food before bed, this late feeding hour seems to suit him when it is hot.

Never leave your dog in a parked car. The interior can become uncomfortably warm in no time, and there have been many cases of dogs dying in cars.

Don't forget to de-flea your Border, and check for grass seeds, which can get into eyes, ears or paws and can cause pain if not dealt with immediately.

Tar on roads melts and can burn their pads. I was horrified to see one of the dogs had bleeding paws; commandeering an abandoned supermarket trolley, we wheeled him off to the vet. It was during one of our hot summers, and the vet said he was about the sixth dog she had seen that day with the same problem, caused by hot pavements. So for the next few days a very spoilt dog was wheeled around in the trolley. He loved it.

If you are going out, provide shelter from the sun; if the dogs are in the garden, make sure all chemicals, weedkillers and sprays are locked away.

If your pet seems to be suffering from heat stroke, don't throw water over it, as the shock might be bad enough to kill. Take the dog to the vet immediately. You can put a towel moistened in cold water on its back or head. Show dogs are often seen sporting damp cloths before they go into the ring.

Winter

Salt put down on pavements and roads can get in between pads and cut them, so it is advisable to wash paws gently after a walk.

Teeth

It is always distressing to have to have teeth extracted from a dog because they are decayed. Like humans, dogs need to keep their teeth clean but, like humans, some dogs have stronger teeth than others. There are various remedies and, if you use toothpaste, Logic makes a brand that doesn't need a brush. You put some on your finger, brush it round the teeth (not forgetting the back ones) and, as it is mildly abrasive, the action as the dog licks it off is supposed to clean the teeth.

Toys

Dogs are like children; they like their own toys and have their own favourites.

Trying to be clever, when Nylabone gave me some lovely toys to try out with my dogs I took several out of their packaging together. I thought if I put them on the floor the dogs would choose the one they liked best. Of course, you've guessed: they both wanted the same toy - and still do. Let one go to the corner where their toys are stored to pick up one to play with, and his brother will wake up from a deep sleep and come bounding up to try and play with the same toy; then sit watching until he can dart in and take the toy away.

Amongst their favourite toys is a Nylabone® Plaque Attacker™ dental floss; this is extremely successful, and has been chewed and chewed. It is good to see this rope being used because the special strands are a doggy form of dental floss which helps remove tartar from teeth. The manufacturers say it is non-absorbent and can be washed, boiled, autoclaved or sterilised. Though why bother? It will be dirty again within a few minutes.

'I've got it this time!' Wyvern on the beach with his Nylabone® Plaque Attacker™ Dental Floss.

Wyvern in particular will come and sit by my side, just staring at me. Eventually I sense his presence, and then great tail waggings, as he leads me to the toy corner. I have to pick up the Nylabone dental floss, and he loves to tug on this. Borders' teeth and necks are so strong that I can lift him up and even swing him from side to side and he won't let go.

This game could go on for hours, but I get tired out after five minutes and leave him worrying the rope. I am told that this is wrong; I should assert my authority by taking the rope away. If only I had the strength!

Widget is calmer, and likes nothing better than to get something called a 'Dental Dinosaur' between his paws, crunching away on this. Sometimes they will chew away at one of the ordinary Nylabones, especially if another dog visits and shows interest, but the favourites come out time and time again.

Be careful with toys given to dogs; Borders have such a strong bite that some of the squeaky toys in particular can be dangerous, as the dog can chew them to pieces in moments. Anne Roslin-Williams, in her book on Borders, emphasises that nylon socks are not good toys; the filaments get trapped in the Borders' stomach. But the Nylabone product is made of a different type of nylon.

Insurance

On the relatively few occasions when Borders need the services of the vet it always seems to be for something expensive to treat, so health insurance makes sense. After some problems with another company when it took months to settle a simple claim, I now use Pet Plan, recommended by The Kennel Club. If you want more information you can call their Freephone number: 0800 212 248

Did you know?

Covering Husky Dog racing in France, I came across the sponsors, Royal Canin. They make prepared dog food, and pressed lots of samples on me; I didn't like to be rude and say my dogs don't like this type of food, so I took the packets. You've guessed it - they loved it.

However, I am mentioning them because they have some good handout free sheets on such topics as Puppy Nutrition, Energy and Dietary Related Problems. They also have a fact sheet with useful information, such as that dogs are 10 times more likely to be allergic to a new carpet or certain grasses than to food ingredients.

Charities for Borders - and others

National Canine Defence League: (See section on **Identification**)

Border Terrier Welfare: (See Chapter 2)

Royal Society for the Prevention of Cruelty to Animals (RSPCA): Every year this society rescues hundreds of abandoned puppies - luckily seldom Borders. However, anyone who loves dogs must be sickened by cruelty to any animal, and recently, under the slogan 'Money can buy him Love', the charity launched an appeal to help fund their work. Twenty pounds will help keep an RSPCA Inspector out on Britain's roads for a day.

Wyvern is a typical friendly Border, and one day I noticed him socialising with a German Shepherd that was wandering outside the local grocers. Wyvern was perplexed, which made me take a second look at the German Shepherd. I found he was covered in sores. His owner came and, when I asked how the dog had become so ill, said: 'He's perfectly all right!' and refused to say any more. We followed the German Shepherd home and, feeling foolish, I phoned the RSPCA. They came, taking away the dog but not telling the owner who had informed on him, and eventually he was prosecuted. The RSPCA kept me informed, so I didn't feel like a 'nosy parker'.

Petsavers: This is the Clinical Studies Trust Fund of The British Small Animal Veterinary Association, dedicated to improving the health and welfare of all pet animals. Founded by a group of veterinary surgeons to advance the science of small animal medicine and surgery, the charity leads the fight against diseases such as cancer, blindness, and viral infections.

Projects the association has funded include a cancer therapy scholarship at the University of Cambridge, and the results of their work are quickly passed on to vets in practice so that all pets can benefit.

Fitzroy enjoying a day out.

Visiting
the vet

A Croxton Smith called Borders 'Knights In Russet' and in *The Field* of September 1942 he says their record is so honourable that

> ... no one would deny them the right to be admitted to any order of chivalry. They are terrors for their size, and should they have a bad mauling one day, they are in harness again as soon as their wounds have healed.

My Winston (more formally Clystland Bow Bell) would have agreed with him. His best friend was Bennett, a Standard Poodle/Irish Wolfhound cross. The two played happily in West Park in Chelsea, sometimes sharing their romps with Chloe, a lovely Old English Sheepdog.

One day Chloe came into season, and Winston was extremely interested, as was Bennett. Winston, the size of Bennett's head, decided he was the man for Chloe and started to fight Bennett for her. A friend rushed us to the vet and Winston, lacerated and bleeding, gazed defiantly up at her.

'Why don't you take on something your own size?' she asked him.

One friend who had arrived to find our doorstep covered in Winston's blood, with a trail across the street, was just about to call the police to say murder had been committed when, luckily, we returned. Needless to say, Winston tried to get out to find Chloe on his return. He and Bennett made it up, but we warned all our friends to let us know if any of their bitches was in season.

Incidentally, it was this incident that showed me why Borders are described as 'blue'. Winston had to submit to having his head shaved so that the vet could get at his wounds, and the skin underneath was definitely a shade of blue.

My two go to The Ark Veterinary Clinic in Pont Street, London, where the Veterinary Surgeon, Dorte Beierholm, has a beautiful apricot Persian, Mookie, and an Alsatian. The first time we met Mookie, Wyvern led me into the surgery. My two love visiting and always dash in to see Dorte. This time, however, Mookie was making a stately inspection of the reception room, which was rudely interrupted as Wyvern strained at the lead, trying to give chase.

He was given a strong lecture that chasing your vet's prized pet wasn't the best way to build up a good patient/doctor relationship.

Some time later, Mookie acted as a barometer when Wyvern was very ill. Walking in Battersea Park I looked round and couldn't see him; retracing my steps, I was met by some strangers who recognised me and the dogs and had come to look for me. They pointed out where a pathetic bundle was huddled up, and it was obvious he was in considerable pain but couldn't say what or where. My guess was that he had investigated a bitch and the owner had kicked him hard with steel-capped boots.

With great care, I took him to Dorte, who spent hours examining him, X-raying and testing, but couldn't find out what was wrong. She said that the trouble with Borders is they won't show pain, so she couldn't find out why and where it hurt. It was obvious that he had been very badly bruised internally, and I had to leave him at the surgery and was told to phone, not visit, as he had to have complete quiet. Each morning there was no change - until one day a joyful nurse said: 'He's taking an interest in Mookie and tried to get at her.'

He was obviously on the road to recovery and I could take him home. We never did discover what had caused this condition, but to this day he has difficulty in jumping. Unfortunately he still chases bitches.

Anne Roslin-Williams, in her book *The Border Terrier*, says, 'In extreme pain or fear it will not show this by screaming but by a general stiffening and the straight ahead stare.' Sometimes mine show pain by licking their lips.

Some Borders love to fight each other. Luckily this seems to be rare, but Mrs Hamilton, writing to Mrs Twist in 1942, mentions she had a sweet little bitch who had lived happily with Renrut May and her daughter Mayfly for months when 'one night without warning or previous scraps, they killed her in the night'.

My Winston and Wellington got on really well in general. However, on certain occasions they would be walking along quietly on the lead when suddenly one must have said something insulting to the other, and I would have a screaming ball of terriers at the end of leads. My inclination would have been to let them scrap it out and teach each other a lesson, but Londoners were so shocked to see the fighting that I had to separate them. Then it would be months before a repeat performance.

Poison

This has been a problem for years; in a report in *Dog World* in 1945 Mr Hancock reported that he had lost his bitch, Daffin, who picked up poison while out on a shooting trip.

One has to be careful, as Borders regard almost anything as food. Wellington once went rooting around at the back of a hotel. That evening, as we went down to dinner, he seemed very quiet. This was so out of character that suddenly, in the middle of eating, I went up to see him - and found him in a coma. He was rushed to the nearest vet, who managed to save him. The hotel had put down poison to kill rats and nearly killed a Border instead.

Traps

Thankfully there are fewer and fewer of these dreadful instruments, although what farmers will do if hunting is stopped...

Borders frequently used to get themselves into trouble in traps; one was Vanda Daredevil (aptly named) who belonged to Mr Fielden. Missing for five days, he was eventually found with his leg caught in a trap; the foot had turned septic but, thanks to careful veterinary treatment, he recovered.

Ailments

Before you buy a puppy, do realise that it is more than possible it might be in an accident or have an infection. Kennel Cough is one ailment that dogs in London seem to pick up from each other, and you hear the dread words from the vet before they tell you what is wrong: 'Are you insured?'

Dogs must have their inoculations; it is heart-breaking to have a dog suffer from some of the horrid diseases that would have been no problem if only the dog's vaccinations had been up-to-date.

Immediate treatment needed

Battersea Dogs Home publishes a list of some of the emergency conditions that require immediate veterinary treatment: cardiac failure, bone fractures, respiratory difficulties, whelping (birthing) complications, haemorrhage, prolonged diarrhoea, wounds, convulsions, shock, urine retention, heat-stroke, pain, burns or scalds, hernia strangulation, coma or loss of consciousness, swallowing a foreign body, fractures, grass seed in ear, skull damage, intussusception, and others. It makes one shiver just to read these. But - touch wood! - Borders are generally healthy.

Car Accidents

If you live near or by a main road, before buying a puppy do realise that it is going to cost you money (a lot!) to fence in your garden. Borders love digging, and will dig down under a fence for some way if they want to get out. So take a walk around the garden and get an estimate for a good fence.

One day Wellington, aged seven months, just took off when playing with his friends in the park. Slithering through the railings, he jumped down two metres and ran across the road right under the wheels of a - luckily - light van.

We arrived on the scene to find a white-faced van driver and a little body on the road. He was still alive so, in fear and trembling, we rolled him gently onto a coat to be carried to the local surgery, accompanied by most of the street. Laid out on the vet's table, he didn't look too good. We all crowded in, much to the vet's annoyance.

'Who owns this dog?' He glared at us. 'What this dog needs is peace and quiet!' He ushered everyone out.

Eventually I was allowed to stay so as to be able to relay the official bulletin to everyone. Luckily, after an X-ray, the vet said nothing was broken; he was so young that the bones had probably just bent. So we took the van driver off to recover, and he was driven home after many doggy stories in the local pub.

Actors

Some Borders would qualify for the Royal Shakespeare Company without any trouble. If they think they can get extra food or sympathy out of owners, their thespian qualities are much in evidence.

Trak Fryer was describing what happens when their beloved Border puppies go off to their homes, and how gloomy they and their Borders feel. Coming in one day they found Top Dog lying in front of the fire apparently crippled in his back legs and unable to stand unaided.

> A quick check of bones and joints can find nothing wrong - so off we rush to the vet. Borders have a reputation for stoicism, but this is rather misplaced in this individual who gives the same performance for a thorn in the foot as for a major injury. In fact, once when he was seriously hurt, he was given his dinner (which he wolfed down) and walked about for about for half an hour before they noticed!
>
> Tonight the vet is as puzzled as us by the mystery and 'bring him back tomorrow if he's any worse' is the best he can do. An even gloomier evening is spent punctuated by carrying Our Hero out at regular intervals for the necessary functions.
>
> The next day Boy Wonder drags himself painfully up the bed and gazes up with sorrowful eyes. When this produces no response, he shakes himself, wags his tail, jumps off the bed, leaps the puppy barrier and demands to go out...
>
> We celebrate April Fool's Day several times a year.

Snake bite

Living in countryside where adders lurked in the bracken, we were used to seeing them slide around. One day Widger had a fight with one and was badly bitten. In those days one relied on local lore, rather like homeopathic medicine today. He was rushed to a Gypsy, who sucked the wound and bound it up with some herbs, and he had to stay for a week before we could collect him. Today vets have injections, but if you don't know the area and there is bracken, heath or moorland, or open sunny places in woodland, do watch out.

Friends who live in Kent say they have been warned not to walk their dogs on a local heath in the hot summers, since several dogs have been bitten. Luckily the dogs all recovered after treatment, but one of their owners whose dog disturbed a snake was badly bitten and spent 10 days in intensive care before she recovered.

Adders are sometimes known as vipers, and have a dark zig-zag stripe down their back, with an inverted 'V' mark on the backs of their heads. I always seem to find them in bracken, so now avoid this plant whenever it is hot.

In America snakes are more of a problem, and one of Alison Mountain's Borders died saving her owner's life when a poisonous snake prepared to strike. The snake was killed, but not before it had bitten the Border.

First aid kit

Basically the things you use for yourself are often used to treat dogs. Your vet will probably sell a simple kit if you don't have all the basics. Many human medicines are used for animals. Once when I was staying with a vet I had an eye infection. He examined the swollen eye. 'This is what I give to the cows so it should work on you,' was his ungallant remark. It did.

You should never give a dog any drug unless it has been prescribed specifi-cally for that dog. Dogs need much smaller portions, and some human drugs have dreadful effects on dogs. A dog can't tell you if it has an allergy to tablets. However, Acriflavine, disinfectant (suitably diluted), lint, bandages and cotton wool are always useful.

Sleep

This is essential for dogs as well as humans; in fact more so, as a dog deprived of sleep will soon die. Dogs sleep during the day as well as at night, so make sure your puppy has somewhere quiet, warm and free from draughts which is its own special quarters. Border pups will often suddenly flop down when chasing around and fall asleep where they fall, so beware of stepping on them!

Adult dogs also needs somewhere that is specially their own - even if they sleep on your bed at night.

Blue Cross

If you have been unlucky enough to lose your job, or there are other reasons why you can't afford to pay for veterinary treatment for your dog, the Blue Cross (see **Useful Addresses**) has four hospitals and clinics (three in London, and one in Grimsby, South Humberside) and a mobile clinic in Dublin, all dedicated to helping animals.

This charity was founded in 1897 as 'Our Dumb Friends' League' and stayed open during both World Wars. In fact the League actually served in Flanders in World War I, running veterinary units at the front for army horses and dogs.

Their hospital in Victoria was opened in 1906 and, during the blitz in the last

Border Terrier in World War 2. (By kind permission of the Blue Cross.)

war, it stayed open even during the worst of the bombing, treating over 110,000 stray dogs and cats. Then in the dreadful floods of 1952 the League was there helping lost and trapped animals; and during the next decade it helped re-house pit ponies replaced by machinery.

More than 50,000 free treatments a year are now provided by these hospitals and clinics, and in 1993 Blue Cross performed 6456 operations. In Victoria, London, they have the original animals' hospital with resident veterinary surgeons on call 24 hours a day, and they will take any animal; they just ask that if you can afford to pay you contribute the going rate.

There is another side to this charity, as some people have been lucky enough to find out. Pets have owners, and the Blue Cross's work is very much for them as well as for their animals. The free veterinary treatment provided in cases of hardship is just the tip of the iceberg. Their ambulance drivers check on the welfare of elderly owners, often struggling to cope on their own, and sometimes the only human contact these pet owners have is with the drivers.

Today Blue Cross is appealing for help to rebuild their hospital in Victoria, last refurbished 25 years ago. One way of helping is to become a Friend.

Cryptorchidism and monorchidism

As far back as 1955 a Sub-Committee of The Kennel Club met representatives of the British Veterinary Association (BVA) to discuss the subject.

The BVA had received reports that the incidence of cryptorchidism (failure of one or both testicles to descend to their normal position in the scrotum) in dogs was increasing and was being observed so regularly in a considerable number of breeds as to give rise to concern. I have owned two well-loved dogs with this condition, so I know from experience that the report was right when it went on to detail problems such as increased fat deposits and eunuch-like characteristics.

Tumours are a problem, and one of my dogs was operated on for this when a few months old. Ever since, he has treated strangers with suspicion. He has to know you well before he will give the usual affectionate Border greeting. After all, a stranger took him off and left him feeling very sore, so this Border is understandably cautious.

Worms

Considering the way Borders sniff around gutters and rubbish dumps it is perhaps surprising they don't pick up more dreadful diseases. However, worms are one horrible thing that every concerned owner should guard against. At your dog's annual 'MOT' at the vet's, you will be told about worming, and all that remains is to ensure your dog takes its tablets. Not so easy!

Borders have a habit of holding a tablet in the back of their mouth, and spitting this out an hour later when your back is turned. If you only have one dog this is not too much of a problem - except getting it back in again. But with my two, one of them swallows as good as gold and the other doesn't; and I can never find out who is the culprit. Life is made easier if you use a multi-wormer, as then you only have one tablet to administer.

Toxocariasis

Headlines in the press and comment on TV suggests that this disease, caused by contact with the eggs of the roundworm *Toxocara canis*, is causing blindness in thousands of children. However, Bradley Viner, Public Relations Officer with the British Small Animal Veterinary Association, says there is a slight risk, but there aren't many cases - 'considerably less than 50 a year. These could be avoided by regular worming and clearing up dog mess'.

In an article in *Smart Dogs* (July 1995), Nick Mays states that 29 cases of confirmed Toxocariasis were reported in 1991, only five of which resulted in eye lesions (not blindness) in children. In 1995, fourteen of the reported cases had resulted in eye lesion, only seven of these involving children. He also included the following quotation from Christine Murphy of the Public Health Laboratory Service (PHLS) Headquarters in London:

> The PHLS records an average of 40 cases of confirmed infection [of Toxocariasis] per year resulting in severe clinical infection. Some of these cases involve eye inflammation, but blindness is very rare.

Lesley Scott Ordish, founder of PRO Dogs, realised that much of the public's anti-dog stance was based on fears that dogs carried *Toxocara canis*.

PRO Dogs (see **Useful Addresses**) had been set up because she was concerned about the growing intolerance to the dog in society. As *The Guardian* said, 'PRO Dogs is concerned with facts not fantasies, construction not destruction, and education rather than legislation'. PRO Dogs publish a booklet about *Toxocara canis*, edited by a medical and veterinary panel, and with input from Nigel Harcourt-Brown BVSc MRCVS, from which we have been given permission to quote. If you would like a copy of this booklet send £1 and an A5 sae to PRO Dogs.

The booklet says headlines such as 'When a pet can cause blindness' should more accurately be headed 'When a parasite causes partial loss of vision in one eye', because even in these very unusual cases, side vision is usually preserved and fortunately only one eye is involved.

In 1978 Mrs Scott Ordish was invited to take part in an ATV programme, attacking the dog, in which one of the rare child victims of ocular Toxocariasis was also to appear along with his parents. The father had caused comment in the press for his statement that he would like to see all dogs put down.

> It was reassuring to meet him (the child) and know that he had suffered a far less alarming disability than had been represented. He had no problems in things such as reading the blackboard at school, and could see everything that was going on in the studio on the small monitor screen.

As this particular family had never owned a dog, but had a cat, it seemed likely that in this case the infection could well have been via the family cat. Yet, once again, the immediate press and public reaction had been against the dog!

Since then she has done all that she can to gather facts to counter anti-dog comment with reference to Toxocariasis.

Steve Dean, the well-known veterinary surgeon who has the Tyrian Kennels, recommends The British Parasitical Society's book *Toxocara and Toxocariasis*. He believes the red fox is also to blame; it carries *Toxocara canis,* and people complaining about dog dirt left in public places do not realise that this very often comes from the fox. Foxes have no compunction about leaving their mess in the middle of grassy lawns, and Steve says anyone who doesn't realise this is 'barking up the wrong tree'.

What he says is born out by my Borders, who just sniff dog mess but love to roll in fox mess; as soon as I see them rubbing their shoulders on the ground in local parks I know foxes have messed and that my dogs will stink of that specially pungent fox odour; so it's straight back into the bath.

If there is a problem with *Toxocara canis* in over-populated areas, then doctors in London should be inundated with cases. My London doctor says it is a 'very, very minor problem' and one colleague who has many children as patients thinks it is much more likely to be cats that carry this.

MOT

Your puppy will need to be inoculated against various diseases, including distemper, and return for a booster injection yearly. These diseases are highly infectious, especially among young dogs, and they attack the nervous system of dogs, foxes, badgers, ferrets, stoats and mink. Puppies between the ages of three and twelve months are the most vulnerable. So every year your dog should go in to the see the vet, just as you take the car in for its MOT, to have a check-up and its annual boosters.

Quarantine

When King Edward VII went abroad, he took Caesar with him, and there are reports of this terrier putting to flight foreign livestock. However, during the First World War, troops returning from the trenches with dogs they had befriended re-introduced rabies into Britain, so that now we have quarantine laws to prevent further outbreaks.

It is hateful to have to put dogs into quarantine for six months when you come back from overseas but, if ever you have seen someone dying from rabies, you will know how lucky we are that this horrendous disease isn't found here. Doctors tell me this is the only disease from which there is no known cure and it is an appalling way to die. You never forget it if you have seen a rabies victim.

However, vets in Europe are pioneering a new microchip for dogs which might end quarantine restrictions across the European Union. A dog could be vaccinated, blood-tested and tagged in any EU country, then taken across any border with its own 'passport' testifying that it has had the vaccinations. Our Government's paper on *Health Controls on the Importation of Live Animals* takes note of these, but says 'Quarantine remains the system recommended by the World Health Organisation as the most appropriate way for rabies free island countries to safeguard themselves from this disease.'

The paper takes note of the system recently introduced into Sweden of vaccination, blood-checking and unique identification of animals but says 'the Government believes that a system for the importation of dogs and cats based on vaccination could only be considered if it could be effectively controlled in practice and we again note that others, including the BVA, have expressed concern on this important aspect', and concludes that it would be premature to introduce immediate changes. A group called Passports for Pets is lobbying MPs for a change in the law. Even the British Veterinary Association, previously ambivalent on the question, now welcomes the microchips, saying these could play 'an important part in alternative arrangements if Britain were to replace its system of quarantine with one based on identification'.

I have had anti-rabies injections for some time as I have to travel to countries where rabies is rife. Although these don't offer complete protection, if bitten one has much longer in which to seek help, and doesn't need so many injections. Cynically, it seems that the poor dogs aren't really central to this argument. On one side are the drug manufacturers who stand to gain from injections, and on the other the Ministry of Agriculture that wants to leave everything as it is so as to make less work. And dogs can't vote!

Snacks

Many Borders can't take milk in its normal form, but my vet said to heat it to blood temperature and give it to the dogs when it is cooled. Mine have it as an occasional treat and, given this way, it doesn't upset their stomachs.

One has to leave dogs outside shops, and it always infuriates me to see signs saying 'No dogs' and nowhere to tie them up. Leaving them outside can cause unusual problems, too. I came out to find an old woman just about to feed the dogs with a large bar of chocolate. A polite request not to do this bought forth a stream of invective and a threat to report me to the RSPCA for being unkind to my dogs. I would have loved to have seen the inspector's face when and if she reported me!

Chapter Six

Breeding

Borders

I am grateful to Steve Dean BVetMed DVR MRCVS for contributing this chapter to the book.

Breeding a litter of Border Terriers can be a most rewarding activity or an unmitigated disaster. There is no magic formula for success, but a little planning, knowledge and forethought will at least minimise disasters resulting from human error. What follows is an overview of the whole process, from mating to rearing puppies. No description, however, can replace experience and it is hoped that those interested in breeding will be encouraged to seek further information and advice.

THE MATING
First steps

Even before selecting a suitable mate for your bitch (see Chapter 2) you should consider the following points:

- Does your bitch have a serious fault, either an inherited anatomical defect or a deviation from the Breed Standard? If so, it is highly likely to be reproduced in her puppies, so it would not be sensible to breed from her.
- What about the litter? Can you find homes for all of the puppies?
- Can you manage to rear a litter? If you are not sure, seek advice from experienced breeders before the mating goes ahead.
- If you think breeding is a good way to make some money, beware; the sale of puppies will bring in some cash but, when you do your sums afterwards, you could well be disappointed as far as profit is concerned.

The only valid reason for breeding is to improve the breed. If you cannot do that, it would be better not to breed at all.

Heats (seasons)

If you have decided to go ahead, you must now wait for your bitch to come into season (on heat). Most Border Terrier bitches come on heat twice every year, although some manage three, and a few only one.

A heat starts with a swelling vulva, followed by a bloody discharge. After seven to ten days this discharge will become pink or clear and she will be ready to mate. Her willingness to mate will last for four to nine days. Taking the first day of bleeding as Day 1, the best time for mating is between Day 10 and Day 14. However, there are many bitches who do not obey this rule, having longer or shorter heats than this. The cessation of bleeding is one good indicator that the bitch is ready for the stud dog. The best indicator, however, is the bitch's behaviour; she will 'stand' during the period of ovulation (producing eggs). 'Standing' is best described as when the bitch pushes her rump towards a likely suitor, straightening her hocks and turning her tail to one side. It's an obvious pose when you see it.

A happy, healthy litter of Border Terriers.
Photo: C Ricks

The visit to the stud dog

While the male will be interested in the bitch from the moment her vulva swells, an experienced stud dog will generally bide his time until she is ready to accept his attentions. Until the time is right, the bitch will often forcibly resist the dog's advances, just as she will when she comes out of heat again. The experienced stud knows when the bitch is ready to mate.

Recognising the heat can be a problem for the pet owner. Lack of experience and the absence of other dogs make it difficult to judge when the bitch is ready. An experienced stud dog owner will be able to give general advice, and a visit to the stud dog at around the right time will reveal much, but what if the stud lives many miles away? Here the veterinary surgeon can help. A vaginal smear will detect the right time in most cases. There are also blood tests that detect the moment of ovulation. These are expensive but useful for the novice.

The physical practicalities of mating dog and bitch are not always easy, either. Assuming that the process goes well, the bitch will accept the dog and stand and the dog will make attempts to mount the bitch. When he succeeds, the time taken to mount her, enter and ejaculate will be about 30 seconds. At this point, the bitch's vagina clamps around the base of the dog's penis and a 'tie' is achieved. This tie lasts

10 to 20 minutes as a rule and, during this time, the dog produces various additional secretions to aid fertilisation. This is a fairly passive process and the dog will often dismount while still tied and turn around, so that he is rump-to-rump with her. This can cause astonishment to the novice, but it is quite natural.

What can go wrong?

It all sounds so easy but things can, and do, go wrong. Pet bitches are often quite nervous, which overrides their natural tendency to be cooperative. Additionally, many arrive at not quite the right time, which compounds the problem. The vaginal tie creates a little discomfort and, if the bitch becomes agitated, she can, at best, break the tie and, at worst, damage the dog's penis. Some bitches like to vocalise during mating, which often means that she screams for the full 20 minutes or more - most distressing for all concerned!

These are just a few of the things that can go wrong, so do not be surprised if the stud dog owner wants to take charge. Be guided by the stud owner, who knows his or her own dog. Forcing a bitch to mate is not advised. A little restraint and persuasion is all right, but muzzles and physical violence should not be employed.

FERTILISATION AND PREGNANCY
On the inside...

If the timing is correct, fertilisation will take place soon after mating. Correct timing is achieved by placing viable sperm in the womb when fertile eggs are available. Day 12 of heat is the rule of thumb for mating bitches and most breeders conduct two matings with a 48-hour interval between. Both matings are achieved some time between Day 10 and Day 14. However, it is quite possible to achieve success with a single mating.

Sperm live for four to six days and eggs, which are normally ovulated between Day 10 and Day 12, take about two days to become fertile. Thus, providing the timing is approximately correct, the odds are firmly in favour of pregnancy, especially when there have been two matings. Fertilisation of the eggs occurs in the fallopian tubes, which pass down from the ovaries to the womb. During the day after fertilisation the eggs pass to the uterus and implant in the uterine wall. During this time the single cell, which was formed by the fusion of sperm and ovum, starts to divide and replicate, becoming a little ball of cells. The cells start to differentiate into differing types: first the spinal cord and brain are formed, then the organs, limbs, skin and finally the hair.

Pregnancy will last around 63 days, although a complete foetus is formed in a little over three weeks. From then until the end of the pregnancy the chief development is growth.

The foetus is nourished by a placenta, which is a system of membranes growing along with the foetus and surrounding it. Cushioned inside the fluid-filled placental sacs, the foetus is largely protected from shock and damage. The placenta is attached to the wall of the womb and supplied with blood vessels from the foetus, which form the umbilical cord. The blood that circulates in the placenta is therefore foetal blood, circulated by the foetal heart. When this blood passes through the area attached to the womb, foetal blood vessels pass close to maternal blood vessels. Exchange takes place at this point, oxygen and nutrients passing from maternal to foetal blood and waste products and carbon-dioxide in the opposite direction. The foetus is wholly reliant on its mother for survival, and any disruption of the placenta may lead to the death of the puppy.

On the outside...

To the casual observer, very little is noticeable during pregnancy, especially in the early stages. Some bitches change in their behaviour, causing their owners to realise that they are pregnant. The first real confirmation can be made by a veterinary surgeon at around 28 days, when the foetuses can be felt when the abdomen is gently palpated. Alternatively, ultrasound can be used to scan the abdomen for foetal shapes and heart beats. Neither method causes any harm to the foetus. Scanning has proved that foetal death and re-absorption are quite common, and it is fascinating to watch the foetuses move.

X-rays can be taken after 43 days when foetal bone starts to calcify and appear on the radiographic image. However, X-rays are rarely used for pregnancy diagnosis these days.

There is very little for us humans to do while the bitch is pregnant. She requires no extra food, but will probably be more comfortable if her food is split into smaller meals during the last two or three weeks if she is carrying a large litter. Vaccinations should have been given before mating, and it is a good idea to worm her, with an effective product, in late pregnancy. Some breeders give supplements and vitamins during pregnancy, most of which cause little harm, although extra calcium is not recommended as it is likely to increase the risk of eclampsia. This nervous disorder, caused by low calcium levels in the bloodstream, is more likely to occur in bitches who have been given high levels of calcium in late pregnancy.

Preparing for the whelping

During the last two weeks preparation should be made for the 'event'. A whelping box will be needed and the bitch should sleep there for the last week or so to acclimatise her to the new surrounding. Provision of warmth should be considered and stores of newspaper and other bedding prepared. Obtain some suitable powdered milk and a bottle and teat, just in case you need it.

Whelping is guaranteed to make even experienced people nervous, mainly because there is no way of predicting how it will progress. The date in our diaries is likely to be wrong, for Day 63 of pregnancy is an arbitrary estimate based on the first mating. It is entirely normal for it to vary as much as five days either way.

You will no doubt hear knowledgeable comments that the pups will arrive early because your bitch is huge, or that she will be late because she has only one or two pups. In fact, no-one knows for sure; not even the bitch!

Please warn your vet of the expected date of arrival and tell him or her when the whelping starts. Do all this in sociable hours, if possible. A vet would rather go to bed knowing a bitch is whelping, even if assistance is not required in the end. That way, the telephone call in the night is no great surprise and some preparation can be made for it beforehand.

A 'typical' whelping

About 24 hours before the birth the bitch's body temperature drops by one or two degrees. A plug of thick mucus may have been lost up to a week before this. The bitch may be uninterested in food, or she may vomit after eating, and she may be very quiet in demeanour.

The first obvious sign that whelping is imminent will be nest making. This is one good reason to have a whelping box full of newspaper for the bitch to rend and tear. She will be agitated and pant as her cervix dilates. After a few hours (sometimes as many as 12) contractions of the uterus will begin. A bag of fluid may appear and burst around this time. This 'breaking of the waters' is a sign that things are progressing, but otherwise not of great significance.

The real business begins when a pup is pushed into the pelvic canal. This sets off a strain reflex and the bitch will start to push visibly. She may do this in a prone position or she may stand and squat, as if she is defecating. The pup will be pushed through the pelvis and then it passes into the upper vagina. It is worth noting that 40 per cent of pups are born back feet first. This is not a breech birth and should progress routinely. (A breech birth is when the tail is the first thing you see - a problem requiring veterinary help.)

The arrival of a puppy is very close now; a little more effort finally expels it, often inside a membranous sac. The bitch should tear the sac away, clean and dry the pup and bite through the umbilical cord. The remains of the placenta are often eaten, which is quite normal.

Now she will settle for a while, until the next pup is pushed into the pelvis by the contracting womb. The whole process, starting with nest building, is then repeated.

Human interference

The majority of bitches, left alone, would whelp unaided, but the average owner cannot believe his or her 'baby' capable of all this without human intervention. Any

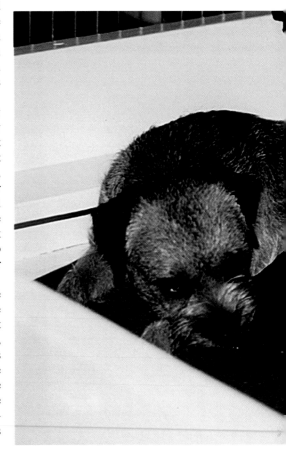

interference should be minimal and effective. If you do not know what you are doing, have an experienced friend with you. Nothing puts a bitch off more than her owner twittering around her in blind, uninformed panic; the emotion is infectious.

Do not react too early. A lengthy wait in the early stages is not necessarily the portent of doom. Nest-making can last up to 12 hours before progress is made. Sit peacefully with the bitch at this time, reading a book or writing a letter, and your calm presence will reassure her. Once real straining starts the puppy should arrive within 30 minutes. If it does not, seek veterinary advice. A call to the vet is also in order if you see no straining at all after six to eight hours of nest making.

Once a pup is delivered, tear the sac away from the head immediately if the bitch has not done so. If the pup is not breathing, rub it vigorously with a clean, dry towel. Return the puppy to the bitch as soon as possible or, preferably, do not take it away from her at all. It is better if the bitch breaks the cord herself but, if she does not, you will have to snap it, preferably using finger and thumb. Only cut it as a last resort, using a thin, sterile cotton or nylon line to tie off the end nearest the pup before you cut.

The pup will need to be dried and kept warm. The bitch should attend to this herself. Do not 'bake' puppies under infra-red lamps; these should be used only to provide background heat.

Be patient between the birth of pups. Up to two hours is normal before another is pushed out, and even longer periods are not necessarily problematic.

Do not be surprised if your whelping does not follow this pattern. Each whelping is unique.

Do not offer food or drink to your bitch during the whelping; it will only be vomited back at you later. Wait until all is finished, and then offer drinks in quantities of six to ten laps at a time. Food offered at this time should be light and in small quantities. (I use scrambled egg.)

In most cases, you will know when your bitch has finished whelping. She will settle, feed the pups and fall asleep.

AFTER THE BIRTH
The veterinary check-up and aftercare

Unless you are very experienced it is a good idea to have the bitch checked over by your vet on the day after the birth, to ensure that all the afterbirths have been expelled, that all is fine internally and that there is milk on tap.

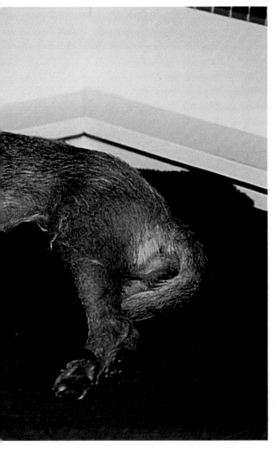

Soiled paper should be removed soon after whelping, but the bitch will continue to discharge quite copiously for the first few days, so keep the bedding clean. You will find that the bitch prefers her bed scruffy while you want it flat and tidy.

One final word of warning: there is no guarantee of success. Whelpings do sometimes go wrong and, fortunately, vets can often salvage the situation if called in time. However, everyone needs to understand that puppies sometimes do die, and so do bitches. These are risks that you take when you decide to produce a litter.

Rearing the litter

The pups have arrived and the stress of pregnancy and birth is behind you, but you still cannot relax. Several hungry puppies are demanding attention and, although their mother should see to everything, you have to make sure that all is well.

Ch Bever Lee Molly Malone CD DG CGE TDI ('Molly') with a two-day-old litter of four. Owner: Lisa Connelly, USA

The first problem is keeping them warm. Pups cannot regulate their own body temperatures in the first week of life. They are born wet, and cool quickly if left alone. Assuming that the family is in an enclosed, heated box, mother can supply plenty of warmth and will lick the puppies until they are clean and dry. A whelping box close to a radiator is ideal, as the temperature inside the box can be adjusted by increasing or decreasing the gap between box and radiator. Cover the open front of the box with a towel, as bitches seem to like the dark, and leave the top slightly open to allow air in and excess heat out.

The way in which the puppies are distributed in the box tells volumes about how hot or cold they are. For example, if they are huddling together they are cold and, if spread out, they are hot. Overheating pups is just as bad as chilling them, so be careful. The bitch will sometimes pant heavily, but this is normal.

Examine the puppies regularly, at least after 12 and 24 hours. They should look sleek and glossy and, when held up, should have little fat bellies. If they do not look like this, you may have problems. Seek help immediately; one hour's delay can mean the difference between life and death for a new-born puppy. The first week is critical; they rarely die after the first seven days.

Common problems with new-born pups

The most common problem is that the puppies are not taking food. If all the pups are affected it is probably because the milk supply is inadequate; if only one or two are affected, there may be an infection or some functional defect.

Individual weak puppies that will not suck are heart-breaking. We all try to rear them, but they nearly always die. When a bitch rejects a puppy it is normally for a good reason. It lies abandoned, cold and limp, and the situation is usually hopeless.

Four-week-old Border pups.   Photo: C Ricks

When your vet checks the bitch, ask him to check the pups too. He will check particularly for hernias, cleft palates and dysfunctional anuses (some do not open properly). Their dew claws should be removed within 48 hours if this is to be done. I know that the law says 'before their eyes are open', and the general rule is four days, but it is much better done before 48 hours.

Caring for the nursing bitch

Having established that the pups are thriving you can turn your concern to the bitch. She will be unwilling to leave her pups, but you should insist on a toilet trip the day after whelping, and at least twice daily thereafter. She may only do a quick puddle at first, but regular insistence will yield better results. This is where eating the afterbirth has a good effect because, being a natural laxative, it makes the first motion easy (but messy).

Give the bitch small meals, four times daily initially. Scrambled egg is my personal favourite but, whatever you use, make sure it is of good quality and easily digestible. In the first week the bitch requires relatively normal amounts of food, but this increases dramatically in the second and third weeks as milk demand increases. Do not be surprised if she loses weight at this time.

Do not worry about the green discharge. It is normal and goes on for some time (sometimes three weeks).

Weaning and socialisation

The puppies' eyes and ears open at 10 to 14 days, and weaning can start as early as three weeks. Border Terriers are just up on their legs at three to four weeks and will need a puppy run on the front of the box at this time. As the pups grow, reduce the heat and remove the towel from the front of the box to allow better air circulation and to keep it cool. After the first week the interior of the box becomes quite hot with the combined body heat of the bitch and several pups.

Wean the pups onto fresh mince, scrambled eggs and then a suitable puppy diet. Worm pups and mother three weeks after the whelping and again at six, nine and twelve weeks.

After three weeks the bitch tends to refuse to clean the pups, so you will need plenty of newspaper and a strong nose.

Start handling and playing with the pups from the second week and let the normal household noises go on around the whelping box so that the pups become accustomed to them. Reduce the bitch's access to the litter progressively from five weeks onwards if she does not do this naturally herself.

Allow human visitors from six weeks, and send puppies to their new homes at eight weeks. By this time you will be quite ready to relinquish them, as they will have become little monsters, destroying everything in their path. This will not dissuade you from trying it all again in the future, however.

At the end

Chapter Seven

Tassel's Red Quintus Kelso ('Kelso'), still full of life on his 13th birthday.
Owner: D Jabroer-ter Lüün, Netherlands.

If they don't have dogs in Heaven I don't want to go there.

Again the Garnett Orme papers came up with just the right poem to a Border Terrier:

> Hill-men bred you; your sire and your grandsire
> > Followed their striding by rig and dale.
> In wild Border weather, through spate and through heather.
> > You learnt to go fearless and never fail.
>
> Your eye is as keen as the gled's on the moorland;
> > You have sharpened your wits by the red hill tod's;
> Come otter, come badger, you'll tackle them gaily,
> > And fight to the death against any odds.
>
> Auld-Farrant you are, and canny and kindly;
> > Who'd guess, as you dream in the firelight's glow,
> At the demon that wakes when hound check and muster,
> > And a fox is to earth, and the Master says "Go!"
>
> Raider? Aye, maybe - true son of the Border!
> > But leal as the reivers, stout hearted and true.
> When there's Boasting and Toasting, my glass will go highest
> > To a game little Border - good hunting to you!

Anon

Pets and residential homes

Walking the dogs one morning, we came across a fellow dog-owning neighbour in tears; it was her last walk with her pet before she had to take him to be put down. Now that her husband had died she was being moved out of her council-owned flat into a retirement home, and pets were not allowed.

For anyone facing the same situation, the Feline Advisory Bureau (see **Useful Addresses**) is compiling a list of retirement homes and sheltered houses that allow people to bring their pets with them into care. Although dedicated to the welfare of cats, the Bureau recognises that people often own a cat and a dog, and can provide a list of homes in return for a stamped addressed envelope and an extra first class stamp to help pay for photocopying. Specify the county for which you need a list. There are about 600 establishments on their list, and they would like to know of any more.

St Joseph's residential home in Bognor Regis is one home that doesn't just allow people to bring pets. 'We encourage them!' says Sister Mary of the Grace and Compassion Benedictine sisters. This wonderful woman says the more animals they have the happier they are.

If you have to go in to hospital for a long stay, The Cinnamon Trust (see **Useful Addresses**) has a network of 900 volunteers who foster pets. Its director Avril Jarvis says: 'We do everything we can to help older people keep a pet. If they can't go out we'll provide walkers.' If the elderly people just cannot look after their animals any more, or have to go into hospital, The Cinnamon Trust helps provide a foster home.

Volunteers foster the dogs; they range in age from young children (who must obtain parent's permission) to people who can't keep a dog, but like to take them for walks. Avril says, 'I get letters from people saying they cried with relief when they knew their pet would be looked after,' and she becomes indignant when she hears of pets having to be put down after someone dies.

Surveys have proved that pet owners live longer and happier lives so, next time your Councillor comes knocking on your door canvassing your vote in local elections, ask what is the Council's policy regarding re-housing elderly people with pets. The thought of getting your vote will concentrate their minds towards a more caring policy.

National Canine Defence League

Membership of NCDL (see **Useful Addresses**) costs just £10 a year, but for that you not only receive a dog disc (details in Chapter 4) but you also receive a Canine Care Card telling people what to do for your dog if you die or are admitted into hospital. You may wish for a friend, relative or neighbour to take care of your dog, but suppose you can't tell them? The Care Card is easy to carry, and sets out your wishes. It also alerts someone to the fact that there may be a dog at home waiting for you.

If you have no-one to look after your dog, the NCDL or Border Welfare will probably be able to help house it in a caring home. This costs money for them to administer, so do discuss this with your solicitor when making your will.

Both charities take the utmost care to ensure that your dog is happily settled in a suitable home. Prospective owners have to satisfy staff that they are suitable and are subject to a careful interview before a dog is passed into their hands.

Sadly, says the NCDL, there are some reasons why dogs are not offered a new home, usually to do with age or infirmity. If this is the case, your dog will remain in the caring and dedicated hands of their staff, and many of the dogs have the freedom of the kennel grounds and can be seen following the staff around during their working day and feeling part of the 'action'.

Border Terrier Welfare

Sometimes a dog is sent to be put down not because it has come to the end of its life, or is suffering, but to suit the whims of the owner.

A typical welfare case for Border Terrier Welfare (BTW) was the puppy that had been bought at eight weeks from a breeder and, before it was eight months old, the owner decided she didn't want it. Taking the puppy to the vet she asked for it to be put down. He refused to do so, suggesting she contact BTW. Gwen Baldwin took her call and was told that the puppy got in the owner's way, upset her social life and she was unable to control it.

BTW swung into action; an area representative visited the woman and took the dog out for a walk. Her report was of a typical bitch puppy, full of energy, with a sweet nature. She has been re-housed and her new owners are delighted with her.

Gwen did wonder why the breeder had sold the woman the pup in the first place.

Luckily BTW does not find too many ill-treated Borders; most are in good condition and perfectly capable of enjoying life with a different family so, if you are thinking of owning a Border, one from BTW might be just the Border that would fit in.

Death

However much one prepares oneself for the fact that dogs won't live very long, it is still devastating when one loses a companion. Mrs Aspinwall says when she has had to take a dog to the vet to be put down it always gives her a lick when she is holding it; as much as to say it knows it is all for the best.

David Lewis was a surgeon in Rochdale and used to dealing with life and death, yet when he lost his dog Kim when it was 15 years old he was devastated. Unwilling to let Kim be forgotten, be contacted the Rossendale Pet Cemetery in Lancashire where Kim now lies buried. In a recent TV documentary he said the cemetery was better maintained than most churchyards, and 'the owners were excellent and understood what I was going through'.

Some vicars and priests will also say a few words at a pet funeral, or even allow the animal to be buried in or near the churchyard.

The Association of Private Pet Cemeteries and Crematoria (see **Useful Addresses**) has a list of members that have pet cemeteries. Send a sae for the list. And if you want help with organising a funeral, Pet Funeral Services (see **Useful Addresses**) will probably be able to help.

Cremation

Most veterinary surgeries now offer a full private cremation service with your dog's ashes returned home or scattered in a favourite spot. This service can be provided for pets that have to be put down, or who have died at home.

One company offering this service is the Lawn Hill Pet Crematorium in Eydon, Northamptonshire. They deal with most pets, and according to the owner, Angela Haynes, one particular request for a terrier was to scatter its ashes on running water. Alternatively the ashes can be scattered at Lawn Hill's spinney, in the

shrubbery, under trees, or delivered back to the owner's home in a special casket or canister. Mrs Haynes says:

> I am always at the end of a phone as sometimes people just want to talk about it. People phone if their pet is terminally ill and we will go through what they would like for their pet so that when it dies or is put down we know just what they want.

Cost of collection from the veterinary surgery or home, cremation and return of ashes is from upwards of £50.

RSPCA Cremation Service

The RSPCA (see **Useful Addresses**) has produced a leaflet *When Your Pet Dies*, which gives helpful and practical advice and offers a cremation service. Send a large sae (plus small donation if you can) to the Purchase and Supplies Department.

Memorials

Many people have erected monuments to pets, from Lord Byron to Sir Roy Strong. If you want to follow their example and commission your own monument there are various companies that can help, or contact the nearest branch of the National Association of Memorial Masons, which you will find in *Yellow Pages*. Elaborate monuments and large gravestones need proper fixing in the ground, and even a small headstone could be dangerous if it fell. Excuse me being practical and pointing out that your current male dogs won't understand the significance of a gravestone and could knock over an unstable one when they lift their legs.

Pet Cemeteries

My Grandfather had a pet cemetery with headstones for all the family dogs at Wellisford, and I think the thing that upset me most when seeing changes made by developers was to find they had bulldozed this cemetery into the ground. My nieces and nephews now have a pet cemetery at their country home, and the little ceremony attached to burying a beloved companion provides therapy for children coping with their loss.

The Victorians were just as much dog lovers as we are today and, when the Duchess of Cambridge lost a beloved pet dog in 1880, her husband, who was Ranger of Hyde Park, obtained permission for her to bury the dog where it used to take its favourite walks. Their friends were allowed to bury their pets there too, until eventually the plot was full up with 300 small tombstones, mostly of dogs, but with a few cats and some birds. One grave bears a quotation from Shakespeare, slightly altered: 'After life's fitful slumber he sleeps well.'

There must be lots of people who have commemorated their pets in stone, but probably the strangest epitaph is that of the woman who had engraved on her dog's headstone: 'To Fifi, who was more faithful than any of my three husbands.'

Coping

If you find you just can't come to terms with your grief, which is understandable, the Society for Companion Animal Studies (see **Useful Addresses**) provides the Pet Loss Befriender Service. They will put you in touch with a nearby befriender.

Dr Roger Mugford is a pet behaviour counsellor and believes that being open with your grief is the best way to deal with a loss. He also agrees that getting a new pet can be beneficial in most cases; some people will want to find a new one immediately, others will want to wait.

Don't forget the other animals in your family will grieve too; when Wellington drowned, his companion Winston wouldn't leave our sides even when we took him on his favourite walks and squirrels danced in front of us. He just stuck to us, trotting along with his head down. So we bought Warrior, and the little puppy's affection gave his thoughts a new direction and bought back our happy Border.

Making a will

If you want to ensure your dog is looked after when you have gone, Battersea Dogs' Home recommends the following wording to make sure that your wishes are easy to understand and can't be mis-interpreted:

> My trustees shall retain cash or investments equal at the time of such retention to £X and apply the whole or any part of the capital or income thereof for the benefit, upkeep, maintenance, grooming and proper exercise of my dog .... during the rest of his/her life, and for his/her decent burial thereafter, and any unexpended part of the said £X shall form part of my residuary estate.

Fitzroy having a rest after a bout of activity in the park.

The last word

Lord Byron was very fond of one of his dogs, and wrote this epitaph:

Near this spot
Are deposited the Remains of one
Who possessed Beauty without Vanity,
Strength without Insolence
Courage without Ferocity
And all the Virtues of Man,
without his Vices.
This Praise, which would be unmeaning
Flattery,
If inscribed over human ashes,
Is but a just Tribute to the Memory of
Boatswain, a Dog
Who was born at Newfoundland
May 1803,
And died at Newstead Abbey
Nov 18 1808.

Wyvern and Widget playing on the beach.

Working Borders

This little gentleman from Northumberland... is all resolution and pluck in a small compass, ready to tackle anything...

A Croxton Smith: *Dogs Since 1900*

Working Certificate

Originally Borders Terriers were bred for hunting, and those that perform well are entitled to a Working Certificate awarded by a MFH (Master of Foxhounds). Although Year Books contain an application form for a Working Certificate, in which 'the Master of a Fox or Mink Hunt certifies that .... worked satisfactorily and is a Game Terrier who will go to ground and stay with the quarry', this is often written on a scrap of paper torn from a pocket book.

Border hunt terriers really earned their keep, and Montagu H Horn once commented on a fox that was found at 8.30 am and ran until 4.00 pm over a distance of 40 miles. The hunt Border Terrier, having run all day, was put down the hole and not recovered until the next day. The fox was dead.

All-purpose working terriers

By the time you read this chapter hunting might have been abolished. No matter what are your feelings about hunting, you have to admire the way that Borders have worked with hunts and, whatever the law says, I can't see Borders giving up their instinctive reaction when an old foe is around.

Unlike most terriers, who go straight in, a Border will assess the situation, and then act cautiously. It is not until it comes face-to-face with its quarry that it faces up bravely to any situation. Frank Wildman, who breeds Ragsdale Borders, says: 'I never hurry my dogs along and most of my best workers have been two years old before they work seriously.'

Huntin' Borders

John Dixon of Rochester, Nr Otterburn, has had working Borders for over 40 years. The Kennel Club said he had to register his affix, but 'people just ring up and ask if you have any pups - I sent one to Colorado.' Today, 'terriers are anything - people follow the hunt in four-wheel drives and take their dogs with them'.

He had been Whipper-In of the Border Hunt and just happened to have the terriers, which were Borders. He was with the hunt for over 40 years, 'since I used to hunt with Jacob Robson when he had the hounds. When he gave up and Ian Hedley took them I was appointed official Whipper-In.'

Like other Border owners he has had problems, and once had trouble with a dog lost in a quarry. Friends came to help, and eventually they used block and tackle and dug the dog out after two days' hard work.

One dog he remembers was Sandy, by Ch Future Fame. There was a fox under a metal road, which a farmer wanted put out of action, as it was lambing time. They dug under the road and found limestone; 'What are we going to do?' asked Ian Hedley, but Sandy worried the fox so much they were able to pull him out.

Chapter Eight

In dry weather the foxes holed up in peat drains; there was one big dog fox holed up in a drain full of water.

> We put Sandy in - could hear Sandy challenge him which echoed up drain. We had to wait a long time for Sandy and the fox to come out. Then he holed again - but Sandy got him out again.

John is a mine of stories; as he says, in the old days 'entertainment was talking in the evening'.

Tracking
It seems Borders can turn their paws to anything. Bent Petersen's Ulrik came top in Tracking Trials in Denmark.

Borders are so versatile, I am sure there are many other jobs they can and will do - and do well.

Gundogs
Although not designed for it, Borders, with their excellent noses, have been known to make good beaters - as long as the guns don't mistake them for game. I have even been told that they make good retrievers, but it takes patience to train them as they will automatically kill anything that is alive. However, if you want Borders to do this work, do remember that most of them dislike loud noises - and that means guns. As it is not the work for which they were bred, if your Borders make it known that they don't like guns popping off it would seem cruel to persist.

Mink hunting
Frank Wildman thinks Borders are the most intelligent of terriers and 'use their brains as well as their hearts'. Copper was one of his Borders, and used to go out with the Northamptonshire Mink Hounds. Some time ago animals were let out of a mink farm and, in many places, they have bred in huge numbers. For this reason, farmers have formed mink hunts to try and keep them under control. One day a countryman asked me what was missing by a river bank. The answer was bird song; mink had killed or chased away most of the birds.

Copper was a keen worker and you could see his annoyance and frustration if the hounds 'lost' a mink. Diving into the River Nene he often managed to catch and despatch the mink before the hounds had caught up. My abiding memories of Copper are of him keeping the huge, clumsy Otterhounds in order, but being unable to hide his frustration when he had to dive in to bring out the mink that the hounds had gone over.

When Frank introduced me to mink hunting, making us members of the Northamptonshire Mink Hunt, his ideas of hunting and mine were slightly at variance. In those days before PC (political correctness) I imagined this would be a cheap way of obtaining a mink coat. Frank loved the sport and wanted to show it off at its best. Soon realising that once a Border had had a go at those vicious little mink there wasn't much left to make a coat (and anyway I would need about 400) we gave up Plan 'A' and went on to Plan 'B': enjoy the hunt.

Many happy days were spent running over the fields, with the odd halt or two at some marvellous pubs. In fact we soon realised that, if we stopped for a delicious lunch, by the time we had finished eating the hunt would have run in a circle and we could re-join it, hoping no-one would have realised we had been absent for the past two hours. Then there was a bit more exercise before someone would say it

was time to call it a day and invite us back to their farmhouse for a superb tea, with fantastic cakes whipped out of the freezer.

When a new Master decided that he preferred Jack Russells, I could see the writing on the wall, although one day when the terrier man hadn't turned up Master asked if we had one of our Borders in the car. (I used to bring them and, when things became rather boring, would take them out and exercise them two fields behind the hunt.) Wyvern was only a year old, and Master was complimentary. But the Jack Russells turned up again next week, and I am afraid that I had joined to see Borders at work, so that was that.

Mink hunts are now based all over Britain, and it remains to be seen what will happen in the future. Now that hunting is under threat, Border Terrier owners are worried that the dog's *raison d'etre* may vanish. As I researched for this book it soon became evident that Borders are adaptable and are working today in many different fields, thoroughly enjoying their new work and making a significant contribution to their owner's lives.

PAT dog Clem (Rudolph?) makes a visit, Christmas 1993.

PRO Dogs

There is no doubt that dogs have a profoundly beneficial effect on the health of their owners, and Mrs Scott Ordish wanted to do something to alert the public to the benefits of dog ownership and counter the 'anti' publicity. This is the reason why PRO Dogs (see **Useful Addresses**) started.

PRO Dogs struggled to become known. One of the sad calls to the charity was from an elderly couple who had to go into a residential home so wanted their dogs re-homed. From this gradually evolved an idea: if dog-owning members of the charity appreciated the need, they would be willing to share their pets. As a result of this, PAT Dogs was born.

If it was to work a stringent testing scheme would be needed, together with insurance. Mrs Scott Ordish could see it working: 'I knew how they missed them - we had a willing response from the dog owners, but the difficulty was being accepted.' However, the turning point came in 1985. 'The Royal College of Nursing asked me to talk at their summer school and bring my dogs.' The Press was there and this produced a large amount of publicity.

Today over 8500 PAT dogs are registered; the largest community service in Europe, and the number is rising all the time. It is gratifying for dog owners, who hate dogs getting such a bad press.

The cost of becoming a member of PRO Dogs is £10. PRO Dogs runs an Information Helpline giving further information about PAT Dogs, how to protect your dog in your Will, who to talk to if you are overwhelmed by the death of a dog, and how to get a free emergency card to carry with you in case of accident. This is given in **Useful Addresses**, along with the address for PRO Dogs and PAT.

PAT Dogs

PAT stands for Pets as Therapy, and Sue Gaywood tells me they have numerous Border Terriers carrying out this wonderful work. In 1983 a pilot scheme was started in Derbyshire, and Mrs Scott-Ordish's idea was on its way with the registration of the first PAT dog, Sabre, a rough Collie. Borders would seem ideally suited to the work of a PAT Dog, being friendly, reliable, temperament-tested, clean and vaccinated.

PAT dogs regularly visit hospitals, hospices and residential homes with their owners, who are all members of the PRO Dogs national charity, so covered by the necessary insurance.

PAT dogs are sometimes the only visitors that long-term patients receive, and they lighten the lives of those who are missing their own pets. They have even been requested to lie comfortably to see out the last moments of one of their human friends, so certainly deserve their PAT collar discs and their yellow PAT identity leads. To be accepted a dog must pass a temperament test and be shown to have the friendly, happy and reliable disposition needed and to enjoy having a fuss made of them by different people.

Carrying their work on further, these dogs are being used in limited case studies to wean patients off drugs to which they have become addicted, with possibilities for further study. Dogs have even been requested to provide evening visits to help patients relax and settle down for the night without needing drugs to make them sleep.

The scheme has been found to have all-round benefits for people living in residential homes, hospitals and hospices. The residents really enjoy the visits, and the staff benefit by having happier and more relaxed patients.

Sue Wheeler has two Borders who work as PAT dogs: Tess and Zippy (so called because she has a mark down her back just like a zip). Sue is a member of the East Anglia Border Terrier Club and lives near Woodbridge where she visits two old people's homes. When asked what makes a PAT dog, and how a dog and its owner enrol, she explained that a PAT dog has to have a friendly and reliable disposition and like having a fuss made of it by different people (sounds tailor-made for a Border). If you feel this work would suit your dog, ask the advice of a dog trainer or someone who knows the system. Then your dog would have to be vetted by the local PAT dog co-ordinator and registered with PRO Dogs (very important so that there is insurance cover if something goes wrong).

Tess and Zippy alternate visits between two different nursing homes. Sue says she took over from someone else in one home and approached the other herself.

The work is very rewarding: one 94-year-old woman's eyes light up when Sue and the dogs arrive.

If you want more information about this scheme, or would like to raise money for them, send a large sae to PAT Dogs (see **Useful Addresses**).

Sometimes, when someone takes pity on a dog because it is going to be put down, it can be the start of a wonderful chain reaction. This happened to Brenda Sandham of Cockerham near Lancaster, whose aunt and uncle had a Border. When they died, Jane, the Border, was going to be put to sleep, so Brenda took her in, and Borders got under her skin. Eventually Jane died, but Brenda acquired another Border, bred from her, and kept two of the puppies, so she now has three: Jaybee, Ozzie and Maggie.

Maggie qualified for Crufts in 1995 but she has a much more important claim to fame; she is a PAT dog, making weekly visits to an old people's home in her village. Brenda appreciates her dogs, and has been a stalwart PAT dogger for some years. Working on the PAT Dog stand at Crufts with Maggie, Brenda seemed to be more concerned that the visiting public should understand what PAT dogs were all about, than worrying about Maggie's ring appearances. Maggie was working on the stand too, allowing people to pat and fondle her, and acting as a worthy Ambassador for these important dogs. During the show Brenda and Maggie slipped quietly away from the stand, and returned with a First and a Second. Then Maggie and her proud owner went back to work telling the public about the joy PAT dogs bring into people's lives.

Brenda thinks it a shame when old people don't have dogs, so she shares hers. She was telling everyone of the joy her three Border Terriers bring to the old people. She also has a German Shepherd but, although this dog is wonderful with old people, the Borders seem less threatening to anyone who isn't used to dogs and are firm favourites with the residents; the puppies are started at eight weeks old, and we all know how adorable Border pups can be!

Her Borders lead very busy lives; as well as visiting the old people, Jaybee performed in *The Wizard of Oz* at Lancaster, taking it in turns to play Dorothy's dog, Toto, with her litter sister, Rosie. They took to acting like ducks to water and fireworks, loud noises and even applause were ignored whilst they put in faultless performances. As the local paper wrote: 'On the Opening night Jaybee was a natural and showed no signs of stage fright.' Demand was so great to see the production that additional tickets had to be made available.

Then Jaybee walked the 195 mile Wainwright Coast to Coast walk. 'It took me about a fortnight,' said Brenda. She and Jaybee stayed in guest houses along the way, where Jaybee behaved impeccably. On this walk they collected for Border Terrier Welfare. All her dogs are seasoned charity collectors, splitting their fund raising efforts with the PAT Dogs charity.

One of the first PAT Dogs was a Border, Bonnie, but she nearly didn't make it. PAT Dogs have to have a sponsor and, when her owner Sue Holleron was looking around for one, it seemed that no-one wanted to know. She had tried a local Brewery with a suitable name, and other firms, but without success. One evening, to universal scepticism, she announced she would write to Cliff Richard to ask him to be a sponsor. She must have caught him at the right moment as he agreed to do this. So Bonnie had her sponsor and Cliff used to autograph photos for her to send to patients.

Eventually Bonnie and Sue went to London to meet Cliff and be shown around the theatre in which he was appearing. After Bonnie had sat on Cliff's lap, Sue said she was never going to bath her until, walking down the street afterwards, Bonnie found an old tramp and cuddled up to him too.

They have appeared on TV, where Bonnie shares bacon butties with the weatherman. Bonnie has even had a gilt-edged invitation to meet the Princess of Wales, but Sue says trying to curtsy to the Princess with a Border under your arms is not funny.

Bonnie's duties included visiting Downs Syndrome children and the mentally handicapped. Sue would go round the schools giving talks on caring ownership, and some schools have community awareness days when various charities come and give a talk. Sue and her dogs also visit the Countess of Chester Hospital, and she is keen for others to join her.

Sue says that she would love to hear from you if you have a steady, friendly dog who loves being fussed over and being the centre of attention (did someone mention Borders?) and can commit yourself to two hours per week every week.

Now Bonnie is retired and one of Sue's current Borders, Biggles, is a little too enthusiastic; he will sit on anyone who is in bed. Sue has high hopes of Holly, however.

Canadian PAT dogs

In Alberta, Sylvia Clark has PAT dogs, and says 'the most compelling reason our Border terriers are in the pet therapy program is because the program works'. There PAT dogs are examined by a vet and have to have their nails trimmed and teeth brushed. Many of the patients in the hospital she visits are from farming backgrounds and appreciate a good working dog.

As she feels her Borders lack 'eye appeal' they wear T-shirts with a catchy logo such as 'Goochie Poochie' or, my favourite because it is so apt, 'mischief maker'. One patient, speech impaired from a stroke, was able to recite all the logos on the T-shirts.

One of the Borders, Pipsqueak, became so attached to 'her' people that when they died she became too despondent to continue in the programme. Since then the dogs have been rotated among patients to prevent undue stress.

To date they have employed nine Borders. Eagle one day dived under a resident's skirt. Red-faced, Sylvia retrieved him and apologised, when she was told sharply to leave him alone. The patient had bumped her leg and Eagle's massage was soothing.

Another time Joss (Farmway Albatross) snatched the lead out of her hand, raced down the hall and disappeared into one of the rooms.

> This was strictly against the rules and I wasted no time chasing after him. Joss was up on the bed exchanging a whisker rub with a patient who was reluctant to let Joss go. He told me to bring Joss more often because he liked an animal with some life to him.

Hearing Dogs for the Deaf

The idea came from America, and in 1982 Favour became the first British Hearing Dog. He was named Favour because the insurance company, Mutual of New York, sponsored the first British dog, and in America when you give money you are said to give favor or favour.

A skinny, white cross-breed with large, warm, brown eyes, Favour had been picked up by the police wandering along the M4. Cleaned up and trained, he was the

first mongrel to gain entry into Crufts Dog Show and, since then, his fellow workers are well known at this show, demonstrating how they help those hard of hearing and the deaf.

Having started out with a police record, Favour added to it as soon as he went to live with Tony Blunt. Within a few days he had located Tony's dustbin, and those of most of the neighbours. He collected a scar across his nose from rooting in tins but did so well as a Hearing Dog that, when he retired, he was presented with a Certificate of Service at Crufts for his devotion to duty.

Today Border Terriers are proving excellent Hearing Dogs, and Border Terrier Welfare have donated four six-month-old puppies. One of them, Toddy, went to a couple who were both deaf and they say he has improved their quality of life immeasurably. If you have a Border litter and want to help by donating a puppy, Hearing Dogs say the ideal situation is if they can select the puppy themselves from the litter, as they have to look for special characteristics.

Since Favour proved so successful, several Borders have qualified as Hearing Dogs, and John V Roberts of Galashiels says his Nick is great! John has written the following section to show what having a Hearing Dog has meant to him:

Maggie and Jaybee with Mrs Gillian Prescott at St John's Hospice.
Photo: Lancaster and Morecambe Newspapters Ltd.

Name: Nick (no kennel name).
DOB: 13.9.91
Differences he has made to my life:

- He has enabled me to hear sounds which I could not distinguish before: door bell, door knocker, cooker timer, smoke alarm, telephone, alarm clock and whistling kettle. He will also fetch me if someone sends him for me.
- He has given me a new interest.
- He has given me more confidence.
- He has given me companionship.
- He has given me a greater sense of security.
- He has introduced me to people and, for a person less extrovert than I am, can indeed lead them back into social contact from which they may have become excluded.

A match made in Heaven? John Roberts with 'born again' Hearing Dog, Nick.

Working

Hearing Dogs learn to recognise up to 60 different sounds. Nick tells me a sound is happening by 'scrabbling' at me. A larger dog will give, or tap with, a paw. I rise and, with an open arm gesture, say 'What is it?' Nick then leads me to the source of the sound or the person who has sent him for me. The exception is that, if the smoke alarm or fire bell has been activated, Nick will lie at my feet instead of taking me to the source of the sound.

Other Border owners are always interested in Nick, who came from Border Terrier Rescue. I am told that he was originally owned by an elderly lady who had him as a pup. She had an older Border too. I believe she originally called him Nicodemus, but Hearing Dogs thought that a bit of a mouthful and shortened it to Nick. (Some of my Christian friends say he must be a 'born again' Hearing Dog.) She became ill and at six months Nick was sent to Border Terrier

Rescue as she could not cope with him. It seems that he 'ran circles' round her and the implication is that he had very little training of any sort as a young puppy.

Hearing Dogs took Nick from Border Terrier Rescue and, after initial assessment, he went to a Puppy Socialiser for two or three months. 'Socialisers' are volunteer people who work on behaviour training. Following more in-depth assessment Nick began his sound training which lasted a further three months. When his sound training was completed he came home with me and had three months more training in my home. Training Staff from Hearing Dogs made regular visits to see us and I had to complete a daily record of Nick's work and behaviour during this time.

Shortly after Nick had come home with me he refused to work! Well, he only worked when he wanted to. A frantic call to Hearing Dogs resulted in their National Training Officer calling in to see us.

The problem was assessed and a 'behaviour modification plan' (sounds grand, doesn't it!) was put into action. For the next few weeks I dutifully weighed out Nick's food each day (he is on Eukanuba) and he had to work for every bit of it! No tea time allowed but of course he wasn't starved as he had his full quantity during the day in 'dribs and drabs' whenever he worked. That cured him!

We also cut back on the amount of fuss he got. No sitting on knees and definitely no titbits when people were eating. I still tend to be on the strict side with him although, when we go to speak at meetings, he often gets spoilt in spite of me telling folk that he shouldn't have titbits. If the meeting is in a village hall or similar (Women's Guild type meetings) Nick has developed an uncanny accuracy in locating the kitchen immediately we arrive. He knows where the tea and biscuits come from!

When I first had Nick I was living alone. Now I live with a partner, Shirley. We are both busy in our independent ways so I am often in the house alone or out in my motorcaravan. Nick works in the 'van as well as at home.

His birthday is on 13 September. That's the day he takes me to the pub for a treat!

He certainly has made a difference to my life. Apart from being my ears he has brought me new interest. I have always been an extroverted person and try not to let my now profound deafness get in the way of socialising. However, many people who become deaf in later years feel very cut off from the world and find it extremely difficult to cope with the isolation and loneliness.

A Hearing Dog is very much a therapist. As you know, dog owners will often stop to speak to other dog owners. If someone has a Hearing Dog with them it creates even more interest and draws the deaf person into conversation and personal contact. So, a Hearing Dog not only works for a deaf person in respect to sound, coming to them and 'scrabbling' (if a small dog) or tapping them with a paw (if a big dog), but they are also a new interest, they are company of course, and they can help the deaf person pick up social contact again.

People, particularly those who have lost their hearing later in life, often become very frightened and are very much aware of what they do not hear! I find this. When I am out in my motorcaravan and perhaps 'wild camping' (to which I have no alternative in the winter months) I get very nervous about things which may be happening outside my 'van; vandals or people messing about. Nick, I know, will tell me if there is any monkey business going on. Deaf people isolated in their own homes can be very frightened. A dog will often give them just that 'extra secure' feeling and help to eradicate their nervousness and anxiety.

The alarm clock is his favourite sound. He works so well for this first thing in the morning. He sleeps outside the bedroom door at home or on the driver's seat if we are out in the motorcaravan. As soon as the alarm goes off he is up, out of his bed, scrabbling and, if that doesn't work, jumping on to me, adding a good lick for extra effect. He knows he will get a treat from his jar, which is always by the alarm clock.

Sometimes when in the motorcaravan I hide his treat jar (a marmite jar with holes punched in the plastic top... lets the smell out, keeps the goodies in!) under my pillow. It's a great game first thing in the morning.

Wonderful, you may think. However, since we moved house last year and came to live in the Borders, he works especially well. Next door (we are in a 'semi') live a lorry driver, Stuart, and his wife. Stuart gets up very early to go to work, anytime after 5.30 am. Nick feels sure that I should know when Stuart's alarm clock goes off, which is anything up to an hour and a half before mine. In he comes to let me know! He doesn't get a treat for that!

It can be useful, though, because I know he will let me know if there is anybody outside the house.

Once when Shirley and I were visiting friends near Gloucester he worked extra specially well. Our friends are David, a bachelor of mature years, and his mother, Vi, who is 92 and has just had a leg amputated.

David and I had gone shopping locally and I had left Nick in the house with Shirley and Vi. It is a very rare occasion for him to be left. Shirley was upstairs making the beds; Vi was downstairs in the kitchen/dining room with Nick (where there's food there's Nick). Suddenly Shirley heard something bounding upstairs, a crying noise from Nick and then him alerting her. Nick turned tail again downstairs and Shirley, realising Nick was telling her something, followed. When they reached the kitchen, there was Vi, precariously stuck between the easy chair in which she had been sitting and her wheelchair into which she was unsuccessfully trying to get.

She is a determined soul and hadn't shouted for help. However, Nick had realised that she was stuck, unable to move either way (in fact a few moments later and she would have fallen onto the floor) and in a real predicament. He had no hesitation in fetching help, even though he is not trained to work for Shirley.

Other uses

Nick does have other uses. He is trained to fetch me if someone sends him for me. All Hearing Dogs are trained to do this as it is no good a hearing person shouting in the house to or for a deaf person. The 'fetch' is certainly a very useful command and people can 'get' me wherever I am. I've no place to hide now!

I went to collect a cheque on behalf of Hearing Dogs and was bemused to see the donor had made it out to Talking Dogs for the Deaf. Well, I certainly do understand some of Nick's doggie language!

The other week we were holding a fund raising coffee morning at home in aid of Friends of Russian Children. (Better not tell Hearing Dogs that. We were sort of roped in when I forgot the word 'No!') There were many people there and the door bell was ringing constantly. Nick as usual came and alerted me... for the first two or three times. He then went on strike. He just curled up by the radiator and went to sleep. There was no glimmer of reaction to the door bell and I could hear his doggie brain saying: 'Why should I keep on working this hard when there are all those people here who are quite capable of answering the door bell? No good having people and working yourself.' As soon as we were back to the normal routine he was working perfectly well again.

The duck pond

Well, he won't forget that in a hurry. We were out for a walk and at the duck pond we came across a lady feeding the ducks. Nick, forever after food of any description, went and sat appealingly at her feet alongside the ducks. If you can't beat 'em, join 'em. He got some too. I called him away to carry on our walk. After a while we turned round and retraced our steps. As we came back to the duck pond the lady had long since disappeared and the ducks were in the middle of the pond pecking at the ice, which was solid for about four or five metres from the edge, but there was one part not frozen in the middle of the pond. Nick, recognising his friends and, more importantly, that there might be food where they were, went hurtling across the ice, only to come grief as it gave way just before he reached the ducks; in he fell with a great plop! A very surprised, wet and bedraggled Border emerged from the water, scrambled back onto the ice and, at my call, came as fast as his legs would carry him back to *terra firma*!

Caravanning

Nick loves his motor caravanning and, on those all too rare but delightful warm summer evenings, will sit outside for hours on his long rope, patiently alert, waiting for any sign of rabbit. He even does this in the depths of winter and sometimes I have to exercise considerable persuasion to get him to come inside.

Out and about

As in all Borders, there is a streak of obstinacy and dominant character in Nick at times which has to be watched. He is small enough not to be a problem when we are out and about in public places or on public transport. But he doesn't like shopping trolleys. He thinks they are out to get him. (I know some people like that too.)

So many people who don't even know their Pekes from their Poodles simply go into raptures about his 'appealing little face'. Well, as I say to them, it's a well-known fact that many dogs are like their owners! Nick gets stroked and made a fuss of by all sorts of people. (I've tried lying on my back with my hands and feet in the air but no one strokes my tummy!) He is, of course, a member of a hardy breed. Feeding is no problem and I find he is economic too: all dog, and only half the running costs of a Labrador!

Would I advise others with hearing problems to have a Border?

Hearing Dogs for the Deaf trains all sorts, shapes and sizes of dog, and this is good as the dog can be well matched to their deaf recipient.

The 'manageability' of Borders in respect to their size, ease of grooming, hardiness, loyalty, intelligence and also their economy in respect of food bills are all substantial points in their favour. Although they do need exercise, a deaf person who is perhaps somewhat physically restricted in the amount of exercise he or she can give a dog will find a Border can be perfectly happy with less exercise than a larger breed. In the open country I find that Nick is off here there and everywhere, sniffing and searching, happily doing 10 times the distance I have travelled.

© **John V Roberts**
Galashiels, 1995

Assistance dogs (UK)

Most shops, hotels, restaurants and other public places readily admit Guide Dogs, but sometimes there are venues that don't understand what other work dogs do and why they need access to venues as well.

To help obtain recognition, Guide Dogs for the Blind, Hearing Dogs for the Deaf, Dogs for the Disabled and Support Dogs have established an organisation which they called 'Assistance Dogs' to improve access for people who depend on dogs for mobility and independence. It is not a fund-raiser, but has obtained from the Department of Health an agreement to allow Assistance Dogs access to places where food is sold. Until recently, this was restricted to Guide Dogs for the Blind.

One reason why the Department is keen on assistance dogs is that all are covered by Indemnity Insurance and each of them will have reached and passed the extremely high minimum standard levels of training required by each charity. If you own a venue that welcomes all assistance dogs you can phone 01844-355898 for a logo sticker to stick on doors and windows.

Nick, proudly wearing his 'Hearing Dog for the Deaf' jacket.

Showing
Borders

The late F W Morris researched into showing Borders, and wrote that 'the first Border to appear on the show Bench was Bacchus at a show held in the Bacchus Hotel, Newcastle-upon-Tyne in the 1870s. He was exhibited by Bill Hedley, a native of Rothbury, who was employed by the brothers Watson, of Newcastle, as kennelman of their famous kennel Bedlingtons. Hedley exhibited his Border Terrier in the Variety Classes and failed to catch the Judge's eye. Mr Morris believes that this was the last seen of any Border Terrier at a dog show for many years.

The next record of a Border being shown was of one owned by Mr George Davidson, which he showed without success in a Variety class at an agricultural show about 1880. Captain Hamilton remembered seeing four Borders at Kelso Show in 1896, when the judge was Bobbie Chapman. They were all red and he thinks three were undershot.

According to Miss Garnett Orme, the first show to accord the breed a separate classification was Bynness in Northumberland, soon followed by Bellingham and Hexham. However, none of the experts with whom I have spoken knows anything about this show.

The first Challenge Certificate (CC) for a Border Terrier was awarded by Mr S Dodd on 30 September1920 at Carlisle Show to Tinker, a 15-month-old dog, owned by Miss Bell Irving.

The first Champion (Ch) to be 'made up' was Teri (born 21 April 1916) in 1921. He was a red dog owned and bred by Mr T Lawrence.

The first bitch to become a champion was Liddesdale Bess (born 9 August 1917), a red owned by Mr W Barton and bred by Mr J Davidson.

The first MFH Working Certificate was awarded to Titlington Jock (born 12 August 1915), who hunted with the Coquetdale Foxhounds and was bred by Mr A Drummond.

To receive a Challenge Certificate (CC) your dog has to be entered in a show where these are on offer. You will see this mentioned in the schedule, or advance programme. Sometimes these may only be on offer for a dog or a bitch, but it is usually for both. Just because they are on offer doesn't mean that they are automatically awarded to the Best Dog or Best Bitch in the show. The judge has to think long and carefully of other Borders they have judged, and see if in their opinion your dog is worthy to join the ranks of the very best.

To become a champion your dog has to win three CCs under three different judges. One CC has to have been awarded when the dog was over 12 months old.

However, before you set off in pursuit of your first CC, it is worth considering that the well-known breeder Mrs Wilkinson says her best dog would look at her at shows and plead: 'Push off, I'd rather be hunting rabbits!' It is very boring for Borders, who like to socialise and to be doing something. They have to sit quietly for hours whilst owners gossip; they are not allowed to chat to other dogs, but have to sit or walk quietly when they would rather be socialising in the ring.

Classes

According to the size of the show, some or all of the following classes will run:

- Minor Puppy
- Puppy
- Junior
- Novice
- Graduate
- Post Graduate
- Limit
- Open

There will be a dog and bitch winner for each class, the only time dogs and bitches meet (officially) during a show being when the Best Dog and the Best Bitch are matched for Best in Show (BIS) if only Border Terriers are being shown or Best of Breed (BOB) if other breeds are represented. Whichever of them does not win becomes Best Opposite Sex (BOS).

There can also be Veteran classes, which are great fun and in which you see some elderly Borders in the peak of condition. There might also be a Brace class for matched pairs and a Working class for Borders who work with hunts.

Stakes

At the turn of the century dogs at shows were tied to stakes set in the ground and, when I see Borders slumped over the edge of the bench, bored out of their minds, I bet they wish this still happened. At least they could see what was going on either side. One writer called the benches 'chicken boxes on legs'.

Perhaps judges would then let dogs play together in the ring; you would soon see which dogs had sociable Border traits, which ones moved well, and which had bad habits. The dogs might then look forward to shows.

The first time I took a friend who wanted to buy a dog to a show it was at Hickstead in summer. The temperature must have been over 30°C (85°F), not ideal for showing off Borders, who love cold weather. Macho Man looked at me, then at the lethargic dogs slumped on the benches, and said:

'Are you seriously suggesting I am going to own one of these?'

However much I protested that if he saw them in winter he would see what super dogs they were, he wasn't convinced. We were just about to leave when a Border slunk past, saw an Airedale within reach, and launched himself, snarling and growling, obviously keen to settle an old score. There was pandemonium, with the Border giving an excellent account of itself and all the owners in a state of shock.

'That's a Border? OK - that's the dog for me!'

So the day wasn't wasted.

Awards

Today dogs compete for the honour and glory, not for the money. However, it wasn't always so. At a show at Rothbury in 1921 prize money was £3 for First; £2 for Second and £1 for Third. In real terms this is much better than what is on offer today, the BIS at Crufts winning £100.

In Britain a dog exhibited at a recognised show must be registered at The Kennel Club, which issues CCs in pairs in proportion to the number of registrations in each breed. The certificates, one for either sex, go to chosen shows which are thereby upgraded to Championship events. After each breed has been judged, unbeaten exhibits are called into the ring and a CC awarded to the Best Dog and Best Bitch of the breed at that show. As I have already said, three CCs, each from a different approved judge, mean that your dog is a champion.

So when you see 'Ch' in your dog's pedigree, it means an ancestor was a champion dog. In old pedigrees, such dogs as Miss Bell Irving's Tinker and Mr J Dodds' Ch Grip on Tynedale and his son Ch Station Masher are often named.

Three early Borders (by kind permission of The Kennel Club):
Left: Rummager, 1933. Owner: R G Morison
Centre: Ch Portholme Manly Boy, 1951. Owner: Mrs S Mulcaster
Right: Bicknoller Red Hackle, 1948. Owner: Miss M Richard

Another descendant, Ch Kineton Koffey, was one of the most famous Borders to appear at Southern shows. He was one of the first champions to gain a working certificate.

Famous names today are Brussel Sprout and Shady Knight from the Dandyhow kennel and Brannigan from the Brumberhill kennel. Mrs Aspinwall's Farmway Borders are also justly famous, as are Mrs Wagstaff's Brehill Borders, along with many others. The only thing they have in common is that every dog's owner is sure theirs is the best - and, to them, it is.

Whatever happens to the breed, all true Border lovers hope that they keep their characteristics, however much one moans that they will fight 'anything in sight on four legs'.

Showing step-by-step

Over 2000 dog shows recognised by The Kennel Club are held each year in the UK, so there is bound to be one near you. Ask the advice of your breeder, who will be into schedules and other buzz words of which you know nothing - yet. He or she will tell you when and where suitable shows are being held.

First your dog has to be registered at The Kennel Club and there must be a record that ownership of the dog has been transferred from the breeder to you. The dog will probably be registered by some fancy name, and no - you can't just register it as Gip or Pincher, even though they are good old Border names. Can you imagine the confusion if that was all there was to identify your dog? I have discussed this under the **Names** section in Chapter 4. There is nothing to stop you calling your Border any name you like, but it must have a proper, unique and individual name for registration.

If your dog hasn't been transferred from the breeder's ownership to yours, fill in the back of the official registration certificate and send this to The Kennel Club.

Sometimes a breeder will sell you a puppy they have already entered for a show. It is only fair to try and take the dog there to show it, and your breeder will be there to help you along.

If you are going to do this showing seriously, try to take some Ringcraft classes beforehand; your vet or pet shop will probably know of some locally. You will learn a great deal from others, and they are great fun. They also accustom your dog to ring etiquette.

Your teacher will probably suggest you enter for an Exemption show. These are used as training grounds for young dogs. Watch what the others do and, if the bug has bitten, the next steps up the ladder for your and your dog are Sanction shows and then Limited shows. These are often held in the evening, and you have to be a member of the organising society, but you pay the usually nominal membership fee at the entrance. These shows are generally more fun and less professional.

Judging

What do judges look for? According to Madelene Aspinwall the entrant must look like a Border, be well balanced and elegant, move well, and have a thick skin, a good coat, nice, tight little feet and a good length of body. 'A nice Border should look like a hunter.' The winner will be the dog who, in the judge's opinion, conforms most closely to the Breed Standard.

Open shows

Another step up? Then it's Open shows for you and your dog. 'Open' because they are open to everyone and much bigger than the shows you have entered up to now.

This is when you have to do justice to your dog. You have a 'showing' outfit so that your dog looks good against you, a special showing lead and a benching lead, and perhaps even a cage for the dog to sit in when it is on its bench. Usually Borders prefer to sit on the bench and see what is going on.

Championship shows

Do well, and there is yet another show level to go. This is **the** one; a Championship show where, if your dog does well, it will qualify for Crufts by winning or coming second in a lower class, or first, second or third in the Limit or Open class. Your dog may do well enough to be awarded a Challenge Certificate (CC) if the judge decides that he is good enough against the dogs competing that day and a good example of the Breed Standard.

For a dog, gaining these qualifications gets entry into The Kennel Club Stud Book. CCs and Reserve Challenge Certificates (RCCs) qualify in all bands in addition to the class awards as listed:

Open Class: First/Second/Third
Limit Class: First

If a dog wins one of these places it is awarded a Stud Book number and qualifies for life for Crufts.

There is also a Junior Warrant which is issued on application by the registered owner at the time of qualification in respect of a dog that has obtained 25 points between the ages of 12 and 18 months. It is generally awarded to a young dog that shows potential.

For First Prize in a Breed Class at a Championship Show where CCs are offered for the breed, three points are awarded.

For First Prize in a Breed Class at a Championship Show where CCs were not offered for the breed, or at an Open Show, one point is awarded.

On the day

When you arrive, dogs are judged first, then bitches. It is done this way so that the males won't be distracted by the smell of Kennel No 5 or whatever is the 'in' scent for bitches.

You will need to learn how to show your dog and, again, your breeder's advice will be invaluable. You have to purchase a special lead for showing and have some treats such as liver or biscuit, which you carry in your pocket, letting your dog know it is there so that he will look interested and catch the judge's eye.

Entrants (the dogs) have to become used to be handled, including showing their teeth. Ask a friend to do this over and over, until your dog accepts it as another manifestation of the extraordinary way humans behave, and doesn't object. If you have attended Ringcraft classes, your dog will aready be accustomed to it.

BOB/BOS/BIS

If you are very, very lucky, and after a great deal of hard work, you may find your dog becomes Best of Breed (BOB) for that day, or BOS (Best Opposite Sex). BOS does not indicate some kinky canine behaviour, but means that if a dog is deemed BOB, then BOS is given to the best bitch, and vice versa.

Finally there is BIS (Best in Show). For this your dog will be judged against other breed winners, and people often wonder how a judge can match one dog against another to find a winner. Actually, they don't. They have a mental picture in their mind of the breed standards for the dogs in front of them, and then go through this point by point to see how each dog measures up. Then the dog that measures up closest to the best example of its breed will be BIS.

Crufts

Although only British-based dogs are able to enter, Crufts is probably still **the** dog show. Bryn Cadogan, who has also judged abroad, says the organisation is excellent, and thousands of people congregate every year at the NEC Birmingham to visit the show.

In about 1890 a Mr A F Sherley, believed to be veterinary surgeon to Queen Victoria, started a pet medicines company called Sherley's that is still operating today.

The much-covetted Challenge Certificate (CC). When your dog has obtained three of these, under three different judges, he or she will be a Champion.

Sherley had a close involvement with the early management of Crufts Dog Show and it obviously made sense for this form of sponsorship to help the dog show, while the dog show helped sell the medicines.

Charles Cruft left college in 1876 and took employment with James Spratt, who had started to sell 'dog cakes' in Holborn, a prosperous area of London. He became a travelling salesman, venturing onto the Continent where, in 1878, French dog breeders invited him to organise the promotion of the Canine Section of the Paris Exhibition.

Back in England in 1886 he took up the management of the Allied Terrier Club Show at the Royal Aquarium in Westminster. Five years later he booked into the Royal Agricultural Hall in Islington for the first of a series of shows under his name, which he ran until he died in 1938. The following year his widow ran the show, but she eventually found the responsibility too demanding, and sold the show to The Kennel Club. Mrs Twist remembers exhibiting at Islington but

A Border Terrier on his bench at the show.

The Midland Border Terrier Club stand at Crufts.

eventually the show moved to Olympia, and then to Earls Court. When it grew too big even for this exhibition hall, it moved up to Birmingham in time for the Crufts Centenary Show in 1991, and has been there ever since.

Discover dogs

By the time I reached the Discover Dogs area at Crufts I began to think seriously about wearing rollerblades next time. But the long trek was well worth while; representatives of approximately 160 breeds have booths in which to display typical examples of their dogs, and they answer questions from the public. There was a crowd around the Border stand, which was well set-out with some super photographs, and an efficient team to talk to visitors about Borders.

Jill Collard, one of the volunteers who mans the stand, says two of the most popular requests were for advice are about stripping and information about temperament. Next time volunteers might be very welcome, both to answer queries and 'lend' dogs.

Jealousy

Most Border owners are very nice people, otherwise their dogs wouldn't tolerate them. However, jealousy rears its ugly head everywhere, and it is said that every judge is biased, unless your dog has won. You are excited at your first win, and suddenly other owners aren't as friendly as they were last week, and you feel very out of everything.

Just talk to the dogs and they will put everything in to perspective. Then realise that the jealousy manifested is a back-handed compliment. There is jealousy in every field (journalism as well as dog shows) but, if it happens to you, remember that it will lessen and you will find out who are your real friends. Don't let it worry you; it happens to the best, and means that those who are jealous are worried that you are going to do better than they can. Good luck to you!

Anyway, there are going to be some people who won't speak to me after this, as I have probably left out a Ch or a CC awarded to their dog, or they may wonder why I have put in another kennel and didn't mention theirs, which has many more Champions. As I said before, I made an arbitrary decision to include those kennels that bred my own Borders' ancestors and those whose owners had helped me with information for my book. So many thanks to all of those people who didn't mind what time I telephoned them and even answered my questions when they were much more interested in what was happening in the show ring.

Ch Rubicon Renewed enjoys playing in the garden as much as he enjoys being in the show ring.
Photo: Robert Smith

Obedience
& agility

with Borders

Improvisation: Fitzroy in Battersea Park.

All that and more out of the back of a small motor car.
Photo: J C Farrer

A chance meeting at the Southern Border Terrier Club's Christmas Party led to Johanna Farrer offering to write the section on agility for this book. She has two Borders, the dignified Pepper, and Boojum, who gets her name from The Hunting of the Snark. Under the apple trees at her country cottage she has set up a wonderful Agility course that she made herself from inexpensive materials, collected from skip hunting or bought for a small amount at DIY stores, and much of her course has been built out of re-cycled material. Pepper is now too old to take much interest in agility, but Boojum only has to see a jump being carried out and she is raring to go. While we discussed how to build the obstacles she was trying to stand quietly, but you could see she was longing to go round the course.

Chapter Ten

Johanna first saw agility being demonstrated at the Olympia Horse Show and thought it would be great as something for her Borders to do. Since she often has to travel between the country and her London home, an agility course had to be easy to transport, and in fact all the jumps and most of the other equipment fit into the back and onto the roof of her not-very-large car.

When Boojum sees the course being taken out to the car she knows fun time will soon be happening. Agility is her favourite activity.

Talking about training, Johanna says agility dogs have to be obedient. When her first dog was only eight weeks old, her vet told her that discipline had to start right then; even a tiny puppy's first play had to be on her terms, not his, and obedience would spring from that early beginning.

When not working with her Borders, Johanna plays the viola in an amateur orchestra - but the dogs aren't allowed to join in!

Other Borders can do it! We were staying for an NSPCC event at Nuneham Courtney, the house (now a hotel) where the real Alice in Wonderland and her friends used to picnic. Outside our bedroom window the police had built an assault course for their dog handling demonstration scheduled for later that day and, at 7.00 am, it was irresistible to dogs and humans.

Creeping out, we couldn't see any police around, so we let Winston off his lead. He ran up to the first obstacle. He had never seen an assault course before, but sailed over the jump, thought the tunnels were the greatest fun, and even conquered his fear to run up the ladder and across the plank - but decided to jump down the other side as his legs were not long enough to negotiate the treads. After this we discovered the police had a practice course on the common behind their training school at Hendon, so we went up there for fun.

Agility is good fun for the dog, and helps owners keep fit. Usually one sees larger dogs such as German Shepherds and Border Collies competing, but there are classes for dogs less than 38cm (15in) high.

Researching this chapter was the greatest fun for the dogs, who met Johanna's dogs down in the Sussex countryside and were introduced to agility. Now we want to start classes in London, so if anyone is keen please let us know.

This is the article which Johanna kindly wrote for this chapter:

FUN, GAMES AND COMPANIONSHIP THROUGH OBEDIENCE AND AGILITY TRAINING

There is a saying that the Border Terrier's ancestry includes lion, fox, hedgehog and monkey. This seems an apt description of some of the breed's characteristics. A Border Terrier is likely to be courageous without being aggressive (if handled properly), intelligent and resourceful. (After all, when underground he has to cope on his own trying to bolt the fox.) He values his independence; you may well find a command gets the simple answer, 'Message received, over and out!'. He is also full of physical energy and an exuberant desire to have fun in whatever way it might be had, authorised or not, but he can also be prickly and uncooperative.

Anybody embarking on what might well be a 15 or more years' commitment to more or less energetic daily walks in open country or amongst other people and dogs, and to sharing living quarters and daily life with a Border Terrier, may well wonder how to harness the energy, and how to turn determined desire for independence into allegiance, and canine resourcefulness and enterprise into fun, games, and a companionship to be shared and enjoyed by dog and owner alike. Many good books have been written about obedience training, and this is just an attempt to point out some of the basic ideas that might help you and your Border Terrier to reach that stage of happy companionship. Agility is seen here primarily as not a competition sport but a training sport, and in the context of handler/dog relationship.

Any Border Terrier worth his salt will try to dominate you: to dictate which door to open for him, when to take him for a walk, when to stroke him, when to give him a titbit. And as you look into his pleading eyes, how easy it is to give in! But beware; if you do give in you will soon be fighting for survival. Your shoe will be his, your bed will be his and your time will be governed by him. Bred to work with the hunting pack, a Border Terrier has a strong pack instinct. He gets on with other dogs, but a hierarchy has to be established. If you, the owner, want more than survival, even more than temporary truces in an endless series of skirmishes in which you and your Border Terrier again and again compete for supremacy, you will have to establish your status as pack leader on a permanent basis. The more you succeed, the more you will begin to realise the deeper meaning of the term 'companion dog'.

Obedience and agility training, then, will not be discussed here in the orthodox way, with competitions and certificates in mind. In the title I combined these words with the concept of fun, games and companionship because they are a means of giving you and your Border Terrier a fuller and more enjoyable life together. Bred for work, a Border Terrier usually thrives on work, and for him there is no distinction between work and play as we humans see it, as long as you, as handler, set to it the right way. Such work (or play) not only makes the dog mentally more alert and physically fitter but also enforces his acceptance of you as pack leader and makes him watch you more closely. You get to know him much better, too.

All this will take time, a great deal of time. You will have to keep working at it, and you must be endowed with much determination, care, love, a firm resolve never to lose your temper, and - most importantly - a sense of humour. There are a thousand ways a Border Terrier can make all your efforts look completely futile and absurd, and you will just have to grin and bear it. But when eventually you have a Border Terrier who wants to please you, who wants to enjoy himself with you in civilised play, cheerful obedience and controlled but enthusiastic agility, then you will have created a much stronger bond between yourself and your dog.

I see the progression in the following four stages:

- The leadership contest.
- The well-mannered dog.
- The obedient dog.
- The agility dog.

The leadership contest

Here are just a few questions that might make you think. The earlier in your Border Terrier's life you start working on this, the better. If you work at it in cheerful play you may soon be able to give a positive answer to most, if not all, of these questions:

1   Does your dog react positively and instantly when you call his name?
2   Does he relax when you turn him playfully but firmly on his back and gently pin him down by his throat and tummy? Only when he relaxes does he accept your dominance.
3   Can you touch him anywhere, and inspect, for example, his teeth and ears?
4   Can you take any toy from him at any time?

5   Can you take food from his bowl while he is feeding?

6   Can he resist snatching titbits from your hand?

7   Does he move out of your way when you approach the doorway he is lying in?

8   Do you feed him when it suits you, or does he whine loudly enough for you to feed him before you, the pack leader, have eaten?

9   When you enjoy a rough game with him, can you stop his playful aggressiveness with just one gesture or word?

10   If you ever allow him to sit on your lap, does he wait until you invite him, or does he just jump up when it suits him? Does he jump off again willingly on your command, or do you have to push him off?

Much praise - when deserved - and titbits or toys are very important rewards. However, Border Terriers being a particularly greedy breed, you may well find that a titbit tends to stop your dog in his tracks, whereas a toy and a quick game will stimulate him. Instead of deciding to hang around and ask for more food he will think, 'I am having fun with my pack leader.' If you work with gentle determination at becoming pack leader, in play rather than in formal training sessions, you will soon have the desired results, and you will have succeeded, not by thinking of your dog as a slightly inferior human, but by teaching your Border Terrier to think of you as a greatly superior dog.

The well-mannered dog

Good manners in this context are good habits, patterns of behaviour suited to certain frequently-recurring situations, which you, the pack leader, can now get your Border Terrier to accept. These good manners will make life run much more smoothly for both you and your dog. Here are some examples:

1   When on the lead your dog does not pull, but adjusts to your speed and direction (this is not meant to be 'walking to heel'), and he waits patiently while you talk to a friend.

2   When you open the car door or your front door, your dog waits for your release signal before running out.

3   Your dog stands still when you take off his lead, and again waits for your release signal before rushing off.

4   Your dog barks only when there is a good reason to do so.

5   Your dog does not jump up at people.

6   Your dog does not want to fight with other dogs, but is happy calmly to walk away with you from any potential challenger.

Not many commands are needed for this training; it is mainly a question of a quiet discipline, to which you, too, have to submit. A Border Terrier is a creature of habit, and will not only be a safer dog, to himself and to others, but also feel happier and more secure within this framework, and through this discipline his acceptance of your leadership will be reinforced.

The obedient dog

The good habits your Border Terrier has developed so far are a kind of obedience already, rather in the line of pleasing the pack leader by not doing the wrong thing. The obedience you are trying to gain now is a far more positive and active one: you will

Total concentration.   Photo: J C Farrer

want your Border Terrier to do as he is told as and when you ask him. Quite a different matter! You now have to use quite definite commands, such as 'Sit!', 'Come!', 'Wait!'. The commands have to be short and clear. The more words you use, the greater the dog's difficulty in filtering out the words that matter to him just then. A Border Terrier's concentration span is much shorter than a Border Collie's, for example, and it is by nature less intense. It is therefore all the more important to look upon training as a game which you and your Border Terrier play together. You should stop before he gets bored and always finish with an exercise he has done well, so that you can praise him. This will encourage him to want to work again next time. A Border Terrier will work best if he knows he will please his pack leader. It is not worth trying to cow an unwilling Border Terrier into submission; anybody who ever tried to extract a tennis ball from a Border Terrier's mouth using threats or force will endorse this statement.

Your means of communication are voice, gestures and body language. Your Border Terrier will be quick to read your movements and gestures, and quick, too, to interpret your commands. Your voice can give a positive slant to almost any command: 'Wait!' is a promise of something exciting to come, 'Close!' is an invitation to walk next to the pack leader, 'Not now!' is the promise, in the near future, of the game, meal, or open door he is asking for, 'Fetch!' is the permission to run and get the working toy and present it to the pack leader, who will be pleased, and even 'Finished!' at the end of a game, when followed by a 'Well done!', can be 'Let's start something else!', not a depressing 'That's the end of that!'. When you really want to say a flat 'No!' - think again. No Border Terrier wants to be stopped doing what he is busy with, but he may cheerfully accept a command that will make him do something else: 'Come!', 'Sit!' or 'Fetch!'. A Border Terrier does not like negative thinking.

Even a Border Terrier can become an obedience dog.   Photo: J C Farrer

Border Terriers have the reputation of being self-willed and difficult to civilise, and there is no substitute for a good dog training class, both for your Border Terrier's socialisation and for his, and your own, stimulation. However you set about it, you will have to work at it yourself, and the great bonus is that the more you work with the dog, the more fun you both have, and the stronger grows the bond between you.

The agility dog

Years ago, when I rang a well-known trainer to ask for an introductory lesson in agility, I was told, 'Yes, do come! What breed is your dog?' The answer 'A Border Terrier' was greeted with a long pause, then a quiet, 'Well, we shall see what we can do.' This inauspicious start was followed by enthusiastic training, some successful competing, and innumerable hours of fun for my Border Terrier and myself. Since those days Borders seem to have become somewhat more prominent in the agility world.

Agility is seen in this context as an exciting and exhilarating extension of your Border Terrier's obedience training. At its best it is total and instant obedience at speed, demanding physical fitness, courage and quick thinking of the dog, and requiring teamwork between handler and dog that sometimes seems to go beyond logical explanation. Just the sort of challenge on which a Border Terrier thrives! It is a sport that started in 1978, and the basic idea is very simple: you have a set of obstacles which the dog has to negotiate according to certain rules, in a prescribed order, and as fast as possible. The height of the jumps depends on the size of the dog: Border Terriers are classed as 'mini' dogs, measuring no more than 38cm (15in) at the shoulder. Therefore no jump must exceed 38cm in height. For initial training purposes or for old dogs you may prefer jumps well below that standard competition height. There are five basic types of obstacle:

1 Jumps (pole, suspended tyre, long jump for example).

2 Contact equipment over which the dog has to walk without failing to touch the designated contact area on each end.

3 Tunnels, rigid and collapsible.

4 Weaving poles: a straight line of five to twelve equidistant vertical poles through which the dog has to perform a kind of slalom, having entered from the right hand side.

Focusing on the next jump while still in mid-air.
Photo: E J Garden

5 A table onto which the dog has to jump, usually about halfway through the course, in order to lie still, in the down position, for five seconds. (This may be replaced by a pause box: a simple square on the ground.)

The table can be replaced by a simple pause box.   Photos: J C Farrer

The weaving poles.

A Border Terrier should be fit, not overweight, and at least 12 months old before starting any agility training. He obviously has also to be controllable before being let loose to enjoy himself over the obstacles. You will do best to join an agility club (but make sure they cater well for mini dogs), or you may ask for private lessons. It is important, not the least for the dog's safety, to have an experienced instructor for the initial training of dog and handler. At a later stage you and your Border Terrier may well want to do some training on your own. Commercially built obstacles are usually designed for heavy club use by all sizes of dog, and are therefore very expensive. Later in this article I shall give some hints on how to construct basic training obstacles to be used by your Border Terrier.

You are most likely to find that, after not more than two hours' instruction, your Border Terrier will be successfully negotiating all the obstacles except the weaving poles and enjoying it hugely, but this is only the very beginning! The real fun starts when you try to string together a set of obstacles and, later, get your dog to complete a full course at speed. He will have to obey instantly (for example, to react at once to the 'Down!' on reaching the table, or if you see him take a wrong turn). He must be able to work on your left and right, learning new commands for types of obstacles, for slowing down, and for left and right turns, to give just a few examples. He will have to read your movements and gestures (the pointing finger indicating the next obstacle, and the way you move or turn making him accelerate, slow down, or turn, even when you are far behind him, as a dog's perception covers well over 180 degrees). He will register the change in the sound of your voice as you turn behind him, too. While being wildly enthusiastic, he will still have to be totally obedient to you, even at a distance, constantly focusing on you, yet making instant decisions, such as when to jump, how to align himself to the see-saw, and how to find the correct entry to the weaving poles. You, too, will have to be fit. You will also have to learn to give clear commands and control your body movements, conveying only those messages on which you want the dog to act, and never taking your eyes off him. You must remember the course all the while and you will probably be running your very fastest. You will be surprised not only by how many mistakes you can make, unintentionally sending wrong or muddled signals to your dog, but also by how many surprises your dog can spring on you. You will have to accept that an agility dog, even more than an obedience dog, has an infinite number of ways to make you look utterly ridiculous.

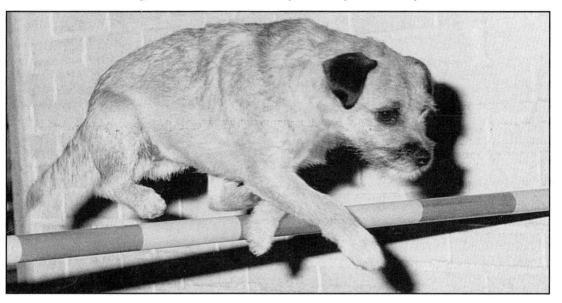

Life in the old dog yet! Thirteen-year-old 'Katie' shows how it's done in The Netherlands. Photo: E Jabroer-ter Lüün

Why can agility training be so hugely enjoyable to both a Border Terrier and his handler? Being a working dog, your Border Terrier is likely to thrive on this mental and physical challenge. Tough, fast, with great nimbleness, quickness of turn, sure-footedness and enterprise, an alert and obedient Border Terrier can derive immense pleasure from this activity. If you can harness all this energy you can think of your Border Terrier as a small 'big' dog, able to work even at a distance from the handler, at speed, yet under total control. There can be few better ways, other than 'real' work, of keeping your Border Terrier fit, alert and happy and enabling you, the handler, to get to know him even more intimately than before. You will probably find that the hours of training, play-work for both you and the dog, the mutual watching and observing, and the exhilaration brought by every small bit of progress, or perhaps even a smooth, fast clear round, create a still stronger feeling of partnership between you and your Border Terrier, which will make itself felt in almost every aspect of your everyday life together.

Perhaps a short word on competitions is appropriate here. There are two basic kinds of competition: agility and jumping, the latter having no contact equipment. There is no doubt that competing adds spice to your training, and that a trophy or rosette is a welcome mark of success for the handler. However, the competition standard nowadays is such that you are unlikely ever to become really successful unless you make agility a way of life, with much mid-week training and many week-end competitions. You and your dog will have still to be willing to give your best after very early starts, long car journeys, and long hours of waiting for your turn, in all sorts of weather. You might find evening competitions at club level more to your liking, but these seem to be few and far between. If you decide to compete, then do remember that it has to be fun for your dog. No dog will do well unless he enjoys it. It is also worth being aware that, although your Border Terrier may make a genuine mistake (for example, mistime a jump), a large proportion of mistakes is actually caused by the handler. Even when your Border Terrier gives way to his instinct and runs out just before the end of a potentially prize-winning round, following the scent of a dead rat in a wood pile by the ringside, you must accept this with a smile, mentally resolving to work that much harder to get your dog even more single-minded about his agility. And if, after such a defeat, you go home still thinking that yours is the best dog in the world, then you know that you, the handler, have passed the real test, and are competing in the right spirit, where the fun of working with the dog counts for more than any outwardly visible success.

The construction of basic training obstacles

As I have already said, commercially manufactured training obstacles can be very expensive, and it is relatively easy to construct your own. Before you start making them, however, there are a few points to consider:

- The obstacles described below are not built to competition standard.
- They are for the use of mini dogs only. Those for bigger dogs would need sturdier construction, and uprights too high for an over-enthusiastic dog to be able to jump over them, running the risk of impaling himself.
- It is important that you take your dog's collar off when he is doing agility to prevent him from getting caught on anything. If in early training sessions you need to use a lead, the collar used must always be a fixed one.
- If you work your dog on public land make sure that he will not be at risk from glass, other sharp objects, ruts or very uneven ground.
- When you train on your own the training tends to be quite intensive, and it is particularly easy to forget to stop before the dog (or indeed you!) get tired or bored.

Using the obstacles described below you can build useful practice combinations and courses. You can pack quite a few pieces of equipment into a car. My Vauxhall Corsa can take eight pole jumps, the long jump, the table (legs unscrewed), 10 weaving poles, the tyre and frame (taken semi-apart) and the see-saw trestle, all behind the dog kennel, the see-saw plank going on the roof. The tunnel has to sit next to the kennel. But with even just the pole jumps, the long jump, the table or pause box, and the weaving poles you can set up very useful and varied training combinations and courses.

Pole jump

The lower pole supports are for initial training, and for the old dog who is still keen. Make sure the supports on either side of any jump point in opposite directions, so that

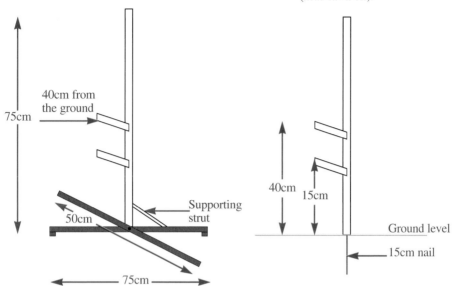

Model A
For standing on the ground.

Model B
For pushing into the ground.
The spike consists of a 15cm (6in) nail
(head sawn off).

75cm

40cm from
the ground

50cm

Supporting
strut

75cm

40cm 15cm

Ground level

15cm nail

the pole can be dislodged easily from either side. The poles are plastic plumbing tubes, 3cm (1¹/4in) diameter, 120cm (4ft) long, but if your garden is small you can make them shorter. Giving the poles a little weight by inserting a small wooden stick or a piece from an old garden hose is useful on two counts: the dog notices if he dislodges a pole, and the poles are less likely to be blown down if there is any wind. Electrical insulating tape provides the colour (for human appreciation rather than canine!) (See page 123)

Long jump

Three elements, made of 15cm (6in) wide planks, the width of the elements decreasing with their height, so that they can fit into each other for ease of storage and transport. Highest element not more than 23cm (9in) high, the lowest 15cm, supports cut at an angle of 30 degrees. The longest element should be 120cm (4ft) wide, but for your purpose it is more important to consider the size of your garden and storage space. The maximum overall length of the long jump is 75cm (2ft 6in). (See page 134)

Tyre

I bought a strong metal draughtsman's table trestle from IKEA (current price £15). The car tyre has an opening of 33cm (13in). This is not regulation size, but is large enough for your Border Terrier. The centre of the opening should be 50cm (1ft 8in) from the ground. The tyre is bound with parcel tape so that the dog cannot get caught in it. Make sure the fixing ropes do not endanger your dog should he run underneath the tyre. (See page 129)

Table

A chipboard square, as near to 3ft as you can make it, sealed against the wet, with four screw-on legs, not more than 35cm (14in) long, and a non-slip mat fixed firmly to the top. I use thin plastic matting bought at a yacht chandler's.

Pause box

The alternative to the table. A 120cm (4ft) square, made up of 2cm (⁷/₈in) diameter plastic plumbing tubes. If you glue the corner pieces each to one of the tubes you are less likely to lose them in storage. (See page 124)

Weaving poles

Half broom-handles, the spikes consisting of 15cm (6in) nails (heads sawn off). Painting the poles a bright colour makes them easier for your dog to see. I use a calibrated string for setting up the poles equidistant at 45cm (18in) intervals and in a straight line. Tighten the string between the two end poles, stick the intermediate poles into the ground in line with the string where indicated, then remove the string, replacing the end poles. (See page 124)

'A' ramp

Two doors (mine came from a neighbour's skip) are connected by two strong hinges to form a right angle. Two skewers act as removable pins, so that you can separate the doors and carry them one at a time. The retaining chains, too, each have to unhook on one end. The anti-slip slats are 25-30cm (10-12in) apart, the lowest one being at least 15cm from the ground. The bottom 105cm (3ft 6in) (the contact areas) on either side are a different colour. Adding a small amount of sand to the paint and waterproofing gives the dog's paws a better grip. (See page 133)

See-saw

A metal table trestle with a round top bar, again from IKEA (current price £11), supports the centre of a second-hand scaffolding plank. The two are securely locked together as shown. You can secure the trestle legs with tent pegs for extra stability, and a string does away with any chance of the trestle splaying. A weight, tied to the plank, enables you to change the balancing point of the see-saw so that your dog never quite knows what to expect. Again, sandy, non-slip paint is recommended. The different coloured contact area on either end is 90cm (3ft) long.

Diagram of locking mechanism of see-saw pivot point

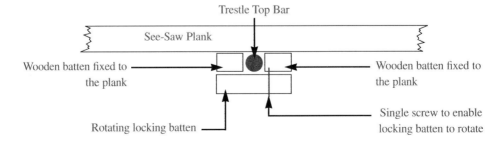

Rigid tunnel

I bought a children's play tunnel. It is really too short, but it will do. The ends have to be fixed to the ground with tent pegs and rope so that it cannot move. (See page 134)

Dog walk

You have to have a great deal of space to put this up. Three second-hand scaffolding planks are securely hooked together, the central one being supported by two strong trestles 140cm (4ft 6in) high. You will need sand added to the paint as for the 'A' ramp. Anti-slip slats on the outer planks are also useful, but the lowest one must not be less than 15cm from the end. Each contact area is 90cm long. This is certainly the most cumbersome, and arguably the least important, piece of my home equipment. (See page 134)

The agility course

You can now try, at least in your imagination, to let your Border Terrier tackle the agility course in the diagram on page 132-133. Make use of all the authority you now command as pack leader, the obedience your dog now happily grants you, and the special skills and teamwork you both have developed in your agility training. Enjoy yourselves!

At the start:

Position your dog behind the starting line and leave him there. He has to wait while you take up your position by the mouth of the tunnel. This gives you a head start on the dog, enabling you to avoid having to run that initial distance at full Border Terrier speed. Your dog will be ready to start, and extremely keen to take off and follow you, but he has to remain where you left him, although the first two jumps and a considerable distance will separate him from you.

No 1 and 2 (Single pole and suspended tyre):

On your command your dog starts and jumps over the single pole and through the suspended tyre, although it would be much easier and more terrier-like to run underneath each.

No 3 (Collapsible tunnel):

Most terriers like dark holes, but the collapsible tunnel is made of heavy cloth and, particularly in wet weather, may be heavy to push through. You must not run on until your dog is safely committed to the tunnel or he will follow you along the outside of it.

No 4 (Single pole):

Your dog emerges from the dark tunnel quite flat. Quickly adjusting to bright daylight he has to gather speed and height in time to jump.

The 'A' ramp: approaching the contact area.
Photo: J C Farrer

No 5 (See-saw):

A sharp turn leads to the see-saw. Your dog has to align himself to run up the plank without missing the contact, tip the see-saw in a controlled manner, wait until the far end of the see-saw has touched the ground, and then run off, touching the second contact area. You must not, by even the slightest body movement, rush your dog towards the weaving poles. Just a glance can make him jump off prematurely and miss the contact.

Training or play: what's the difference?
Photos: E J C Garden

No 6 (Weaving poles):
Your dog has to find the correct entry to the weaving poles while you are on the opposite side, and then concentrate on weaving right to the end of the line. You must not anticipate the next jump, or the dog will not weave right to the end of the poles.

No 7 (Single pole):
On the way to No 7 your dog gets ahead of you, giving you a chance to move across behind him. While he is jumping No 7 you tell him to turn right, and send him over No 8. You must not move across until he has committed himself to No 7 or he will follow you.

No 8 (Single pole):
As your dog jumps No 8 he is getting further ahead. You tell him to go on and to locate the table and lie flat immediately.

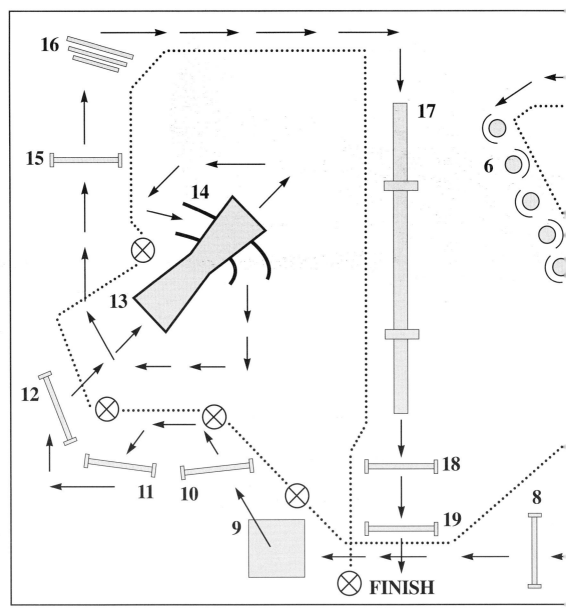

No 9 (Table):

Your dog has to lie in the Down position for five seconds, stopped dead in mid-flow. You have this much time to catch up, possibly reinforcing your 'Down!' command, and to position yourself on the far side of No 10. Your running past must not cause your dog to get up, let alone jump off.

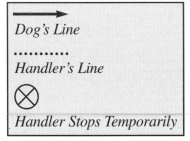

Dog's Line

·········

Handler's Line

⊗

Handler Stops Temporarily

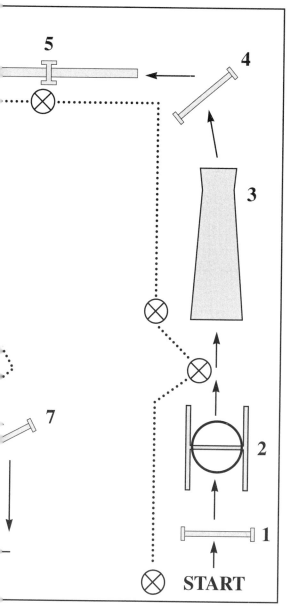

No 13 and 14 ('A' ramp and rigid tunnel):

A rigid tunnel is always tempting for a Border Terrier, and you have to draw your dog away from the tunnel opening and send him up the 'A' ramp. While the dog climbs up you run to the far side to make sure the dog touches the contact area and does not just jump off. You make the dog turn tightly around you and send him into the tunnel. Your dog has to be willing to follow the tunnel, although it leads him seemingly right away from you, and you now turn towards No 15.

No 15 (Single pole):

As your dog emerges he will see No 10, 11 and 12. He might want to run towards them. You have to call him even while he is still in the tunnel, so that he becomes aware of the new direction in time to turn to No 15 the very moment he emerges.

No 16 (Long jump):

A long jump presents no problem for a Border Terrier. The dog will accelerate enthusiastically, but has to be steadied again almost at once for the tight turn to No 17, and the correct alignment for the dog walk.

No 17 (Dog walk):

Unless the dog walk is rather unstable or the planks very springy there should be no problem on the way up. But you will know that you have nearly finished the course. Your dog might sense this, and great care must be taken not to convey any sense of hurry to the dog as he reaches the contact area of the down plank. It is easy to think 'Only two more jumps' and, instead of slowing the dog down, your movement will cause him to rush on, missing the contact.

No 10, 11 and 12 (Single poles):

You call your dog over No 10, send him over No 11, and call him back over No 12, moving to the right but always staying on the same side of those jumps.

The long jump. Note the rigid tunnel in the background.   Photo: E J Garden

The dog walk.   Photo: J C Farrer

No 18 and 19 (Single pole jumps):

You send the dog ahead to cross the finishing line as quickly as possible but, after jumping No 18, your dog will catch sight of the now familiar table (No 9), and he will be tempted to veer towards you and then jump onto the table instead of continuing to No 19. Your 'Go on straight!' signal will have to be particularly clear and strong.

After the finish:

The rules do not require the handler actually to cross the finishing line, but beyond it, as soon as you have caught up with your dog, is the right place and time to give him plenty of praise and to let him know how much you enjoyed running the course with him.

Boojum in real competition mood.   Photo: Bill Bunce MM

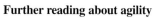

Further reading about agility

Some books on agility are listed in the **Bibliography**. The ordinary bookshop is unlikely to get you any of these books: you may do best to contact the publisher direct. Some agility shows have Agility Club shops, in which these titles are usually available.

Agility clubs

If you want to find out about agility clubs it is best to get in touch with The Agility Club or The Kennel Club, both of which are listed in **Useful Addresses**.

© Johanna Farrer, July 1995

Travelling
with Borders

Other dogs may hate travelling, but most Borders take it in their stride. As I was checking in for the helicopter flight to the Isles of Scilly the receptionist advised me to carry my dogs, because 'dogs usually cause problems and won't go up the steps'. Needless to say, mine treated this remark with the contempt it deserved, trotted by my side and, after an exploratory sniff, climbed confidently up the steps into the helicopter. The only thing they objected to was being shut into dog boxes once inside, as they couldn't see what was going on. Every so often a little paw waved through an air hole with a 'don't forget we are here' gesture.

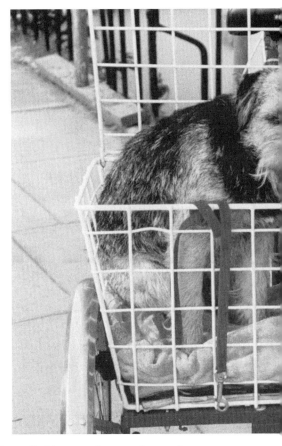

If you start a dog travelling at an early age he will usually enjoy the ride, especially a Border, who likes to know what is going on. Friends say they prefer to take their Borders with them on holiday if possible because, however friendly and helpful their neighbours, it is a responsibility looking after a Border who might go walkabout at any moment.

MEANS OF TRANSPORT

Car

When you are travelling by car, make sure the Border is restrained so that it can't jump out of the car window when passing a cat. I learned by bitter experience when Widger did just this. If a dog is wearing a harness he will not be thrown all over the interior if there is an accident. There are good dog safety harnesses made now to fit in any car.

A dog guard will stop your dog from climbing over the seats, but won't stop it being thrown around if the car stops suddenly. Some friends use theirs in another way: their well-behaved dogs sit on the back seats, and the kids are put in the rear behind the dog guard 'because they are not as well-behaved'. This is not to be generally recommended, however.

Another means of transporting dogs is the dog cage or dog box - a box made of wood or plastic with a wire mesh front. This can be strapped securely to the floor of your car, and can double as a bed for your dog in the house.

Luggage? If your dogs belong to the Caesar Dog Food Club they can get their own special Awayday Bag. Actually this is useful because you can keep all the bits and pieces in it that get lost between one trip and another. There is even space where one day, hopefully, one will be able to put the dog's passport.

Cycling

It is a good 30 minutes walk to my local park and I could think of many things to do with that time, but taking a taxi was much too expensive an option. When I saw a tricycle parked in Knightsbridge it seemed as if this could be the ideal solution to my problem. Cycling to the park would take less than 10 minutes.

I sat the dogs on a piece of paper and measured them, drawing round their behinds, and took the pattern to Phoenix Cycles in Battersea's Parkgate Road. Mike, the owner, who is a cycling enthusiast and supplies everything from tiny folding bicycles to Penny Farthings, was quite prepared to order a tricycle. I stressed that the paper pattern had to go to the manufacturers so that if the dogs didn't fit into the basket - no sale.

The cycle arrived, whereupon the dogs tried it for size and settled in immediately. They are tied in with their leads in case they see a cat but (touch wood!) once in the basket they behave impeccably. Riding through town they look at everyone with a regal air, totally ignoring any dogs that bark at them in envy; this sends those dogs into greater frenzies, but mine just put their noses in the air.

When I have to leave them outside shops, I come back to find the dogs the centre of an admiring crowd. As I cycle past groups of tourists there is a gasp - then cameras are focused on the pair sailing past in their basket. Widget and Wyvern take it all in their stride.

Wyvern and Widget in the tricycle basket custom-built to fit their behinds!

Some revellers tried to wheel the tricycle away at 3.00 one morning. Several streets away they were stopped by the police, who asked where were the dogs that usually rode in the basket, and then made them wheel it back where it came from.

Train

It can make sense to let the train take the strain now that railways no longer make a charge for dogs, and there are many good deals going for weekend and off-peak travel. British Rail says that dogs must be well-behaved and go in the guard's van if anyone objects. Sometimes the service is extra-luxurious; when Inter-City invited me to bring my dogs and give an opinion on their service to Penzance, we arrived to find a very worried PR lady deeply concerned because she was going to have to tell me that dogs were not allowed on seats. Tactfully explaining that they were not usually allowed on seats, I went to lunch, leaving the dogs tied up next to another journalist, who didn't want to eat. When I came back it was to find the dogs down the other end of the carriage in the middle of an admiring crowd who, far from objecting, were making a tremendous fuss of them.

The regulations say that dogs are allowed to travel with their owners only when this does not interfere with the comfort of other customers. Their owners must ensure that the dogs do not occupy accommodation in trains to the inconvenience or exclusion of customers. In no circumstances must dogs travel on the seats and they must not be allowed in sleeper or restaurant cars except, by special arrangement, for guide dogs travelling with blind or deaf persons.

Should a customer object to the presence of a dog in customer accommodation the owner must remove the dog; in such cases, if accommodation cannot be found in another train, the dog may be conveyed in the luggage van. When dogs are carried in the luggage van (other than those contained in a receptacle) they must be

Widget and Wyvern posing with National Express staff.

secured with collar and chain and efficiently muzzled. (A supplementary feature says, 'Offensive breeds, as defined in law, must be muzzled.')

There is no charge for up to two dogs per customer. However, if you have to have your dog on a seat, it must be in a cage or box, and then you will be charged at the excess luggage rate. Dogs are not conveyed in guards' vans of InterCity 125 trains but may be accommodated in TGS vehicles.

If your train journey includes a ferry crossing (to Ireland, for instance) there may be a charge for the dog on board, and only small dogs are carried on trains on the Isle of Wight.

If you are going on a long journey, it is worth knowing that some of the time-tables show arrival and departure times at major stations; your local enquiry office should be able to provide information. Trains such as the Plymouth to Aberdeen have 10-minute and 15-minute stops at Birmingham and Edinburgh respectively, provided there are no delays. When you get on the train, have a word with the senior conductor to alert him that you will be leaving the train to exercise dogs. He will be able to tell you if the train is running to time and how much time there will be.

Madelene Aspinwall recollects how dogs used to be sent by train for mating, especially up north, where Ronnie Irving's grandfather Wattie was station master. The dogs would be mated in the waiting room and sent back on the next train. Perhaps when British Rail is privatised some enterprising person might fix up Motels for Mating!

Coaches

National Express will take dogs on non-Rapide services, that is those with no refreshment service. They are carried at the discretion of the company, and you must inform them when making a booking. There is a nominal charge of £1 per single through journey. As a courtesy I phone the day before to confirm that I am bringing a dog, just in case the scheduled driver has an allergy to dogs. Sadly the drivers often ask me tactfully not to let the dogs on the seats, making me wonder at other dog owners who have obviously done this. (Telephone: 0990 80 80 80)

Incidentally, National Express will take Guide Dogs on Rapide services, and also state that they accept Hearing Dogs.

If you want to travel on one of the thousands of private coach and bus services around Britain, there is a TBC hotline (Train, Bus and Coach) 0891-910 910. They seem to have every time-table ever printed, and made out a complicated itinerary for a cross-UK trip with the dogs in a few minutes.

Air

British Midland Airways accepts dogs as passengers and says that they are quite frequent flyers. They go in the hold, which is pressurised and heated, and must be in a carrying cage or box. The airline cannot guarantee that the dog will go on the same flight as you, as this service is subject to availability, but says, 'We have never had to separate dog and owner yet.'

WHERE TO GO

Two favourite places for the dogs are the Isles of Scilly and the Lake District.

Isles of Scilly

In the Isles the only place where the dogs had to be on leads was in the Capital, Hugh

Town; and they are not allowed on the island of Tresco. Otherwise they roamed around acres of heath and sands with no-one in sight, only rabbits and birds for company. Instead of buses we hopped on and off boats between islands and became seasoned locals. John, one of the boatmen, has a Border Terrier, and everywhere we went locals stopped me to ask what was I doing with John's dog.

One magical day we went to Bryher, where a beached whale's carcass provided a wonderful pongy place for the Borders to explore, until I had had enough. We then set off to walk around this tiny island and explore its delightful beaches. When I was tired I just sat on the shore and the boatman who had taken us there popped over and took us back to St Mary's, the main island. Another day we tracked all over the island of St Agnes and then hired a boat to visit the seal and puffin colonies. The dogs sniffed at the seals as they came bobbing alongside the boat but then showed their disgust at my interest by curling up at the boatman's feet and going to sleep.

Lake District

Don't believe those scare stories of massive traffic jams in the Lake District. Many hotels back onto the fells (hills) and you can walk out of the back door and be away from the crowds in two minutes, giving the dogs and yourself wonderful exercise as you follow the thousands of miles of trails. Walking all day, you may not see anyone else for hours.

Most people in the Lake District seem to own dogs, including the staff at tourist attractions, so dogs are welcome almost everywhere. In fact at the marvellous Brockhole Visitor Centre they fall over backwards to look after their canine visitors. Notices in the car park ask visitors with dogs to leave their car under the trees, so that the interior is cool for the dogs when they return. Entrance and car parking is free unless there is a special event.

Brockhole is the ideal place in wet weather as well as fine. Dogs are allowed off the lead in the gorgeous parkland which stretches down to the lakeside and, if it is wet, you can take advantage of a special dog area with hooks and water bowls, with bottles of fresh cool water for topping up. The dogs can sit there whilst owners browse around inside the bookshop, select videos about the area and have their own private showings, and eat delicious home cooking.

Helen Lister is one of the executives at Brockhole and has dogs of her own. These lucky animals are given a special birthday cake made of dog biscuit and cream cheese, and she also makes dog 'brownies' from liver, cornmeal, wheatgerm, garlic and eggs. Baked in a toffee tin, these are cut up and given as treats, and are excellent if a dog has been off its food. Not much chance of that with most Borders!

Another free attraction is Whinlatter Forest Park, England's only mountain forest. Thousands of people go there every day and within five minutes of leaving your car you are out of sight of anyone else. Many locals drive up here to exercise their dogs early each morning, so you can arrive at crack of dawn and find many cars already in the car park. As we walked around a corner we fell over rubbish strewn all over the ground. 'Who'd have wildlife?' joked the warden, telling us this was caused by foxes.

If you are into orienteering you can try out the first Trail 'O' course, and at the entrance to the forest is a well-thought-out visitor centre. This is a marvellous place if it is raining, although once under the trees you are sheltered from the worst of the elements. In the grounds there is a giant reproduction of a badger sett, complete with horrible sounding noises. You walk through the underground labyrinth and suddenly come face-to-face with a giant brock with vicious looking claws. It makes one really appreciate a Border's courage in facing up to such a challenge.

Geraldine Grave, who works at the visitor centre at Whinlatter, has two Borders: Nap aged 15 and Tyam (Cumbrian for two) who is seven. She also has a rescued Shih Tzu who thinks she's a Border. Sheep are all over the place, but her dogs don't chase them: Nap got a hiding for chasing sheep when he was young and Tyam takes his lead from the older Border. They are great swimmers and love to go in Bassenthwaite Lake, the only lake in the Lake District. (Local joke: How many lakes are there in the Lake District? Answer: Only one - the rest are meres and waters.)

Geraldine's husband, Hedley, who has worked at Whinlatter for over 40 years, is a keen photographer, and the dogs pose whenever the camera appears. Nap is now deaf 'until you open a Mars Bar'. Whenever the tea cups appear this spells Digestive biscuits to the dogs.

Mirehouse, just north of Keswick, is the home of the Spedding family. It is one of those lovely homes where there is something to interest everyone, from Dad to the kids. Anyone who is into photography will be fascinated to see early photographs by Julia Margaret Cameron, and Border owners will be intrigued to see in one of the drawing rooms a collection of 1920s photographs, some of which feature Michael.

Michael was a Border who belonged to General Wilfred Spedding and used to accompany him to council meetings. Spedding adored Michael, Michael adored his master, and they went everywhere together. According to the current Mrs Spedding, the General was very keen on having an airport in Keswick, and a photograph in the small drawing room shows council members, many looking very disinterested, standing in front of a huge bi-plane, with Michael stealing the centre stage.

Mirehouse is open to the public on Wednesdays and Sundays, but Clare Spedding, the owner, welcomes guest at other times, provided they pay the basic group fee of £45. She is a marvellous guide, with an especial feel for what interests children, and for a fascinating glimpse into family history for the past hundred years it is well worth a visit.

ACCOMMODATION

On hearing that I was researching for this book, several Border breeders said they had difficulty finding hotels that accepted dogs. Most B & Bs will take dogs but, as one owner said, 'If we decide to push out the boat and celebrate, it is very difficult finding a good hotel that welcomes dogs.'

As a travel writer I am invited to stay at hotels, and sometimes ask if I can bring my dogs to test out the facilities on behalf of readers. There are some lovely hotels that really welcome dogs, but do check when you book; a hotel can change hands and new owners might have funny ideas and stop taking dogs.

When I asked one hotel if they accepted dogs, the manager's reply was: 'We are delighted to welcome dogs as guests, but sometimes a little less enthusiastic about the people that they bring with them!'

Much more sensible than the newly opened hotel whose brochure spoke of being 'in the heart of the country - just right for country walks and then back to tea by our log fire'. Obviously just the hotel for us, thought I. Wrong! When I phoned to check, the receptionist responded with shock and horror: 'We couldn't allow dogs on our new carpets.' I can't wait for the guests to trample through the countryside and then muddy their pristine Wilton.

However, I have learnt, even if a hotel says dogs are welcome, to ask if there are any resident cats, having been woken up one morning at 5.00 by my Borders demanding to be let out of the ground floor French windows leading into the garden. They had obviously heard the hotel cat stalking past, and proceeded to give very vocal chase, waking everyone up.

Arriving back at another hotel where the dogs had been left quietly in the bedroom, I discovered them sitting on the receptionists' laps: 'We knew they were alone in the bedroom so thought they needed company. Anyway they're helping us post the bills!'

Chambermaids can be startled by a welcoming dog, so tell the housekeeper you have dogs. If I leave them in the bedroom when I go down to breakfast I usually leave the 'Do not Disturb' sign on the door if I haven't been able to alert the staff.

Hotels that accept dogs often say they give less trouble than human visitors. Dogs are usually sensible, and accept the fact that they are to sleep on the carpet in a corner, and are not allowed on beds; not only for reasons of cleanliness but also in case the next occupant is an asthma sufferer.

Dogs can let you down, however well-trained. A friend was dining at one hotel when the manager came up to tell him his dogs were 'howling their heads off' and the guests in the next bedroom had complained. Rushing upstairs, sure enough he heard that Border 'song' echoing down the corridor. Opening the door he could see tails wagging, until the door opened fully and they saw Master there. He travels a great deal, staying in the best hotels, and, when he thought back, he realised that his dogs must have twigged that at night chambermaids patrolled the corridors, turning down beds, and often leaving a chocolate on the pillow. These maids, suckers for a sad-sounding Border, would come over with cuddles and chocs and generally provide excellent service. Today the dogs are banished to the car whilst he is dining.

The AA Hotel Guide has a symbol for Dogs Not Welcome. However, they say if the symbol isn't there, it doesn't automatically mean the hotel will accept dogs; it may depend which manager is on duty. Therefore, it is advisable to ask first.

Consort Hotels, an hotel marketing consortium, will tell you which of their member hotels take dogs if you phone them with your itinerary (01904-620137).

London

Friends that bring their dogs to London say the dogs love it, especially if they are males. A lamp post every few yards must be dog heaven, and the lovely smells and chance to socialise in the parks make a welcome change.

Basil Street Hotel

The nicest Colonials, such as Sir Edmund and Lady Hillary, all know the Basil Street Hotel, but it is one of those secret places that never advertises because it doesn't need to. Full of fascinating antiques, with a dining room that is home to the local trendies who appreciate good cooking and good wines at kind prices, it is a lovely place to meet friends.

Is is situated only two minutes away from Harrods and five from Hyde Park, and everyone in the family is catered for. There are several old-fashioned services such as shoe cleaning and turning down the beds and most of the staff have been there for ever.

Buchans Restaurant, Battersea Bridge Road, SW11

This restaurant has a very sensible system; dogs and their owners can dine in the front

Wyvern playing with the author in London's Kensington Gardens.

area, with wooden floors and tables. Those who want elegance sit in the back room with starched linen tablecloths. They have a wonderful Sunday lunch with a roast at £12 for three courses (1995 prices).

The Heart of England

Ettington

The first Chairman of The Kennel Club was Mr Sewallis Evelyn Shirley of Ettington, near Stratford-on-Avon. His family had lived on the site since Saxon times, and held the estate since the Norman Conquest. His obituary described him as having the 'guiding mind [that] first conceived the idea of evolving law and order out of the chaos... which then surrounded the exhibition of dogs. His personal influence enabled him to gather other workers around him, who were eventually to be the founders of The Kennel Club in 1873'. If you travel to Stratford from Oxford you see his old home on the right, six miles short of Stratford: a huge house set in its own park.

Shirley's unusual Christian name comes from the Domesday Book, which recorded that Saswolo or Sewallis held this manor from Henry de Ferrers. It was his grandson, another Sewallis, who became 'de Shirley' when he moved to the village of that name in Derbyshire, whilst retaining Ettington.

Shirleys had been local MPs since 1296 and Shakespeare records their martial prowess when Prince Hal talks of 'the spirits of valiant Shirley, Stafford, Blunt'. Another Shirley, Robert Shirley Lord Ferrers, found his way into the Guinness Book of Records, with 17 children by his first wife, 10 by his second and 30 illegitimate children. His descendant Laurence Shirley was the last aristocrat in England to be executed for a felony; hanged with a silk rope, in deference to his rank, for murdering a receiver of rents.

Sadly Sewallis was the last Shirley to live at Ettington. Following family tradition, he was an MP for Co Monaghan for 12 years and, when he died in 1904, the house went through various owners. Eventually it was sold to a hotel company and, believe it or not, dogs are not allowed!

The Feathers, Woodstock
We stopped here because we had heard the lunch-time bar snacks were worth it, and they were. Afterwards we went for a walk with the dogs in Blenheim Palace grounds, and it seemed stupid to press on when such a delightful hotel was waiting. The receptionist had been so friendly when we asked if the dogs could have some water outside.

As long as dogs have their own bedding they are allowed in the hotel bedrooms. The chef prepared a delicious meal just right for dogs; we had asked for scraps but it looked good enough for us to eat. We hid the chocolates that are provided in the bedrooms before we went downstairs for our own dinner. Don't forget to book, as locals fill the dining room. Seven choices per course, saddle of hare being the speciality the night we dined. Chocaholics are well catered for!

The George Hotel, Stamford
Princess Anne stays here, and so do my dogs. I hope she enjoyed it as much as we did, as we sat in the courtyard and ate marvellous bar snacks. Some of the bedrooms are huge, some much smaller, but as there has been an inn here for over 900 years you have to expect some crooked staircases and very different bedrooms, all well-furnished.

The hotel is easy to find; just look for the huge sign across the road. There is a lovely restaurant with memorable food, and this is the place to have real roast beef, served from the trolley.

Lion Hotel, Shrewsbury
You can almost feel Brother Cadfael slip-slopping past the old windows as he goes about his business. Shrewsbury has more half-timbered houses than any other town in England, and this is one of them. It is an ancient coaching inn and, in the days when the local gentry came into town for a mini-season, its ballroom (some say designed by Adam) was much in use.

Most of the bedrooms have been added on recently, sympathetically too and, although small, they are well-furnished. However, you can still stay in the suite where Charles Dickens stayed. The chef produces some delicious dinners, often using local produce such as salmon.

Manor House Castle Combe
Cirencester 21 miles
This is a very appropriate hotel for animal lovers, as it is in the village where the Dr Doolittle film was shot. Every time you go through the picture-postcard main street you seem to hear Rex Harrison singing 'Talk to the Animals'.

In the main hotel there is a welcoming feel of old furniture, panelling and open fires. Most of the bedrooms have four-posters, but the 'cottages', converted from the old stables and stores, are also nicely furnished and it is easy to let the dogs out in the morning. In the restaurant the menu doesn't just describe 'duck': it is named as 'mallard'.

New Hall, Sutton Coldfield

This hotel doesn't take dogs, but is in this book because its Guest Relations Manager is Rupert, a Labrador. Apparently he receives more faxes and bookings than the official reception. Staying for Crufts, I had put the dogs into the Top Hat Kennels, and drove down the drive with its notices warning guests to beware 'low flying pheasants'. With a name like New Hall, this of course is the oldest inhabited moated house in Britain, and in the morning, looking out over the moat, one wished one had long hair to let down *à la* Rapunzel. Although the hotel is part of the Thistle Country House Collection, they were sensible enough to ask Caroline and Ian Parkes to run it as if it were there own. No corporate touches are allowed to intrude, but the setting and service are so superb that you will find the nicest pop stars, ex-Presidents and *incognito* notables enjoying the gardens and superb cooking. Do look out for the staff uniform, which is attractive without being 'twee'.

The rooms in the old house are a historian's dream; those in the newer part fit in beautifully, and are much bigger than the average bedroom. If you have to go to Crufts this is the civilised place to recover.

No names...

A friend had asked for advice on where to hold her wedding reception, and I had recommended a friend's hotel near Oxford. Normally they don't take dogs, because there are some hotel cats, but this time Dudley said he would be happy for mine to stay, and put us in the newly-opened cottages.

The peace of the evening was shattered when the devils came across a hedgehog; they will go in and grab spines in their teeth, then shake it to make it open up. I managed to shake them off, and bundled them under my arms up into our room. On the way I felt bleeding, shoved them into the bath, and spent the next two hours picking out spines whilst they were feeling pleased with themselves.

If anyone was staying in that hotel and found a weird woman on her hands and knees peering at the stair carpet at midnight - I was the culprit, minutely examining the brand new Wilton to see that there were no blood stains.

Randolph Hotel, Oxford

This is an institution and Rocco Forte's sister has just done up the reception rooms in their original Victorian style, so they gleam with gold leaf and jewel colours. A fitting setting for guests such as Elizabeth Taylor. Bedrooms are extremely comfortable with goodies galore in the bathroom. Officially the hotel takes 'small pets by arrangement', so tell the dogs to behave!

Oxford has some wonderful restaurants but, if you are too tired to walk, the hotel houses Squires Restaurant, with silver salt and pepper shakers. Sipping a drink, do take time to look at the wonderful cartoons on the bar walls; you can get postcards of these.

Whately Hall, Banbury

This hotel is really welcoming to dogs. At dinner time chef sent over a huge plate full of doggie goodies, beautifully garnished with parsley. Sadly my two didn't appreciate this attempt at decoration; they just wolfed it down. Dean Swift wrote part of *Gullivers' Travels* here and, with the panelled rooms, you feel his spirit is still around, this illusion being helped by the fact there is a secret staircase and a priest's hole.

East Anglia

The Swan Hotel at Lavenham

Its leaflet says 'built 1400 approx. Renovated in 1991', and this gives a good idea of what it is actually like, except that the renovation was done sympathetically, with many lovely old rooms looking out onto a garden. Lavenham was one of the wealthiest centres for the wool trade and has a magnificent 'wool church', St Peter and Paul.

Playing on the beach near the Swan Hotel, Lavenham.

A novel form of transport at Woolley Grange, Bradford-on-Avon.

The village itself hasn't altered much in the past 400 years, and The Swan was developed from three typical timbered houses. Once described as 'The Capital old-established free public and posting house' it had stabling for 50 horses. More recently a Roll of Honour commemorates pilots of Bomber and Flight Command who made it their unofficial headquarters. Oh, and they welcome dogs and serve delicious food!

On the beach in Northumberland.

West Country

Woolley Grange, Bradford-on-Avon

Bath: 7 miles.

With a welcoming Springer Spaniel and the head housekeeper ex-Buckingham Palace, this hotel wraps you round with superb service. Children will love it; they have their own Woolley Bears Den where marvellous nannies look after them all day. Your bedroom will probably have an open fire, and plenty of goodies in the bathroom.

The Restaurant is a delight, for food and décor, and the dogs definitely enjoyed their stay, with a chance to snuffle round the gardens and take walks in the surrounding countryside.

The Border Country

Headlam Hall, Co Durham

Darlington 8 miles.

As we arrived there was an almighty crash, and a Labrador shot into view looking as sheepish as only a Labrador that has been naughty can. This was Hilda, the hotel's resident dog who, searching for something to stave off the pangs of hunger, had managed to overturn a huge, two-metre-high rubbish bin. Labradors must be related to Borders, the tricks they get up to satisfy hunger.

Hilda is happy to show off her village to visiting dogs and, on the promise we wouldn't let her anywhere near anything remotely resembling food, the hotel staff allowed us to take her for a walk around the little hamlet of Headlam, tucked away in the Durham countryside. It is ideal dog-walking country; even the cars seem to nose carefully round bends as though expecting dogs to be in the middle of the road.

As we walked we collected several canine friends; did they like Hilda for her personality, or because she had access to delightful snacks? We'll never know. But Headlam Hall welcomes dogs and their owners, and the Robinsons put you up in the Coach House in the garden, with an indoor swimming pool (for humans not dogs).

Langley Castle, Nr Hexham

This is more a keep than a castle, but incredibly impressive, with walls more than two metres thick and a collection of 14 garderobes (mediaeval loos). The remains of these can be seen on the walls and no one knows why there are so many.

The castle belongs to an American family who love all things British. They saw this castle advertised in *Country Life*, flew over, fell in love, and turned it into a gem, accommodation comprising nine large bedrooms with modern bathrooms (not garderobes). However, it hasn't been over-chintzed so is reasonably priced.

The heart of the hotel is a huge drawing room; all corridors from bedrooms lead to this, so you get to know your fellow guests over a drink in front of the log fires. From the roof there is a marvellous view over the surrounding countryside, and Catherine Cookson lives nearby.

Linden Hall, Nr Morpeth

Newcastle-upon-Tyne: 21 miles.

There are 'cottage' bedrooms where you can stay with your dog. This hotel, built around an elegant Georgian mansion, belongs to the prestigious Grand Heritage Hotels marketing group. There is plenty of room to exercise the dogs in 450 acres of grounds and you will need exercise yourself to take advantage of the breakfasts; kippers, kidneys and every sort of egg and bacon you can imagine. Food at dinner is good too.

In Northumberland there are many 'Border' connections and, when Widget ate something poisonous during the day, they didn't panic but phoned the local vet, giving us clear directions how to get there. We found everything waiting for us when we arrived.

Lord Crewe Arms, Blanchland. Northumberland

Consett: 30 minutes.

Blanchland is in the middle of wonderful walking country, near Consett in Northumberland. Huddled around its abbey, the hamlet is caught in a time warp, and it is easy to listen to stories of when the Scots came raiding over the Border but couldn't find the village in thick fog. Thinking they were saved, monks in the abbey set the church bells ringing, thus guiding the raiders straight to the settlement.

In the village is the Lord Crewe Arms with the Dorothy Forster bedroom, reputed to be haunted. Knowing my mother was a Forster the hotel gave this room to my parents, only to have to change it when their current dog howled his head off. A local poet wrote:

> Tis whispered that 'Spirits' abide in the 'Crewe'
> (perhaps better seen when you've had one or two)

and none of my dogs will go into this room; a previous owner of the hotel told me his dog always waited at the bottom of the steps when he went into the Dorothy Forster room.

Don't be put off - my dogs love the rest of this delightful hotel, parts of which date back 700 years, and the management is very welcoming to dogs. The dogs particularly like the Hilyard Room with its huge fireplace built with a priest-hole, reputed to be where Tom Forster, one of my infamous ancestors, once hid to escape capture by the King's forces in 1715.

Nearby are the moors, where the dogs can do their 'Jack-in-the-box' progression through the heather. My grandfather used have a shooting lodge, sadly now burnt down, at Riddlehamhope.

Sunlaws House, Kelso

When I phoned for the first time to ask if the hotel took dogs, a happy, laughing Scots voice said, 'We do, yes.' This is a wonderful hotel for humans and animals. It is part of the Duke of Roxburghe's estate and one feels some of the best pieces of old furniture in the suites must have come out of the ducal attics. The less-expensive bedrooms are attractive too, but in modern style.

Log fires welcome you, delicious cooking using local produce is served in the superb restaurant, and the staff turn down the beds at night.

Floors Castle is the centrepiece of the estate. It was here that the film *Greystoke* was made in 1983 and, according to Professor Milton, Borders featured in the film. Anyway, the castle is well worth a visit, as is the delightful town across the picturesque river.

Tankerville Arms, Wooler, Northumberland

Dogs are always welcome here, as long as they bring their own beds. Right in the middle of 'Border' territory, Anne Park and her team are welcoming to dogs, children and well-behaved owners. The Copper Bar is a haunt for farmers on market days, and in the evening there are usually locals sitting by the open fire.

Nearby are the incredible white cattle of Chillingham, relics of ancient herds. You have to leave the dogs in the car if you want to see these cattle, as any strange noises and they are off, but their story is so extraordinary that it is worth the effort to find them. All around is magnificent countryside, the Cheviots providing the border between Scotland and England.

Yorkshire

Boar's Head, Ripley, Yorks

Telephone: 01423-771888

This was originally The Star, a coaching inn on the Leeds-Edinburgh run, providing plenty of convivial enjoyment. In 1919, however, the owner, Sir William Ingilby, a strictly religious man, objected to the pub serving drinks on a Sunday, and ordered it to be closed on the Sabbath. This so incensed the landlord that he packed his bags, and no-one took his place.

For 70 years Ripley village remained dry, until Sir William's grandson, Sir Thomas, re-opened the pub as The Boar's Head (the family crest). However, if anyone gets too convivial the village stocks are right outside! Sir Thomas is fond of a glass of malt himself, and takes a great interest in the hotel, personally selecting the Wine List. The cellar contains more than 200 bins filled with wines from all over the world. Paul Tatham, the manager, knows and loves Borders, and in each bathroom is a wooden boat thoughtfully provided by Lady Ingilby to make guests feel at home.

A novel mode of travel: 'Blue' on a steam-roller. (Owner: Mrs Valerie Furness of the Quatford affix)

Cumbria and The Lakes

Crown Hotel, Wetheral, Nr Carlisle
Situated on the banks of the River Eden and looking up towards a castle, this hotel is in the middle of a lovely village. The main part is an elegant Georgian building, with sympathetically built modern bedrooms at the back. If you wonder why you can't open the windows more than a few centimetres, this is because the rooms are low down and, when this modern wing was opened, the management found that some guests were helping themselves to televisions, bedding and even beds. The windows were ideally placed for a car to be driven alongside and loaded up with stolen goods.

The dining room is in a lovely conservatory which overlooks romantically floodlit gardens.

Leeming Hotel, Ullswater
Penrith: 7 miles.
The dogs definitely approved of the Leeming Hotel. As far as they were concerned it had all 'mod cons'. As we took a stroll through the grounds all seemed quiet. 'Let them off the lead,' invited the Manager. Whoosh! A rabbit was seen hopping across the lawn and the dogs disappeared joyfully into the bushes. This was something like; at last a hotel that realised what was essential for Border guests!

Once we had re-captured the two happy guests we continued around the gorgeous grounds. Wordsworth would be delighted with the daffodils and other flowers that spill out everywhere. It is a Forte Hotel, but most un-Forte.

Approved kennels
If you have to leave dogs in kennels and don't know which one to choose, the best recommendation is from another owner. This is where it is useful to belong to a breed club, as other members will always be happy to tell you of good kennels. Get the names of one or two and visit them.

Noise is usually a good sign. Do the dogs seem happy, wagging their tails as you go past? Does the owner insist you bring the dog's vaccination record, and refuse to allow your dog in if you don't? Ask to see the quarters your dog would occupy. Are they big enough? Is there a warm place to sleep in? Do all the dogs have clean drinking water? Will the dogs have adequate exercise every day?

The following kennels have been used, and very much approved, by my dogs. The dogs trot into them and don't even look back at me. I have always asked friends and our vet for their advice and, as I arrive at the kennels, the 'hairs on the back of the neck' tell me if everything is OK. The moment when the dogs wag their tails at the kennel maid or man I know everything is all right.

Top Hat Kennels
Coventry Road, Hampton-in Arden, Solihull, B92 OHH
Having to cover Crufts, I had decided to take my dogs because we were going on to a friend who loves to see them. I didn't know what to do with them during the day until a friend who works at the NEC said she always left her dogs at the Top Hat Kennels and Cattery. Brian Morrison and his staff were so kind and welcoming that I asked if the dogs could stay overnight, to save having to go backwards and forward. It was a rest for me not having to get up early before Crufts to give them walks, and the dogs appreciated their holiday there.

Haxted Kennels

Haxted Kennels in Sussex have a wonderful dog collection van that comes to your front door in London, picks up your dog and returns it after its holiday, for a fee of £15 extra. Last time I went to collect Wyvern he came in draped around the kennel maid's neck, so I knew he had enjoyed himself. Don't forget to book well in advance, particularly for the summer and Easter holidays.

SPECIAL INTERESTS
Otters

If you want to go and see what a genuine 'otter face' looks like you will be glad to know that it is becoming easier to see these enchanting creatures. As a child I used to watch them in the rivers, seeing them flash through the water like furry electric eels. However, they almost disappeared from their haunts. Although hunting might have depleted a few stocks, the real culprit was river pollution from organochlorine pesticides, primarily dieldrin, poisoning the animal's food chain. I remember that Mel Freeman, who worked for the Anglian Water Authority, wouldn't allow his family to drink tap water. Years before designer waters became fashionable they always drank bottled water. So think what pollution was doing to the otter! However, *English Nature* say they are coming back and recommends reserves where you will almost certainly be able to see them 'at work and play'.

The Otter Trust is at Earsham, Nr Bungay, Suffolk (Telephone: 01986 893 470). Nearby is The Swan Hotel at Lavenham (see **Accommodation: East Anglia**).

In the West country there is an area that markets itself as Tarka Country, and also the Tamar Otter Park and Wild Wood, Petherwin, Nr Launceston Cornwall PL15 8LW. Contact the West Country Tourist Board for details.

On the Isle of Skye is the Kylerhea Otter Haven on Forestry Enterprise land. Five years ago Ron Johnstone wondered if people from cities would appreciate the chance to see an otter in the wild, and set up the haven. There are specially built observation hides where you can generally see these creatures at work and play.

Polo

People who play polo usually have a dog or two chucked into the back of the Range Rover along with the polo sticks, helmets and all the other gear. At Cowdray Park, doyen of polo clubs, they ask that dogs are kept on leads during play. At other times dogs can run around the huge fields, under supervision, having a wonderful time. Spectators are encouraged to tread in the divots at half time, and this is when dogs and their owners socialise and a good time is had by all.

Going to a polo match is a lovely way to spend a summer afternoon. You can go early and take a picnic, then take the dogs for a walk in wonderful grounds. Clubs welcome non-members in their cars, on bikes or on foot, usually charging about £5-£15 per car (occupants free) according to quality of play. There are about 50 clubs spread around Great Britain and the Hurlingham Polo Association (01869-350044) can tell you your nearest ground.

Terrier racing

This is a very popular sport, and almost certainly bound to be part of the entertainment at many of the country shows in the North Country. Some Shows where this will probably be featured are:

- Lune Valley Mink Hounds Show, Lythe Valley (May).
- Calderbridge (May).
- Brough Hound and Terrier Show, Kirkby Stephen (June).
- Penrith Agricultural Show (July).
- Coniston Country Fair (July).
- Lowther Horse Driving Trials and Country Fair (where you can usually see Prince Philip duelling with George Bowman in the Driving Championships) (August).
- Vale of Rydal Sheepdog Trials and Hound Show (August).
- Hawkshead Show (August).
- Threlkeld Sheepdog Trials (August).
- Grasmere Sports (August).
- Patterdale Dog Day (one of oldest dog shows) (August).
- Hesket Newmarket Show (September).
- Wasdale Head Show and Shepherd's Meet (October).
- Buttermere Shepherd's Meeting (October).

FRIENDS FROM ABROAD

Writing recently in *Dog World*, Anne Roslin-Williams mentions taking a friend visiting from Sweden to South Wales. On the way they saw the Ledbury Foxhounds exercising, so out came the camera. Then she took her friend terrier racing, 'which was terrific fun. There were lots of Borders... competing. Margareta will have some rather unusual holiday snaps to take home, better than the Tower of London any day'.

I do so agree (although the Tower is a magnificent sight) and for years I have been trying to get tour operators and Tourist Boards to focus visitors' attention on our country pursuits rather than the honeypot towns like Chester and York of which, although they are a wonderful sight, I am sure all most visitors see is the back of the neck of the tourist in front of them.

If you have friends from abroad and want to show them our agricultural shows, sheepdog trials, Cumberland wrestling, caber tossing or any one of the many countryside pursuits at gatherings which are unique to Britain, contact your local Tourist Information Centre (TIC).

There are over 800 TICs in Britain, 250 of them open all year round and connected by computer to other TICs. Most local TICs should be able to key into the English, Northern Ireland, Scottish or Welsh Tourist Boards' List of Events, which has thousands of outdoor events listed all over the country. Say when your friends are arriving and to which area you want to take them, and a list of suitable events should be offered.

'Ready - steady - go!' Terrier racing is a very popular sport.

If you would rather contact the regional Tourist Boards direct, the ones most likely to have Border Terrier and other related events are:

Cumbria Tourist Board	Telephone: 015394-44444 Fax: 015394-44041
Northumbria Tourist Board	Telephone 0191-375 3000 Fax 0191-386 0899
Yorkshire and Humberside Tourist Board	Telephone: 01904 707691 Fax 01904 701414
Scottish Tourist Board	Telephone: 0131-332 2433 Fax 0131-343 1513

If you are travelling around, don't forget the major TICs are linked to BABA (Book a Bed Ahead) and will be able to book you into accommodation in your price range that will accept dogs.

We tend to think Tourist Boards are only interested in promoting to overseas visitors, but two thirds of our tourism revenue comes from the British holidaying in Britain. The Government, which would like help with our balance of payments, wants to encourage more of us to stay in our islands. For this reason, TICs warmly welcome locals as well as foreigners.

PRICES

You have probably noticed that I haven't given prices; as soon as you mention these, up they go! However, the hotels I mention often have Weekend or Special Breaks, when the prices are half of those quoted in the hotel guides, so do ask. There used to be a wonderful book published by the English Tourist Board giving all these special offers, but the Government decided that it would be better for the Regions to do their own publicity, so now you have to ask each of the regions for their *Breaks in the .... Region* brochure.

There are 11 regions - don't blame me for all the extra work and telephone calls! Incidentally, the original book made a considerable amount of money for the English Tourist Board, but I am so angry about the mindless politicians that try to ruin (sorry, run) our tourism industry, that I'd better not say any more!

Wherever you go and whatever you do, your Border Terrier will be only too happy to join in.

Border tales

Chapter Twelve

Joe Bowman

In 1920 W C Skelton wrote down Joe Bowman's *Reminiscences*, in which Bowman recounted that his dog Turk once save his life by drawing off a charging bull. Joe was huntsman in the Ullswater Hunt for 35 years, being appointed in 1879, and on one occasion Joe and his friends were having a 'sing-song'. Ten healths were drunk and Grip was seen to leave the room during each health. At the end of the evening 10 dead hens were discovered.

More stories followed:

> I think I did not tell you that we got a Terrier now and then when I was young from Willie Tysons of Black Hall, Eskdale. A brindle bitch, Fury, from these was in great demand in finding sheep in snow drifts at which she was very clever.

Shepherds will tell you that Borders have very keen noses; particularly when there is a bitch in season anywhere nearby.

Sir John Renwick

He was one of the most famous of the well-known Renwick Border owners, and a noted sportsman who exhibited his dogs for over 50 years. His first Borders were exhibited in 1890 and he always said there was no terrier to compare with a good Border as a huntsman's dog. His terriers had to be game and have a good look, and many of them became champions, including Ch Newminster Rose.

The story is told of one of his Borders who, having won Best of Breed at the Bellingham Show, two days later bolted a fox out hunting, together with five more.

Copper

Arriving at the mink hunt one day we saw a huntsman go to have a word with the vet when the hound trailer arrived. The door was let down, and Frank Wildman's Copper pranced down. Left behind were three hounds, much the worse for wear; whatever they had said to Copper, he had objected and given them 'what for'.

Copper was a tremendous worker, and so muscular that he was box-shaped. He didn't stand any nonsense from hounds that didn't do their job properly and, with a shake, would launch himself into the river in pursuit of the mink when hounds had made a nonsense of the chase.

Seen on the *Creative Image* stand at Crufts.

Bill Gillott and Sam

Bill Gillott, of Weegee Border Terriers from Melton Mowbray, has written *Border Terrier Records,* giving details of famous Border Terriers and their Show records. Sadly, this is now out of print, and Bill says he won't be reprinting for another 10 years. If you want to see a copy many breeders will have one. One day Bill was at the Belvoir Hunt Terrier Show, where there was terrier racing. The Borders won every race in which they were involved so, for the semi-finals, it was decided to give other terrier owners a chance, having one race for other terriers, such as Jack Russells, and one for Borders.

The Borders were let off, chasing a fox pelt; long before the end they had caught this, and six Borders fastened themselves onto the skin. The owners managed to pull off all the terriers except Sam, who just would not leave go. Eventually a huntsman suggested they blow in Sam's ear; no-one would volunteer to disturb Sam, so the huntsman blew into the ear himself. Sam was furious, let go of the pelt and bit the huntsman on the lip, just to show him what he thought of that.

Harry Singh

People might have wondered whence came the affix Vandameres. In The Border Terrier Club's year book it explained that this was contraction of Windermere, and belonged to the late Harry Singh, a well-loved and well-remembered owner.

There was a lovely story about him: a Championship Show Judge, he was about to visit Hickstead, and one of his Northern colleagues asked him if he knew how to get there. 'Look here, man, a' got to England from India, so a' tink a'll manage.'

Matron's pet

James Rothwell remembers his preparatory school Matron, Miss Wigan, at St Michaels in Tavistock. She had a Border Terrier bitch with a very sweet temper, who hated to see boys fighting. If two boys were having a set-to she would jump up between them trying to make them stop, and wouldn't leave them be until they had.

According to James's father, David, there was an adjutant of a Gunner Regiment whose Borders had been trained to sing to the Regimental march and used to perform on mess night.

Nigel

When Ros Foale was in the Royal Marsden Hospital she was told she had a serious form of cancer and became deeply depressed. Nothing seemed worth bothering about until David Brown, the Senior Chaplain, decided to see what Nigel, his Border Terrier, could do.

Let into the hospital, Nigel seemed to know exactly where to go. Nudging his way into her room he jumped onto her bed, wagging his tail and kissing. 'His zest for life is infectious. It gave me the will to want to see my own dog again.'

Ros's dog, Tim, was a PAT dog, so she knew how much dogs could do to help people recover. Her story is typical of the many patients David and Nigel encountered at the Royal Marsden, and it appeared in *Take a Break* and *Dogs Today*.

David is an American who came to England for a short stay. Now, 20 years later, he is one of the few people who hold dual American/British nationality. He is senior chaplain at the Royal Marsden's two sites, his attitude is refreshingly helpful, and Nigel (who sadly died very recently) was often been part of the care given to patients. Hospital staff would turn a blind eye to the crumpled bedclothes and the odd dog hair on the sheets, but Nigel knew he was not allowed on certain wards because of different patients' needs and treatments. However, he was familiar with every inch of the Marie Curie Rehabilitation section and the wards he visited regularly, and was a familiar sight bouncing up and down the Brompton Road. David said:

> Patients suffer from depression, loneliness and isolation. A romp around with the dog can do more to cheer them up than sophisticated drugs. Nigel is extremely intelligent and senses that his job is to shower love and attention on a patient. But if required, he can also sit quietly.

Women responded better to Nigel than men because usually they don't mind showing their emotions. They would often begin to cry, and this was Nigel's cue to give them a big lick and cuddle up to them. He wanted to show how much he cared.

However, he knew the ward fridge was out of bounds. As a puppy he learned how to open the fridge door at home and help himself to whatever he fancied. Master didn't like this, and said some strong words about it. One day David phoned me to say he must be going senile; he had started to think he had done something, only to find he hadn't. He'd think he had bought food and then find he hadn't...

A few days later he phoned to say it was all Nigel's fault.

Realising that if he left the fridge door open Master would know he had been at the food, Nigel learnt to close the door after he had done his raid. David would buy

sausages or bacon but, when the time came to cook them, there they weren't! However, on going into the kitchen one day, David noticed a tell-tale piece of sausage wrapping paper lying under the table, and this made him realise that Nigel had been opening the fridge door, helping himself to whatever he wanted, and then shutting the door so that Master wouldn't know what had happened.

A thankful David phoned to say he wasn't going crazy after all, and what could he do to lock the fridge door? A trip to Mothercare for a child-proof lock, and David's food was safe from Nigel.

Nigel was an adored pet. He went running with David each morning, and every evening it was down to the Princess of Wales pub for his special treat: a packet of plain crisps. Lying on the floor, he would hold the bag between his paws, gently bite off the top and then dig down into the bag, bringing out each crisp one by one.

Madelene Aspinwall with some Farmway Borders.

Terrier's incredible 300ft plunge

The headline in *The Daily Mail* of 8 March 1995 said it all; Fail, a Border/Lakeland cross, had been chasing a rabbit on the cliff top at Humersey, near Skinningrove, Cleveland, when she slipped and went over the edge. Her owner, 13-year-old Darren McConnell, ran frantically down, fearing the worst, but there was Fail at the bottom without a scratch.

Darren said she had been called Fail 'after we lost two terriers down holes. We knew she wouldn't fail and now she's proved it. I don't think any other dog would have survived.'

Apparently *The Daily Mail* couldn't interview Fail; according to their reporter 'she was out chasing rabbits as usual'.

Farmway

Arriving at the home of the famous Farmway Borders, you see a notice: 'Don't worry about the Dogs - Beware the owners!'

When Madelene Aspinwall wanted to show Border Terriers, she wrote to a Mrs Mulcaster who had advertised a puppy for sale in Scotland. Mrs Mulcaster wrote back that the puppies weren't good enough but she had a four-year-old bitch with two CCs she could let her have. So Madelene's mother lent her £30 to buy this Border. What the breeder had not bothered to tell her was that Polly fought everything in sight, so she had to build her a kennel outside. Her first show was WELKS, and to her delight Polly got her third CC and was made up to Champion.

Madelene, founder member and now President of the Dog Training Club in Marlow, trained Petra, the first Blue Peter dog, in whose honour the club has a Petra trophy. When the TV show did the *Dog A - Z* her Fine Feathers went up with a litter to represent Borders, and of course took it all in her stride and performed brilliantly.

Now Mrs Aspinwall represents Border Terriers at The Kennel Club and says that judging abroad is a great treat, as the judges are so well looked after.

Farmway Borders, too, have travelled to many countries. In New Zealand Rosemary Williamson has had Farmway Borders for many years. The first one went by sea and was looked after by the Captain's wife for six weeks. One of the top Borders in the Netherlands is Farmway Flamebird, and Farmway Southern Hawk did a great deal for Borders in Finland.

One day four Farmway Borders were lined up to have their photos taken in the grounds of Cliveden, to appear under the caption 'A winning line in Border Terriers' on the front cover of *Country Life*.

Another time, when a photographer managed to take seven of the Farmways sitting on a garden seat, she was asked, 'Was it superglue?'

Paddy Reilly

Anne Roslin-Williams tells the story in her book *The Border Terrier* of Paddy Reilly, a Border puppy that went to America in 1925. He is credited with collecting $30,000 for the Humane Society of New York, helping the police to capture a burglar, giving warnings of fire, and saving three children and a woman from drowning, and is reputed to have saved a total of 49 human and nine animal lives during his 14-year life. On his death the Greenwich Village Humane League was founded in his memory. If any reader lives in New York and is able to find out more it would be fascinating to know.

Brannigan

Ch Brannigan of Brumberhill was Reserve Best in Show at Crufts in 1988. Winner of 31 CCs and 10 RCCs, he is known as Bodie to Stewart McPherson of Brumberhill Farm at Appleton Roebuck in Yorkshire. Friends at the next farm had Borders, so Stewart decided he wanted one too. He bred Brannigan's sire, who fathered a promising puppy which turned out to be Bodie.

Today Bodie, when not fathering more champions, is rather fond of ratting.

Pepper

Dove Cottage, Grasmere, in the Lake District, belonged to William Wordsworth, and today is open to visitors. Inside is a delightful portrait of what must be an early Border Terrier, called Pepper.

According to Jeff Cowton of the Wordsworth Trust, Pepper was a present from Sir Walter Scott to Wordsworth's children on his visit to Dove Cottage in 1805. Scott was a great lover of dogs and often named his dogs after spices.

Coquetdale Vic

This famous Border was owned by Adam Forster, who did so much for the breed. He once said, 'The best pedigree a Border can have is the marks on its face', and Coquetdale Vic had all the flesh torn from her underjaw whilst working, yet won a Challenge Cup three times in succession; the first to win this particular cup outright.

At that time one of the Club's rule was, 'if any part of a terrier's face was missing through legitimate work, that part was to be deemed perfect'.

Morris dancing

Mike Bush is a member of the Midlands Border Terrier Club, and wrote in their year book to say that he had hoped his Border, Briggsy, would help collect money when he and his mates were performing in a Morris dancing team. He set about trying to train Briggsy, but the dog had other ideas. As soon as the music started up he joined in heartily, singing along to his master's accordion playing.

James White, otherwise known as James Herriot, with his Border. Reproduced by kind permission of Michael Joseph Ltd.

Border bites back

Border TV used to have a Border Terrier as its symbol and used this dog extensively on posters and advertisements. At the time when all the other TV companies had announced increases in their media rates, a famous full-page advertisement in the trade papers read by the advertising industry showed a newspaper billboard announcing price increases, and just the hindquarters of a Border, drawn lifting his leg and aiming for the advertisement. The Border was phased out when owners objected to the strap line (advertising jargon for the motto) 'Border Bites Back', saying that Border Terriers didn't bite.

The advertiser in *The Hexham Courant* obviously wasn't thinking of Borders when they placed an advertisement: 'Dog walker available. Sensible 15 year old seeks occupation. Wages negotiable, depending on size of teeth.'

On the 'box'

One TV advertisement featured a Border supplied by Plushcourt. This was the one where the man walks in with a Border under his arm, sees his girl friend on the phone to 'another', and walks out again.

FAMOUS BORDERS AND OWNERS

Some very famous people own Borders, but as they are as discreet as their dogs often one only comes across them by chance - although there were two Borders recently featured in *Hello!* magazine. It used to be said that a lady was only mentioned in the press three times: at her birth, on her marriage and when she died. But, as it is generally male Borders that get mentioned in the press, here are some of their stories. Unlike better-known dog breeds, the Border gentleman gets on with his life, and leaves flirting with the dog *paparazzi* to flashier animals.

James Herriot

This was the pen name of Yorkshire veterinary surgeon James Alfred White (1916-1995). Born in Sunderland, he studied at Glasgow Veterinary College before joining 'Siegfried Farnon's' team at Thirsk (known as Darrowby in his books).

Although known world-wide for his books, he didn't begin writing until he was 50, after nearly 30 years in practice, and at first the books didn't sell very well. It wasn't until his agent sold a selection of his stories in America under the inspired title *All Creatures Great and Small*, which was an immediate success in the States, that a knock-on effect was produced here, he became a super best seller, and the BBC started its popular TV series.

His books were translated into every European language, as well as Japanese, and his writing made his adopted county so famous that people come from Japan, America, Australia and most of Europe to see where he lived. He loved animals and, like so many vets, owned a Border Terrier, which had its counterpart in the TV series. If you want to see where he and his Border roamed, go to Yorkshire, where the Tourist Board have named part of the Shire 'Herriot Country'.

Herriot never wanted TV filming to be done locally as he knew no-one would get any work done, so the locations were changed to the Dales and the higher parts of the North Yorkshire moors. Anne Turner runs the bookshop in Thirsk and says he would often pop in for a chat and to see how his books were doing. Thirsk plays down the Herriot connection (although there is a Darrowby Café in the main square), yet visitors bring in over £40 million to the area each year.

There is another TV connection here: Nicholas Rhea, the police constable who wrote the books that were filmed as *Heartbeat*, also comes from the district, and he and Herriot were introduced when the landlord of their local asked Rhea to give the up-and-coming author advice.

Bill Cosby

When asked about famous Borders (and their owners) in the States, Lisa Connelly from Bahama, North Carolina, came up with Bill Cosby, the comic, actor and entertainer. He owned Ch Krispin Natty Gann, who appeared on stage with him in his Las Vegas show. Not only was Natty a 'showgirl', she also performed well in the ring and was a multiple Terrier Group winner and one of the top winning Border bitches ever to be shown in the USA.

Incidentally, Cosby is obviously a terrier man, as he and his partner, Captain Jean Heath, also have a well-known kennel of Lakeland Terriers with the Black Watch affix.

Marion Dupont Scott

Marion Dupont Scott, from the famous industrialist's family, was a great supporter of Borders, and the annual Montpelier Border Terrier Rally is held every year at her former home, Montpelier (also the former home of US President James Madison). These rallies grew up out of the birthday parties she used to give for her favourite Border Terrier, Wallace. Her kennels were taken over by Damara Bolte, and her bloodlines can still be found in present-day Borders.

'The Lady of the Lake'

Border Terrier William was a great comfort to his owner, Lady Gow, after her husband was killed so tragically by an act of terrorism and, during his eventful career, William caused quite a stir in Battersea Park.

The park has been invaded by Canada Geese. These eat the grass and greenery, and the once-green lawns surrounding the lakes are now acres of bare earth. The geese multiply at a rapid rate, and are taking over the park, becoming such a problem that a notice was posted in the park warning people there would be loud bangs before the park opened, caused by culling the geese. Of course this notice acted like a red rag to a bull for the local conservationists, who besieged the Town Hall, wrote letters and caused the cull to be stopped.

William, along with other dogs, wanted to restore the *status quo*, and must have decided to organise his own cull. Energetically chasing the geese into the lake, he set out to swim in pursuit. Suddenly they turned on him, and William found himself being attacked by angry geese. When she saw William being attacked there was nothing for Lady Gow to do but swim out into the lake to rescue him, and since that episode she has been known as The Lady of the Lake.

Sadly William has gone to the happy hunting ground in the sky, but his sister Jennie, according to Lady Gow, 'is like Queen Victoria and rules the roost with our other dogs'.

If your dog chases Canada Geese and gets you in to trouble, you might like to know there is a lake in the grounds of Buckingham Palace, not very far from Canada Geese haunts in Hyde Park and Battersea. When a guest asked Her Majesty what she did when geese landed, ready to eat the grass, The Queen replied, 'It is simple. I just set the Corgis on them.'

'Posh dog' Fitzroy Farmway Master Martin having a friendly fight with his friend, Ptolomy.

The Hon Joe

Lord King of British Airways bought Joe for his wife, but the dog often accompanied him to his office in London. Joe settled happily into office routine but when he got bored he used to jump onto the desk and sit in the OUT tray, meaning 'It's time to go home'. Lord King often told friends about this, citing it as an example of the breed's intelligence.

In the dog shop George on Chelsea Green there was a lovely bronze of Joe. Carla Heseltine the sculptress was commissioned to sculpt Lord King, who asked her to do one of Joe; his master was delighted with the result, and gave permission for copies to be made.

Elton John

The Thoraldby Kennels sold a Border to Beechy Colclough, who is in the music industry; this dog was seen by Elton John, who wanted one for himself and asked his housekeeper, Jenny Newman, to make enquiries. Thoraldby didn't have anything suitable, and passed her on to Mrs Lee of Tythrop.

Mrs Lee has been breeding for 14 years. Since she started showing in 1989 she has had two champions and, when she provides a puppy, she insists on knowing it is going to a good home. She therefore refused point blank to deal with anyone over the phone, particularly as Jenny wouldn't say for whom the dog was intended.

Her Majesty Queen Beatrix of The Netherlands with Moby and Dushi.   Photo: ANP Foto

Eventually Jenny Newman came to see her in Aylesbury; being the housekeeper she would be looking after the dog when Elton was working abroad. She picked a dog puppy and everything seemed fine until Mrs Lee received a phone call from Jenny: 'We've got a bit of a problem. We need another one.'

Elton John had returned from abroad and liked the puppy so much that he wanted another one to go to Atlanta. Now there is one here at Windsor and another in Atlanta, Georgia.

Elton asked Mrs Lee if she could keep the dogs for a few weeks as he was going to be away.

'I do charge for running them on,' she said.

'How much is that?' he asked

'£5 per week per dog.'

'Oh, I think I can afford that,' he laughed.

Tythrop puppies are always given nicknames and, quite fortuitously, Mrs Lee's daughter had called that litter after rock stars. The first puppy had been called Brian and the next one that went was his litter brother, Bruce (Springsteen). Brian's registered name is now Rocket Man (after Elton John's hit single) and the other is Bishop's Envoy. The brothers were by Jasper Jinks out of Box of Tricks. As Jasper belonged to Dr Laura Hapgood (daughter of the Archbishop of York), and Terry Waite was in the news at the time Bruce was born, he was given the registered name Bishop's Envoy.

Eventually Jenny called with another 'problem'. This time she wanted a dog for her parents, who had retired.

Fabergé

When Queen Alexandra wanted to give a present to her family, Fabergé would often be asked to provide some little trinket. His exquisite pieces found favour with the crowned heads of Europe and, when friends wanted to give King Edward VII a present, he is supposed to have pointed them in the direction of the Fabergé shop in London, saying they would know just what he liked.

Recently, as I browsed around the wonderful Fabergé exhibition at The Queen's Gallery, one of the stewards asked what my current project was. When I said I was writing a book about Border Terriers, he told me to come with him. 'There are our Borders,' he said, pointing to the exquisite Fabergé carvings of Border Terriers and proving you can find something to interest anyone almost everywhere. The Fabergé animals are well known, and Her Majesty often lends a selection for exhibition, so if you want to see them keep your eyes open.

Posh dog

If you walk in Battersea Park, you will probably come across the only dog I know with his own visiting card. Fitzroy Farmway Master Martin has so many admirers that his owners, Geoff Walker and Harley Carpenter, have included his name on their card.

Their Borders are named after London squares; their last one was called Berkeley and Madelene Aspinwall of the Farmway affix asked if I knew them, as Fitzroy was one of her Borders. He is well known in the park, but his favourite friend is Gamble, a beagle. Gamble and Fitzroy have the same ideas about playing; making a bloodthirsty noise doubles the enjoyment, and people who don't understand dogs look askance at their antics. When Geoff and Harley walked their dogs in Green Park they used to meet Bill Heseltine, the Queen's private secretary, who also owns a Border; Berkeley used to send him a Christmas card each year.

When we met in Battersea Park I was telling them about Johanna Farrer's agility course (see Chapter 10) and we wished that enough dog owners could get together in this park to set up a permanent one. If any reader is interested, please lobby the Friends of Battersea Park.

Royal Borders in The Netherlands

Her Majesty Queen Beatrix of The Netherlands has owned Border Terriers for some six years now, and Princess Margriet has owned them for somewhat longer. They both started with dogs without papers (although the pedigrees were known), until Princess Margriet went to Scotland and bought two Borders from Professor Milton of Baillieswells.

Some time before his bitch, Tigga, had pups the Professor received a phone call from someone in Brussels enquiring about the puppies. He told him to phone back after the pups were born, and the call was returned just when his bitch was in labour. 'Phone back later,' the caller was told. Eventually the last pup was born at 6.00 am, and after a hard night the Professor retired for a quick nap, only to be woken at 8.00 am. A rather frosty response, and again the caller was told to phone later.

Eventually that afternoon the caller came back again. It was Sir Jack Stewart Clark, apologising because the time was an hour later in Belgium. His wife is Dutch and knows the Royal family, and he had been asked to find a Border after Miss Pepper was lost so tragically. The Queen had been very upset and Princess Margriet had decided they wanted a Border from Scotland. Sir Jack had been a director of a company where a fellow director knew Professor Milton, and he had therefore come to him in his search. The Professor has been breeding for over 20 years, starting with the foundation bitch, Foxhill Farthing, who lived to be over 17.

Sir Jack now wanted two bitches, one for Her Majesty and one for the Princess. He was told he couldn't have two, as there only two in the litter, and the Professor was keeping one; so it was decided to have a dog and a bitch.

The next day *Who's Who* was checked to make sure it wasn't a friend playing a practical joke but the names and telephone numbers were correct. 'It was terribly secret; I didn't even tell my children.'

Eventually, after many phone calls, the Princess arrived to see the litter and played with the puppies on the lawn whilst an assistant carried out behavioural tests. The Princess chose the bitch Brandy, and took a dog puppy for The Queen; eventually this one was called Moby by Prince Claus, after a German TV detective. Since then Moby has been joined by another Border, called Dushi.

The Queen goes everywhere with her dogs, and they have featured on magazine covers with their royal owner. Shortly after Moby arrived The Queen hosted 45 Ambassadors at a royal reception and in the middle of the official photograph there was Moby, being cuddled by her. But then Borders fit in anywhere!

... and in Jordan

Madelene Aspinwall says she has sold Border Terriers to all sorts of people, from postmen to Royalty. At the Windsor Show an attractive woman came up to talk to her about Borders. Hovering in the background was a man dressed in a dark suit. The woman asked if she had a litter because she wanted to take a puppy back to Jordan. Madelene Aspinwall thought of Jordan as a hot country, but the woman assured her that they had snow (in July) where she was living.

Posh Dog Fitzroy Farmway Master Martin trying his paws at agility.

There was a phone call from the woman, who wanted to come and see the puppies. At the time, the Aspinwalls were having a new roof put on and there was scaffolding all over the house. An enormous black Mercedes drove up with four men in dark suits, who 'cased' everything. Then up drove a white Rolls, with the woman and a little boy. It was the Crown Princess and Prince Hassan. It all provided a wonderful show for the builders on the roof.

Prince Hassan had to choose which puppy he wanted, and when the papers were being written out Mrs Aspinwall asked, 'What address?'

'Royal Palace, Amman,' was the reply.

THE BORDER CHARACTER
Picnics

Once the weather gets hot, London has an influx of visitors from the Gulf States, enjoying picnics in the park on the grass. Dogs in those countries carry rabies, so children and grown-ups move away as soon as a dog approaches. It didn't take mine long to suss this out, and one day they rushed up to a picnic, scattering the family, and fed on the debris. Now, whenever we see picnics, on go their leads, although I make a point of showing any interested children how to approach and pat dogs.

Reading *The Midlands Border Club Year Book* I discovered my Borders weren't the only culprits. Dave and Trak Fryer live on the Fells, and climbing Cat Bells one day they breasted a rise and came in sight of a young family, with their dog, having lunch on the hillside. 'The Borders were quick to appraise the situation and the family dog sprang to the defence... to no avail. No cross-bred Terrier will keep a

Border from his prey.' Their Borders lunged straight amongst the crisp packets and sandwiches and 'managed a decent snack before being rounded up and apologetically carried off'.

Oh! I do sympathise.

The demon drink

Most Borders seem too sensible to drink alcohol, but there are reports of some liking a favourite tipple. When Winston decided to try a whisky, it was the last he ever touched. A friend put her glass down on the floor and was talking away when the puppy came into the room, sniffed around and, deciding that malt whisky was a good thing, slurped it all up and continued on his way.

Next morning he woke up in his basket, prepared to bound out - and suddenly his legs gave way. Rolling blood-shot eyes, he gingerly started to shake his head, decided that was too painful, and sat there contemplating the world. Eventually one paw crept over the edge, his body was gently levered up and he took about five minutes to go downstairs. The hangover lasted until the mid-day meal, and he never touched alcohol again.

Fitzroy basking in the sunshine.

Smells

Apart from wanting to sniff everything and using their noses for hunting, Borders love to rub themselves in some pretty horrible stinks. Peter and Esmé Mitchell of Llandeilo had moved to a new house, where their Border soon found a polecat's lair under a tree. Of course there was a fight, and the polecat disappeared but left its smell behind. Esmé soon realised what people meant when they talked about 'stinking like a polecat': it took two bottles of Fairy Liquid before their Border smelt even halfway decent. Well, to them anyway.

Another of their Borders had caused trouble killing their ducks. Peter put a stop to this by tying a dead duck around the Border's neck for a day, which so annoyed the dog that it left the ducks alone afterwards.

Neighbours - long-eared and otherwise

As I write I can hear the next door neighbour whistling, not for her dog, but for a pet rabbit. One expects Borders to get into trouble, but it is a bit much when neighbours' pet rabbits show Border tendencies.

This rabbit lives up on the large balcony of the first floor flat next door. I used to hear its owner whistle to it, which intrigued my dogs, but I thought it must be another dog until one day I arrived home to find a note from Annie Irving , my upstairs neighbour: 'Don't go into the garden.' She told me whilst I was out she had seen a rabbit take a flying leap into my garden. In Chelsea one is used to strange happenings so, locking the dogs inside, I slipped into the garden and, sure enough, there was a huge rabbit which, having leapt four metres down from its balcony, was now happily eating my plants.

Eventually the owner came home (before my garden was totally demolished!) and told me that their rabbit thought it had wings, and they were constantly having to pick it up from wherever it had jumped. They had fenced in the other side of the balcony where it used to leap, but didn't think to do my side because it was so far down. Now all sides are fenced, but the rabbit is still trying to escape. Needless to say my dogs think I am a traitor for having allowed the rabbit into 'their' territory, and keep on looking up to the balcony with a 'just try it again' expression.

Annie is a script writer, and so works from home. If I have to go out for the day the dogs are left in the garden, but one day Annie said she was worried they were making such a noise when I was out. So the next day I set a trap, put on my coat, shoved them into the garden and left, locking the front door. Creeping upstairs, I could hear what she meant - there were two Borders singing at the tops of their voices, trying to attract attention. Now Annie leans out of the window when the singing starts and shouts 'Stop it!'; with a tail wag they obey and all is peace and quiet. Annie says it is quite a party trick; friends arrive, hear the noise and then see Annie go to the window and, miraculously, the dogs obey her!

Before any burglars think these dogs are often left when I go out, this happens about once or twice a month. Usually they go with me, and have friends among the hotel doormen all over London whom they visit whilst I am researching.

Climbers

Although most Borders hate cats, they share some things. Their feet should look similar to cats' feet, and some Borders climb trees. As Claire Ricks of Newmarket says, 'Pebbles should have been a cat the way she can climb trees.'

Tree-climbing Borders seem to manage to dig their claws into the tree bark, and the momentum carries them up the trunk to chase their quarry.

According to Borders, cats are put on this earth to give them fun and exercise. For some reason London cats have a kamikaze streak and will often stand their ground when chased. After one of mine had killed a stray that thought it didn't need to climb up the nearest tree I was visited by the Dog Warden. Sitting him down, I fed him specially-bought chocolate biscuits whilst the culprit rolled over for him to rub his tummy.

Eventually, pleasantries over, the Warden asked to see 'the vicious dog'. When I told him he was at his feet, that luckily took the wind out of his sails, but I was read a stern lecture whilst I swear the wretched dog laughed.

One of my Borders had to be watched carefully whenever there were cats around, as he had developed a tree climbing technique. As long as there was a low branch, he dug in his claws and scraped his way up.

They do not always have it all their own way, however. Coming round the corner one day, I noticed one of the stable cats crouching behind a brick wall. This was unusual behaviour, as generally he and his brother stayed together the better to defend themselves from the dogs. In the distance I could hear loud, excited barking, and suddenly a cat shot past the wall, hotly pursued by a dog. As the dog went past the wall, a paw slashed out cutting him across the face. Two cats shot up the nearest tree and turned to gloat over their enemy, who was standing, perplexed, with a 'What hit me?' expression on his face.

Walking in Parks, Border owners are often accosted by conservationists: 'Do you know your dogs have just chased squirrels up that tree?' Most squirrels are too fly to be caught, but one stopped more than a metre up a tree to look back and, probably, thumb its nose at Widget. But Widget's momentum had carried him well up the tree, and that squirrel met its end with a very surprised look on its face.

Wellington and Winston used to clamber along gutters. We lived in Stewart's Grove in London and the back of the Mews house joined a glass garage roof. Because it would be much too dangerous for humans to walk along it, no-one thought to block it off when the Borders moved in.

One day the Borders couldn't be found; search parties went out looking for them, until a neighbour down the street came in with them. They had been visiting her, and thoroughly enjoyed their outing.

Bored with life one afternoon, they had investigated possibilities, which included clambering along the garage guttering. The houses' bathrooms looked onto the garage roof and, as she was taking a bath that afternoon, Anya had looked up and seen two curious faces peering in at her.

After that, if the Borders couldn't be found, one just waited for them to return across the roof-tops.

Sheep

One day we thought our Borders were taking too much interest as we went through sheep-dotted countryside. However careful you are, there is always a risk that your dog will escape as you travel around, and it would be terrible if he went off and worried sheep. It was obviously time to send him and his companion off to the hunt to spend time with the ram. The Ferney Hunt obliged, but said that Winston had lasted longer than any other dog except for a mad Lakeland belonging to the terrier man.

Foxes

People have said they don't like red Borders, as they look too much like foxes and might be mistaken by hounds. Mr Horn in *Our Dogs* disagreed and mentioned that a Mr Welton had sent details of interesting dogs that had passed through his hands. In all his long memory of 'bolts' in the Tynedale and North Tyne countries he never saw a hound mistake the terrier for the fox. He once remembers a fox coming out with a Border attached to its rear, and the dog was never touched. He also says that he never knew a terrier to be hurt when kennelled with hounds. The hounds were a different matter...

As we were walking through the Cemetery yesterday a vixen was nonchalantly ambling through the bushes until she saw us and took off. 'But she will be back to eat the food thrown out by sympathetic householders,' said my friend. It won't be long before we have to pay for expensive dustbins with heavy lids to deter the foxes from turning them over and spreading the contents across the road.

The Hill is a London freebie magazine which recently had an amusing poem apparently written by 'Charlie Fox', complaining Chicken Vindaloo and cheap Spanish Rioja were giving him hangovers. It wasn't all that divorced from reality!

Never give up!

Dog World of 7 November 1924 carried an article by J W H Beynon entitled 'A Good Old Sporting Terrier' in which he recounts 'a true story':

> During a hunt on the River Ayr with the Dumfriesshire Otter Hounds, an otter was located in his holt under a tree root; a young dog out of the famous old bitch Venus - which, by the way, was the first Border Terrier to win the 'Mary Rew' cup - was entered, and a tremendous fight followed, resulting in the expulsion of the otter followed by the terrier, minus an eye; a few days later he was hunting rats as merrily as when he had both optics.

I have often noticed that, if my Borders are in an accident, they don't waste time bothering about the consequences, or what might go wrong; they just get on with their lives. Beynon echoes this, when he makes a plea for

> ... all who have the love and welfare at heart of the gamest terrier in Britain to keep to the pure, unadulterated type; the hard-bitten, sturdy, devil-may-

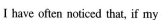

care Border Terrier which knows not fear and is true till death... Don't let the glamour of shows and first prize cards obsess the mind to the exclusion of his unique character and working qualities.

'Unique character' and 'working qualities' are the birthright of the Border Terrier and must be preserved at all costs.

Intelligence

Every Border owner knows their dogs are intelligent and Wizard, belonging to Dave and Trak Fryer, lives up to her name. The Fryers have 10 Borders and love long walks up in the Shetlands, going through the nesting grounds where local skuas can be a hazard to man and beast. Dave used to carry a strong field guide lodged beneath his wool hat to prevent bloodshed when dive-bombed by these birds.

However, once the Borders became part of the walk, the Fryers discovered the dogs became the preferred target. The first few times that they were subjected to these rather startling dive bomb attacks the dogs glared at the Fryers as if it was some trick of their making, but they soon learned to cope by weaving and ducking away from their attackers.

One of their older bitches, Wizard, decided that the whole affair was rather fun. She would carefully spot the attacker wheeling and screaming but would trot nonchalantly on. As soon as the bird was committed to the dive she would gather herself up and leap into the air in a counter attack causing the startled birds to shear off, using language that would embarrass even a skua. Wizard used to enjoy this sport hugely.

If you were the person walking on Wasdale Screes one day and came upon someone shouting curses at themselves - here is what really happened:

Ch Quatford Kardinal. (Owned by Mrs Valerie Furness)

Trak Fryer was descending in thick mist one day, accompanied by two of her kennels' 'worst elements' who had wandered just out of her range of visibility. In heavy mist you tend to walk in your own circle of view. Getting rather fed up with constantly calling them back, she released a stream of invective which, whilst telling them to return to heel, also called into question certain elements of their breeding. Whilst she was in midflight, and could just see them at the edge of her field of vision, a group of rather staid walkers suddenly appeared coming up the path. The dogs became invisible, leaving Trak the recipient of some funny looks.

Romeos

My grandfather used to keep a map on his study wall to record his Border dogs' exploits. In the 1930s his dogs wandered freely across the countryside. There were virtually no cars to knock them down, so it must have been paradise for Borders in more than one way.

Friends would phone my grandfather and state accusingly that their bitches had whelped and the litter were Border crosses. Denying all responsibility, Grandfather would put a pin in the map, and says that the Borders would find their way home from over 20 miles' radius before dinner. Typical Borders!

Travellers

However, none of the Borders seem to have travelled as far as one mentioned in the Southern Border Terrier Club's year book. One year a heartbroken family lost their Border. It loved to visit the port nearby, but no-one there had seen it. Six months later a happy, well-fed dog trotted through the door as though he had never left - and in the harbour was a ship returned after six months' sailing around the world. Least said, soonest mended!

Lost and found

Every Border owner knows the heart-stopping moment when your dog doesn't come to the whistle and you realise it has gone walkabout. However many times it happens and you tell yourself it is part of the breed's characteristics (and after all they have always come back before) you are still frantic. For minutes, hours or days nothing seems to matter as you frantically try to find where they have gone. Friends are always helpful and, when Winston, aged six months, went missing, the whole street turned out to look for him. We went everywhere, but couldn't find him, until eventually a neighbour opposite came home and came out again carrying Winston.

Winston hero-worshipped the neighbour's dog, Bennet, and had gone over to bark at his door. Bennet's new party trick was to squeeze the lock with his jaws to open the door and he had obviously invited Winston in. We just wish Winston had told us first before he decided to pay social calls!

Often the only time one sees any mention of Borders in the press is when they are lost, and found again. Back in 1954 *Our Dogs* reported that Major and Mrs Roslin Williams had a worrying time when Smuttle of Mansergh was lost underground on Feck Fell for 11 days before he reappeared.

Smuttle worked regularly with Kendal hounds and was Best of Breed at Kendal, but was exhausted by his efforts to get out. Thanks to the excellent care he received both from the vets and from Mr Arthur Swettenham, the keeper who walked miles through the snow twice a day to watch the mouth of the hole for him and afterwards nursed him through the worst, he recovered.

Remember Rastus the Border Terrier who was trapped down a hole for six days? When he had been dug out his picture was on the front page of *The Daily Telegraph*. This is a familiar story for any Border Terrier owner.

From childhood I've sat for hours waiting by holes, until a filthy, dirty, happy little devil decides to come up. Even Borders living in London get up to mischief; one of mine, Wellington, escaped and was found by some Americans. They took him home, fed him with a German Shepherd-sized tinned meal, and phoned to say they had found him on a rubbish dump digging for scraps. When I collected him it was obvious they thought he'd been starved and they read me a stern lecture on feeding dogs properly.

Wyvern took himself off across Hyde Park after a bitch: after hours of searching I returned home just in case there was a message on the answering machine. There was - an angry call from restaurateur Pru Leith saying would I collect my dog as he was sitting by the restaurant back door and it was obvious I wasn't feeding him. When I went to collect him the wretched dog was delighted to see me. I just told him I was fed up with chasing him halfway across London.

The Times of 16 April 1994 carried an account of Pip and Rick, belonging to Nigel Ward of Conisbrough, South Yorks, who had been trapped for two weeks down a badger sett. Nigel called to the dogs every day and eventually they became so thin that they were able to free themselves.

Another Border was saved by a ham sandwich. According to *The Daily Mail* of 27 February 1988, Rocky fell 12m down a crevasse at the top of Brithdir Mountain whilst out rabbiting with his owner, Gareth Davis from Abergoed, Merthyr Tydfil. Three RSPCA officers dug down through rock but after a week they were still eight metres short.

A mining rescue team took over with heavy cutting equipment but stopped once they came within view in case the noise frightened Rocky further into the mountain. Then Gareth's friend, Martin Townsend, had a brainwave. Fetching a ham sandwich and a rope, he dropped a noose with the sandwich in the middle: 'As Rocky put his head through the noose to get the sandwich I pulled it tight before he even knew what was happening.' *The Mail* reported that, after a bath and a meal, Rocky curled up in front of the fire at home, his rabbiting days over if Gareth had anything to do with it.

On yet another occasion, the headline in the local paper said, 'Two Crufts winners lost for four days.' Professor Milton, of the Baillieswells affix, had lost two of his Borders. No-one could find them, so he called in the help of the local paper. Thanks to their story, reports started coming in, giving details of the Borders' movements during the past four days.

Eventually a sighting from a farmer had the Professor jumping into his car. He couldn't find them; but when he got back to his car there was the dog, who had jumped into the back seat. The bitch appeared a short while later; there had been a delay as the woman who had picked her up hadn't read the paper until the week-end.

One of the reports claimed that two vicious dogs had come into a garden, and eaten a pet rabbit. Worried that the dogs might get a criminal record, the Professor asked advice from the police, whose opinion was that, before criminal charges could be pressed, the rabbit's owner would have to pick out the offending Borders from an identity parade.

Returners

There are many stories of Borders returning home after being left miles away; W Barton recalls:

> ...Venus ...when she got up in years and done for showing or breeding I gave her to my sister for a pet. She stayed three or four days in her new home and then disappeared. She came back to her old home. It would be 10 to 12 miles across the hill and much more round the road.

Escapologists

Ruth Jordan owned Alfie, who managed to get out of anything. One Christmas Day she had just moved to a new cottage, and the fence wasn't properly secured. She put

Fitzroy after his morning dip.

Alfie out into the garden, but later her heart sank when he didn't return. It was pitch dark, she didn't know a soul around, and had to knock on strange doors to ask if there was a stray dog in their garden. It's one way of getting to know the neighbours.

Heidi was another of Ruth's escapologists. The bedroom door was closed, but the window open. Heidi decided what was happening outside was more interesting, so got up onto the ledge and dropped down from there. Waking up and finding no dog in the room, Ruth hurtled downstairs expecting the worst. As she opened the door, Heidi came trotting round the corner, none the worse for her high jump.

Cats, or consequences arising from them, naturally featured in Ruth's life. Betsy had been let off the lead, and her collar had been taken off, as they were walking in rough fields with many rabbit holes. At the bottom of the field was an old, converted workhouse. Suddenly, Betsy saw a wild cat, and chased it down to the workhouse buildings and up the new fire escape. Momentum carried Betsy up and across one divide, but then she was stuck on the roof and unable to get down. Eventually the RSPCA were called, and Ruth was torn off a strip for letting Betsy chase a cat, and because she didn't have a collar.

Another Sam

Prospective owners should read Sam's story, and realise this is what can happen with a Border. They are independent characters who have their own work to do, and that takes precedence over any demands you might make. Dr Jeremy Cherfas was walking with Sam, his seven-month-old puppy, one Christmas Eve. Taking a detour at the end of their normal circuit they were soon exploring territory new to Sam, in densely-planted Forestry Commission woodland. Every 30 seconds Dr Cherfas looked behind to check all was well with Sam.

Turning for the umpteenth time, he found that Sam wasn't there. Calling and searching produced nothing. Eventually running home to tell his wife, he ripped open Sam's Christmas present: a squeaky toy that would be bound to bring Sam running - but nothing happened. By now it was dark, and Dr Cherfas was reflecting that he was unfit to own a dog; thoughts arose about the slogan 'a dog is for life'. Here he was without a dog that wasn't even going to be for Christmas, let alone life.

That was the moment Sam chose to saunter into view, moderately pleased to see him 'and could he please destroy the toy now?'

Sam has pulled the same trick many times since, and the questions that Dr Cherfas wants answered are: Where does he go when he vanishes, wraith-like? What is he doing? And how come he inevitably turns up a few paces from where he vanishes, and yet is completely unfindable in the meantime?

Sam has done this in pinewoods and on a beach with no cover to speak of. He once absented himself during a personal guided tour round a stately home and park, delaying dinner and inconveniencing an entire house-party, though they were too polite to say so. Dr Cherfas says:

> I'm resigned to these vanishing acts now. The only pattern to emerge is that he re-appears near where he disappears. Whether that means he stays in the area, I have no idea. I do know that if I stay put and stay calm, he will return when he is ready to. At least he always has so far. I have no idea what he does on these escapades, or what prompts his vanishings. It isn't anything as simple as foxes, badgers, or even rabbits, for many's the time I've smelled fox strongly on the air and Sam hasn't turned a hair.

Most owners will be able to sympathise with Dr Cherfas and ask, where do they go, and why?

If Sam vanishes near home he will bark for admittance, no mean feat for a Border. I have known mine sit on a doorstep for two or three hours if I have shut the patio doors thinking they are inside. They will sit patiently waiting to be let in and never think to bark to hurry me up.

Exercise

Borders thrive on exercise, and Joyce Rowe runs marathons with her Borders; first it was Lottie, and when she became too old Daisy went into training and runs the 26 miles happily, 'still wagging her tail at the end'. In her Marathons Daisy raises money for Guide Dogs for the Blind, PRO Dogs and Hearing Dogs for the Deaf. Without exercise, Borders can sulk, and when they are bored watch out!

Nanny

One little Border bitch arrived to help a chocolate Labrador get over losing her litter. Flora was so desolate after losing all of her pups that owner Jayne English decided she needed something small for companionship. Jayne had always liked Borders, so she went off and found Meggie, who arrived and was soon helping Flora forget her troubles, bossing her around in typical Border fashion.

When Flora eventually produced a fine litter, Meggie was there to watch over them, even though she knew she wasn't allowed into the basket with the pups. She would sit for hours with her chin resting on the basket edge.

Eventually the pups became big enough for Flora to leave them alone for a short time. As soon as Flora was out of the basket Meggie was in, baby-sitting to her heart's content, licking the puppies, cleaning them up and being a marvellous surrogate mother. When Flora returned out Meggie would hop with a 'my job's done' shrug of her shoulders.

When the pups grew up Jayne kept Hebe, and now Meggie bosses both Labradors. If she wants to play she produces her favourite rag, shakes it under Hebe's nose, and runs up and down with it until Hebe plays. They have a wonderful time together.

Another owner has a delightful Border bitch who takes the law into her own paws as soon as she considers her pups are old enough to leave. She will wait until everyone's back is turned, then take them out and leave them in the middle of cornfields, returning with an 'I've done my bit!' attitude. Then everyone has to go out and look to see where she has put the pups.

Book hunting?

There are some old books on Borders, but sadly many of them are out of print, and trying to buy these from the specialist sellers at Crufts is enough to give one apoplexy. *A Handbook on Borders* was being sold for £100 at the last exhibition.

It is sometimes possible to find old copies of Miss Garnett Orme's *Border Tales* if you root around in book shops in the Charing Cross Road, or else go to Hay-on-Wye and try the bookshops there.

We were staying in Ross-on-Wye in a lovely hotel, intending to go book hunting after breakfast. Peter and the dogs were off walking and I was enjoying a leisurely breakfast when I began to realise fellow breakfasters were commenting on something outside the picture windows.

At first I thought I was seeing things. There was a large bush in the middle of the lawn, shaking violently. Of course it was Winston and Wellington, who had discovered an earth and were digging up the roots in their eagerness to get to work. Fellow guests crowded the windows, egging them on. I crept out to see what I could do to help and, when they were dug out, carried one upstairs to try to clean it off.

Two hours and three showers later the dogs were clean enough to be let out but the bathroom looked as though it was modelling for trench warfare photos. Luckily the housekeeper was a farmer's daughter and a large tip reconciled the chambermaid to the chaos.

We never got to Hay-on-Wye to hunt for books.

Research

Sometimes my dogs actually help me with work. For some time I had wanted to meet the Romanian Ambassador, Sergiu Celac. I was off to Romania on an assignment, and had wanted to have a word with him, as did everyone else in front of me in the queue. At a New Year's Day Reception I thought I would get a quick word - but no such luck. Eventually I realised I wasn't going to get to meet him, so left. I was just putting the dogs into their basket when I noticed the Romanian Embassy car alongside and the Ambassador admiring the dogs.

It turns out he is a confirmed dog lover and was interested to meet and talk with my two. We had a long conversation, and now if I want an interview I phone up and ask if the dogs can come and visit. We have a five-minute conversation, and then he and the dogs get down to serious visiting.

'Op it

We all want to be public spirited citizens and pick up dog mess, but sometimes this is difficult with Borders, who are very gentlemanly (or ladylike) and go off under bushes to do their business discreetly.

Perry was watching his Border, who took off into Hyde Park's bushes. Following, plastic bag in hand, he fell over a courting couple.

'Wotcher doing 'ere?' asked a belligerent voice.

Not wishing to tell such an aggressive person what he was actually doing, he replied, 'Bird watching.'

' 'Op it. We're not them sort of birds.'

Ch Quatford Kardinal and Quatford Karrina. (Owned by Mrs Valerie Furness)

Borders abroad

Kennel Club records show that in 1930 Netherby's Ricky went to Don E Hewat of North Adams, Mass and was recognised the same year by The American Kennel Club.

The first Border Terrier registrations in the Netherlands appeared in the Dutch Stud Book in 1933, imported by a well known judge, Mr H Jüngeling and the Secretary of the Dutch Kennel Club, Mr J L J J Harms. In due course one became a Dutch Champion, but from these Borders no offspring were every registered.

Mrs Bergman introduced Border Terriers to the Swedish public in about 1938. At one show in Stockholm it is recorded that all the entries had come from her kennel, except for the winner of the puppy class - which she had bred!

Even during the war Borders managed to cross the Atlantic, and in 1942 Dr Lilico sold the bitch Bladnach Blossom to Mr Emerson Latting of the Balquhain kennel in New York. In April 1944 P R Smith writes to *Dog World*, 'I have just received a letter from an American client saying how pleased he is with a bitch that I sent out to him... and intends to purchase a good young dog after the end of the war.'

An informal moment: a Foxforest Border on a fishing trip with his owner in Finland.

James Garrow reported from the USA that Border Terriers were making progress, saying 'I am glad to see that Heather Sandy did so well at the recent New York show. Some time ago Mr William McBain, New York... commissioned Mr Robert Chapman to find him a good Border dog to show and to kill foxes on his farm in South Carolina.'

Austria

There is no special Border Terrier Club in this country; instead the breed, along with 15 other terrier breeds, belongs to the Austrian Club for Terriers. Ten Borders were registered in the Austrian stud book between 1960 and 1972, and then nothing until Rocheby Skipalong in 1986, soon to be followed by others. Currently over 200 are registered.

Good dogs living in this country only have to go a short distance to pick up

titles in other countries. Margarete and Josef Huber's Ch Elfe-Highness vom Lärchenbruch recently slipped over the borders to add German and Hungarian titles to her Austrian, Argentine, European and World wins.

With its lovely scenery, cool streams and snow, Austria is a favourite country for Border holidays, particularly for those from the Netherlands, and in 1996 Vienna co-hosts The World Dog Show with Budapest, so no doubt there will be many Borders on holiday, and then the hills will be alive with the sound of Borders!

Australia

The Border Terrier Club Year Book contains some amusing reminiscences from Frank Jones, including: 'I once judged a massive breed entry of two! for the Queensland Terrier Club, Brisbane.'

Things have improved greatly since then, and now many overseas judges officiate at excellent shows. The NSW Club show in particular is known for being strong in Borders. However, the show always seems to attract torrential rain - a matter for congratulation in Australia!

Belgium

The appropriate breed club in Belgium is The Club Royal de Terriers (see **Useful Addresses**), President: Mme Monique van Brempt, Secretary: M André Demullier.

The Belgian Kennel Club is called the Royal Society of St Hubert, and was founded in 1882. It gained royal patronage under Leopold II in 1887 and, ever since then, His Majesty The King has been Honorary President.

The Society is one of the founding members of the Fédération Cynologique Internationale (FCI) the secretariat of which has been established in Thuin, Belgium, and in 1995 the Society organised the World Dog Show in Brussels, where the British Judge, Bryn Cadogan, judged the Borders:

The quality of dogs was very good, especially from Finland. I thoroughly enjoyed the show, and it is pleasant when you have some nice dogs to go over. Seventy-two dogs were entered and very few no shows - probably because the entrance fee is £52 for the first dog, and £45 for each subsequent one! No prizes as such, just qualifications such as Belgian and International Certificates. [If the dog wins they can put World Champion to their name.] A Finnish dog was Best of Breed: Foxforest Light The Sky. Sadly the Best Bitch, Lyrical of Lexington at Plushcourt from the UK, had to go back into quarantine.

Canada

It was extremely interesting to learn that Mr Patterson of Buck Skin Ranch imported a pair of Borders in 1929 who lived outdoors 1220m above sea level, where the tem-

peratures could drop to - 40°C. I try telling that to mine when they hog the fire, but no notice is taken.

Snow forms a large part of a Border's life. Whereas in Britain we have to dig deep to put fencing far enough down to stop Borders digging underneath the fence, in Canada the amount of snow means that owners often have to build a snow moat around their property to stop Borders just walking over the snow-covered fences.

The Border Terrier Club was started in 1973, and Borders are scattered all over this vast country, which is making it difficult for the Club. Many Border owners slip across the US/Canada border to show their dogs in the States. In Canada they hold Den Trials where Borders can earn a Certificate of Gameness.

Denmark

Sissel Bagge Blindbæk, the Breed Representative in the Danish Terrier Club, reports: 'Border terriers have been part of my life for 11 years now, and I don't regret it one

Ch Foxforest Light The Sky: World Winner 1995.Bred and owned by Seppo Saari in Finland.

minute'. She takes her Border to work at Copenhagen University every day. He, like his predecessor (now an OAP living with her parents), accompanied her there during her studies. There is a wild park next to the campus, where they spend the lunch break. In winter they track the foxes on the snow and have so far 'discovered two earths, that are well hidden in the summer'. Sounds like paradise for Borders.

Corresponding with Club Secretaries from around the world makes one realise how well they speak English. Ms Bagge Blindbæk's report was written in impeccable and idiomatic English, and said:

> The Border Terrier is a relatively new breed in Denmark, the first being reg istered in 1958. In the early 1960s, Countess Abigael luel-Brockdorff

imported the bitch Portholme Monawin and started breeding under the kennel affix Ambrosius. Since then, the breed has increased in numbers as well as in popularity, and registration numbers are about 150 a year.

We do not have large kennels in Denmark - most breeders keep their Borders in the house and raise the puppies in the kitchen or the sitting room. Pups go primarily to pet homes, but quite a few are sold as workers. Very few are sold as actual show dogs. The average championship show in Denmark has an entry of about 20 Borders, so that figures.

Nevertheless, a few home-bred Danish Borders have managed quite well on the Continental show scene in recent years, winning well in Germany, Holland, Austria, the Czech Republic and Poland, as have Danish-owned imports from Britain, Sweden and Finland.

We do our humble bit to keep the Border Terrier a working breed. In order to compete for a CC in a Championship show, a passed working test is required of a Border. The test takes place in an artificial earth, where the terrier must attack a live fox which is protected by wooden bars. Most workers also have their first experience of the fox in this way.

Apart from showing and working, Borders in Denmark do a bit of agility. They are quite efficient at that, but apparently not many people are interested in both Borders and agility. A few have managed well in the obedience rings, but again - people tend to select other breeds for this sport, even though Borders are famous in agility and obedience in our neighbouring country Sweden.

The annual Border Show is usually judged by an English breeder and is held late in summer (August-September). Miss Bagge Blindbæk was excited that Ragsdale Redcoat, belonging to Frank Wildman and herself, won Best of Breed at his first official Danish Show. (So was I, as Redcoat and one of mine share the same father with the lovely name, Why Not.)

Very sportingly she mentions that the Foxforest dogs came over and conquered: 'We certainly don't bear the Finns a grudge - anybody showing dogs of that quality are welcome to beat the rest of us any day.'

Anyone who wants to purchase a Border Terrier in Denmark should contact The Danish Kennel Club or The Danish Terrier Club. Both clubs keep lists of puppies for sale. The sire and dam of the litter must have been to a show in order for the puppies to get on the list.

There is no Border Terrier Club in Denmark, but the Danish Terrier Club has about 150 members with Border Terriers. Amongst them, they elect a Breed Representative who is responsible for information about the breed and arrangements for owners of Border Terriers for such things as shows, stripping demonstrations. The name and telephone number of this representative can be obtained from The Danish Terrier Club (see **Useful Addresses**). You can also apply for membership.

Finland

Bryn Cadogan had said that there are some very good Borders coming out of Finland, and they have swept the board at shows across Europe.

Seppo Saari was delighted to talk about his and his wife's superb Foxforest Borders. Last year in 1994 their Bitch Clear to Fly (Ch Double Scotch ex Ch Digbrack Candy Tuft) won Best of Breed in the World Winner Show in Bern under

Terry Thorn. This year her litter brother Light the Sky was BOB and World Winner 1995 in Brussels under Bryn Cadogan. Their mother, Int Ch Digbrack Candy Tuft, was their foundation bitch and had a litter of six, three of which are winners.

Agility is also popular in Finland, and Borders are often winners, including the Foxforest Borders. One of the nice things about Border owners is that they seem to be like their dogs, possessing a good sense of humour. One of the Foxforest Borders is called Crashboombang - I wonder what made them choose that name? Watching Borders at play perhaps?

There are several important shows in Finland, and there is often a Border Terrier Day in July and the official Speciality Show in September.

Germany

Looking at the attractive dog on the table, the vet said to the owner:

'If you ever breed from this mixture I would like to have a puppy.'

'It's not a mixture, it is a Border Terrier!' was the indignant reply, and that was how Mrs Tillner of the Malepartus affix was introduced to Borders.

Their first Border was 'the best we ever had. It was a birthday present to my husband. Eventually it was so good we wanted to breed from it, and went to shows to pick out a mate.' Whilst there they said they thought they might like to show him, but were told that he didn't have a chance. In true fairy tale fashion he went on to win, and become Champion of Germany. At the 1994 Border Meeting their Malepartus Ravishing Rebel and Malepartus Portly Pearl did very well.

The year 1994 was the Centenary Year of the Klub für Terrier (see **Useful Addresses**), founded in Munich in May 1894. The founder members were Airedale owners, supported from England by a German living in Bradford called Max Gutbrod. Today the club covers 26 Terrier breeds and has over 13,000 members.

Their Centenary Show had an entry of over 800 terriers, from Black Russian to Yorkshire. There was an entry of 42 Borders and Jeremy of the Half House bred by

Ch Foxforest Clear To Fly: BOB WWorld Winner Show 1994.

Minka Crucq from the Netherlands won the dog ticket and was BOB, and Borderhouse Beauty Queen, bred by Tinna Grubbe from Denmark, won BOS out of Junior Bitch.

To celebrate the centenary, Miss Wiebke Steen produced a *Centenary Book* of 450 pages, with old photos and extracts from books and journals, which tells of the ups and downs of German terrier breeding. It also documents the close links between Germany and Great Britain in the dog world. A copy of the book can be obtained from the Klub für Terrier.

Christofer F Habig, writing in *The Border Terrier Year Book*, comments:

> Looking through the pedigrees of the entries at various shows in the last years, it is amazing to realise that we have obviously not yet produced our own quality males in Germany - or we do not seem to trust our own breeding.

The vast majority of the stud dogs have been imports (mostly British). During the Centenary Show, of the 42 Borders entered only 20 had actually been bred in Germany and only one exhibit had two German-bred parents. Only 25 per cent of the sires of all litters registered in Germany between 1956 and 1992 were German-bred dogs.

This must change soon, especially as registrations in 1994 are 60 per cent up from 1993 (a total of 233 in 1994) and 10 German Champions earned their titles in 1994 of which seven were bred in Germany.

In Germany dogs can have a hunting licence, usually for foxes or perhaps wild boar, although Mrs Tillner doesn't let their dogs go after boar in case they get wounded. The dogs are so intelligent that they may have 20 foxes during the winter without too many problems.

Netherlands

There are some devoted Border owners in the Netherlands, starting with Queen Beatrix; tourists can even buy a postcard with a picture showing one of the Queen's Borders.

Mrs Jabroer-ter Lüün writes:

> The first three Border Terrier registrations appeared in the Dutch Stud Book in 1933. They were Sandyman of Kandahar bred by Wattie Irving and bought by a well known judge, Mr Jüngeling. The other two were bought by the Secretary of the Dutch Kennel Club, Mr Harms; one was a bitch aptly named Lady Pioneer, by Dandy Warrior ex Rosa May bred by J Renton, and the other was a dog Southboro Stanzo bred by Mr J J Holgate.

In 1933 Stanzo became a Dutch Champion, but from these three Borders no offspring were ever registered.

It wasn't until 1951 that the next Border Terrier imports arrived in the Netherlands. Mrs and Mrs C Langhout, from the well known Urtica Cocker Spaniel and Bull Terrier kennels, became very enthusiastic about the breed during a visit to Crufts and decided to take it up as their third breed. First they imported Reiver Lad (Ch Tweedside Red Silvo ex Ch Rona Rye, breeder J Renton), but it was the combination Raisgill Rego (Ravensdowne Joker ex Raisgill Ribbon) and Glenluffin Red Queen (Raisgill Recovery ex Glenluffin Pippin) that put the breed on the map in the Netherlands with the litters they had between them.

Two Foxforest Borders in Finland: beautiful dogs in a magnificent landscape.

Kelso on holiday.
Photo: E Jabroer-ter Lüün

Eastcoast of the Windy Spot.

From one of these litters another Cocker Spaniel breeder, Mrs A H Wetzel de Raad of the Tassel's affix, bought the bitch Urtica's Letty and with her and the imported GB/Dutch Ch Golden Imperialist (Fire Master ex Dusty Queen, 1952) she started her own Border Terrier kennels. In later years she also imported GB/Dutch Ch Braw Boy (Ch Billy Boy ex Lassiebelle, 1953) and Dutch Ch Garw Thistle (Sw Ch Llanishen Ivanhoe ex Dundagoo Esmie) but her most influential import proved to be Dutch Ch Winstonhall Dunkie (Ch Winstonhall Coundon Tim ex Winstonhall Dilly, 1962), a dog bred by Miss M M Long that she bought as a pup. He was not only successful in the show ring but also a very prolific stud dog who really put his stamp on the Dutch Border Terrier population.

With one of his daughters, Dutch Ch Biddy (1965, ex Biddy Clipper, a daughter of Ch Deerstone Destiny) Mr and Mrs Bons started their very successful Roughdune's kennels. They also imported Dutch Ch Deerstone Destina (Ch Deerstone Dugmore ex Ch Deerstone Delia, 1967) bred by Mr R Hall and the blue-and-tan dog Dutch Ch Wharfholm Wickersworld (1970), bred by Mrs B S T Holmes by Wharfholm Wonder Lad ex Brookend Arwen.

Others followed in the footsteps of these three pioneers and started breeding Border Terriers. Some of them gave up after some years, others are still active as breeders today.

On 24 October 1971 the Dutch Border Terrier Club (NBTC) (see **Useful Addresses**) was founded, initially with 40 members. From these beginnings the club has grown to a membership of about 800 today, a result of the growing popularity of the breed. Club members breed about 150 puppies a year and there are only a few breeders who are not members of the NBTC. The club has a service called Pup-Info (see **Useful Addresses**), providing would-be owners with information about current and imminent litters.

The club also organises several events throughout the year, such as 'trimming days' where people can learn how to take care of their Border's coat, and 'family days' where all kinds of Border people meet just to have a lovely get-together with their Borders and exchange experiences. The dogs can try their paws at agility, mini-coursing and ring training, and obedience demonstrations are given by members with their 'obedient' Border Terriers.

Then there is the annual Young Dogs' Day, preferably judged by people from the breed's country of origin. These days provide an excellent chance for breeders and owners to watch the development in the breed and to see how their pups compare with the others in the same age-class. The Borders shown on this day range from four months to about two years. The event is usually held at the beginning of September. For the last few years there has been an entry of about 100 Borders!

Every year a (Championship) Breed Show is organised. The dogs are again preferably assessed by judges from Great Britain and the entry is growing steadily, to about 100 during the last few years. The Breed Shows mostly take place at the end of October or beginning of November.

As it is forbidden by law to hunt with terriers the owners are looking for something for the dogs to do as a kind of replacement for the 'real' thing. Many Borders live in the big towns so it is also necessary to have a reasonably obedient dog, otherwise it might be impossible ever to let them off the lead, because of all the traffic and other restrictions when living in these kind of surroundings.

Therefore, nowadays many owners follow obedience courses and some Borders have proved to be very good at it. According to Mrs Jabroer-ter Lüün:

Our obedience is not like the obedience we can see at Crufts for instance, but the dogs do their 'heelwork' walking much more independently beside you. Otherwise the exercises are more or less the same when you reach the highest level of obedience in our country (scent, retrieve, distant control, etc) Although my own bitch has reached this level I must stress that it doesn't suit every Border Terrier and it might even ruin its character if too much pressure is put on it during training.

Another thing Borders are very good at is the Endurance Test. These tests are organised by the Dutch Kennel Club; the dogs that come through get an official certificate and the title can be added to the data on their pedigrees. The test means covering a distance of 20 kilometres beside an 'iron horse' (a bicycle) to be run at a certain speed within a certain time, and there are obedience exercises at the end of it just to prove they are still fit enough.

Then if that isn't enough to exhaust you (not your Border!), both of you can take part in a Triathlon. This consists of:

- 120m swimming with the dog on a lead.
- 12km cycling with the dog trotting beside the bicycle.
- 1200m running.

This may be fine for the dogs, but Joyce Jackly says 'the owners just made it to the finish'.

Then last year 20 Borders were entered for the UV-test (Endurance test) covering a distance of 20km beside a bicycle at a certain speed, not too slow or too fast. They came through with flying colours. On seeing all the Borders trotting past a little boy remarked, 'Look, a group of Turbo Terriers.'

Of course there are Borders taking part in agility and flyball, further means of getting rid of their surplus of energy and keeping them happy.

Mrs Jabroer-ter Lüün says:

I am the proud owner of two Border Terriers, or better... they own me! My Tassel's Red Quintus Kelso and Red Lady Katie have interesting pedigrees, with famous name such as Dandyhow Shady Knight, Farmway Snow Kestrel and Oxcroft Poacher amongst them. As my two sit at my feet it is fun to think I am writing about their distant cousins across the North Sea.

As they are now getting on in age (the dog is 14+ and the bitch nearly 12 at the time of writing) I can honestly say: once a Border, always a Border! For as the years pass by you and the dogs get to know each other better every day and they get dearer to me every day.

She has had a successful showing career, although she had to give up showing Kelso after he had an accident in the Austrian mountains.

Katie has been very successful, obtaining Dutch, Belgian and Luxembourg titles and she is also an International Champion. At her first Winners' Show in Amsterdam in 1984 she came home with Junior Winner, Winner and BOB. She has proved to be a very versatile little dog, as she also reached the highest obedience level in Holland and is very good at agility too.

The dogs always go on holiday with Mrs Jabroer-ter Lüün to the Austrian Alps, and during these seven weeks in summer and two weeks in winter 'they get a chance of being dogs again, and I certainly feel they also need a real holiday after living in a busy town for nearly a year.' They wander in the mountains, drinking from the clear streams or lying in them when they are hot, or rolling themselves in the snow when they reach 2500m. 'Although they're rather old now I've never seen them really tired!' The lucky dogs get a two-hour walk every day on the coast near The Hague.

I wondered how the affix 'of the Windy Spot' came about until Marianne van der Horst-Siraal told me she chose this to stand for the sea and the Navy. She lives near the sea and her husband is an officer in the Royal Netherlands Navy. She gives all her litters names which refer to the sea and the Navy; Beachcomber and Pilot Officer have both done very well, and Eastcoast takes part in

Am Ch Calirose Prize Patrol ('Eddie') at 12 months old. Owner: Lisa Connelly of North Carolina, USA.

Head study of 'Eddie'.

flyball and agility. Again it is interesting to look up their pedigrees and see famous Borders such as Brannigan of Brumberhill, Oxcroft Tally and of course Mansergh Pearl Diver.

The Netherlands countryside is often dangerous for Borders as the soil is sandy; they dig, and then the tunnel caves in.

Maastricht, a charming city in the south of the country, has a dog show (see **Useful Addresses**), and recently hosted the European Championships.

New Zealand

Madelene Aspinwall says there is a real family feeling amongst Border owners in New Zealand. There is a mention in a year book of Jock, an old stager who was 'always to be seen out of the ring sitting on Mary's foot'. What is it about Borders that makes them love to do this?

In New Zealand they have Veteran Stakes for dogs 7-12 and 12+. Rosemary Williamson of Patterdale Borders, owner of Inca Dove and Ring Dove, says: 'What a thrill for me personally, to show a Border again.'

South Africa

As I watched a now-famous wildlife film about meerkats it seemed that these wild animals had many Border traits and were as affectionate and courageous as Borders. Sure enough, in *The Southern Border Terrier Club Year Book* Anna Maydon reports that one of their Borders has gone to a game farm where he has become attached to the resident meerkat, which he carries around everywhere.

Sweden

The Border Terrier Club of Sweden was founded in 1962, and these dogs seem to settle into the country extremely well. Mrs Bergman imported Borders in the 1930s, whom she had obtained from John Renton. Her Happy Thought became an International Nordic Champion, and Saucy Queen became a Champion when she was 11.

During the War Baron Leijonhufvud had imported several dogs from Tweedside and Raisgill, and the breed, struggling at first, eventually became extremely popular.

Today there are always guests from Sweden at the major shows in the UK, and often a Swedish judge; the first was probably Carl Stafberg, who judged at Leicester in 1974. When the Swedish Club celebrated their 30 years at the Jubilee Show they invited Madelene Aspinwall and Betty Rumsam to be judges; Madelene was very proud to show me the beautiful piece of Swedish glassware she was given, which has many happy memories for her.

Here, Borders do well in tracking and agility and have taken top prizes. An annual show is held at Stockholm in December.

By the way, those breeders who have commented on the mosquitoes of Sweden might like to know that I was given some 'Clarins' beauty products with anti-mosquito formulas to try out. I usually end up like a pin-cushion, but this stuff worked beautifully on me, and I didn't scratch once. As it is non-scented men can use it too. Most Clarins after-sun care products contain this formula.

USA

The breed has been recognised in the States since 1929, and is now becoming sufficiently popular to cause concern for breed lovers. As a result the Border Terrier Club of America (founded in 1949) (see **Useful Addresses**) has revised its publication *The Border*, which is a model of its type, given to all prospective owners. The handbook starts out:

> This booklet [is] to help you decide if a Border Terrier is really the dog for you... we know that terrier manners and Border traits are not for everyone... Because of our concern... we believe it is important that you are well informed about the breed before choosing a Border for yourself and your family. A border can live successfully in a variety of situations but, unless you are willing and able to provide for his special needs, you will both be unhappy.

Mrs Laurale Stern, the Secretary of The Border Terrier Club of America, issues the booklet, giving details of the breed, with some lovely photographs on the cover of typical Borders doing typical Border things. (One shows a boy in the bath with two Borders - I wonder which was the dirtiest!) The photographs are not just fun ones of puppies; there are some of older dogs looking very happy.

They also issue a *Breeder's Directory* listing BTCA members who have informed the club that they are active in at least one of the categories listed: Show, Field, Obedience and Tracking. So if you are interested in one of these aspects you can contact a breeder who shares your interest.

To increase breed knowledge The American Kennel Club is trying to increase the educational work of its member clubs. Each club is required to have an education co-ordinator working with judges, a Public Relations officer to inform the public about the breed and also how they can be good canine citizens, and a legal person to inform clubs of laws that might affect the sport of pure bred dogs.

In many areas there are terrier trials with racing, conformation, going to ground, lure coursing, flyball and agility. The American Kennel Club has an Earth Dog Test offers three levels of certification for breeds which are bred to work underground.

The fastest growing dog sport here is agility and many Borders are competing successfully and earning titles. Another sport enjoyed by dogs and owners is tracking, as Borders have good noses, and some go on to receive the American Kennel Club Tracking Dog title. Flyball as a team sport is also extremely popular.

In the US, many shows begin with a hospitality breakfast, covered by the cost of entrance, and owners also enjoy a buffet dinner included in the entry fee. At a recent show the judge, Edd Bivin, caused consternation by asking handlers to let the dogs stand, leads relaxed, close to each other, so he could see the dogs standing naturally. Here stewards walk round the ring at the end of each class with the winners' numbers on a blackboard.

Lisa Connelly of the Carolinas and Virginia Border Terrier Club, Bahama, North Carolina writes that 'virtually all of our Borders here in the States are descended from British imports', and encloses the pedigrees of her own Borders: they have wonderful kennel names: Krispin Wee Bonnie Margaret, otherwise known as 'Maggie' (Ch Woodlawns Mickey Finn ex Ch Krispin Katie Gibbs); Ch Bever Lea Molly Malone, or 'Molly' (Ch Krispin Scotland Yard ex Ch Bever Lea Polly Pureheart) and Ch Calirose Prize Patrol, or 'Eddie' (Ch Otley's Touch of the Desert ex Ch Calirose Collectible)(pictures on Page 186). Their pedigrees contain many famous Border names, such as Cheltor Michael, Ch Duttonlea Suntan of Dandyhow, Farmway Redwing and Snow Kestrel and Thoraldby Magic Chip.

The *Breeder's Directory* informs readers whether breeders offer a stud service, and each year there is a Register of Merit. In 1994 Gold Standard was achieved by Ch Feorrawa Ketka Cagney, Ch Krispin Tailor Made, Ch Steephollow Little Nell and Ch Jocasta Just Hollywood.

The Border Terrier Club of America also produces a magazine, *The Borderline*. A list of books on the breed is also available from the club, as are the addresses of the following regional clubs:

- Border Terrier Club of The Redwoods
- Border Terrier Fanciers of The West
- Cascade Border Terrier Club
- Great Lakes Border Terrier Club
- Lone Star Border Terrier Fanciers
- Northeast Border Terrier Club
- Southeast Border Terrier Club
- The Carolinas and Virginia Border Terrier Club

A video entitled *Stripping a Border Terrier* is available at a cost of $18 from Phil Klosinski, 2647 Jutland Street, Toledo, Ohio 43613

Borders in other countries

Borders are to be found in other countries such as the Czech Republic, Eire, Estonia, France, Japan, Norway, Spain, Sweden, and Switzerland. Wherever they go they seem to settle in without fuss and become part of the family. So if you live abroad and want to become a member of a club, a phone call to a Club Secretary in the UK will usually tell you the telephone number of someone representing the breed in your country, if not a Club Secretary. You could also look up the names of the Overseas Members in the Year Books: The Midland and The Southern Border Terrier Club Year Books each have a special section to make this easier.

Kelgram Kayhasi, 'Luca' for short.

Border clubs

If you are thinking of owning a Border the first vital step is to belong to a breed club, probably the one nearest to you. The club will introduce you to other members, who are always prepared to help new friends and will be able to advise you where to find the best Border for you, be it from a fellow club member, from a breeder belonging to another club, or even from Border Terrier Welfare (see Chapter 3).

Belonging to a club can add to the interest of owning a Border and annual membership is usually between £5 and £10 per year.

Club Secretaries

Any club is only as good as its Secretary, and without doubt Border Club Secretaries are some of the best around. They have been of enormous help to me while I have been writing this book, going out of their way to find information for me to pass on to you.

Most club secretary posts are Honorary (Hon), and this is certainly the case in Border Terrier Clubs. The dictionary says this is 'an office held as an honour only, without pay'. Perhaps it should go on to say: 'honorary' means digging into your own pocket for items such as envelopes, odd stamps and telephone calls. 'Honorary' is certainly assumed to give any member the right to have a go at the Secretary when something is not right, even if it has nothing to do with the Secretary. The 'Honorary' Secretary is also there to volunteer for all the jobs that other club members 'just don't have time to help with at the moment'. Hon Secretaries will take minutes of meetings, and then receive complaints when members say they never said what everyone else can remember distinctly that they did.

Luckily Border Terrier Clubs have marvellous Hon Secretaries who cheerfully give up their time to handle all the work of the clubs and give members an excellent service. It is well worth belonging to one or more clubs, as you will find their help and information invaluable and it adds to the fun and interest of owning a Border.

The following gives details of the Border Clubs in Britain, and an approximation of the membership fee. Do remember that dates of club events change from year to year. The addresses of the Hon Secretaries are given in **Useful Addresses**.

The Border Terrier Club

For some time before the First World War owners had been talking about forming a club. The War put a stop to this, but once it was over the idea re-surfaced and The Border Terrier Club was founded in 1920. This is the oldest Border Terrier club still in existence, and it played an important part in establishing the Breed Standard.

At a meeting of The Kennel Club on 1 September 1920, approval was given for the formation of a club, and gradually the Club 'progressed quietly from small beginnings to the happy and successful participants of the Terrier Group... widely acclaimed throughout the world today', as it says in its year book.

There is an article in the 1995 edition of the club's year book, detailing the foundation of the Northumberland Border Terriers Club. Brian Staveley (Hon

Secretary, Border Terrier Club since 1978) does not know when this club folded, or if it was absorbed into the main club. It was issuing Working Certificates at least up to 1932. Perhaps readers know what happened?

Some owners were against the formation of a club, thinking that once one was formed this would let in the 'show' folk and lead to the breed being spoilt. However, The Border Terrier Club has always insisted that Borders keep to their roots. At the beginning there was some dispute as to size (of Borders, not the club!). The Border Terrier Club had adopted a top weight of 7.7kg (17lb), whilst the Northumberland Border Terriers Club set the maximum weight at 6.4kg (14lb). Eventually sense prevailed and the standard was changed to 5.9-7.1kg (13-15^1/2lb) for dogs and 5.1-6.4kg (11^1/2 -14lb) for bitches. Since then the members have steadfastly defended the Breed Standard, to ensure that the Border remains a working dog, not a show animal.

There was an interesting article in the May 1994 issue of *The Kennel Gazette*, written by the expert W R Irving, giving more background information and some amusing details about Club Committee meetings - or the lack of! However, things quietened down, The Border Terrier Club went from strength to strength, and today it has over 800 members, an excellent year book, and the annual subscription (1995) is £5.

In 1980 the World Conference of Kennel Clubs tried to promote an international unity of breed standards: that all standards should comply with an order of clauses favoured by the American Kennel Club. Border enthusiasts had to add to the Breed standard clauses on 'General Appearance', 'Temperament' and 'Gait' (Movement). However, the Club committee and members kept an eye on the changes to make sure that the original idea behind the Breed Standard remained true to the idea that the Border is a working terrier.

There is an excellent Breeders' Code of Ethics in the year book, which includes the note: 'Members will agree without reservation that any Veterinary Surgeon operating on any of their dogs which alters the natural conformation of the animal may report such operation to the Kennel Club.'

There are many Club functions where members meet up, and in 1994 the Club held a Workshop which was so successful that members are asking for more. So contact the Secretary if you want to come to the next one.

To celebrate the 75th Anniversary, Mrs Eva Rowall and Mrs Eva Heslop (Vice-Chairman) have taken on the mammoth task of making and embroidering a table cloth. It is in royal blue satin-backed cotton with gold braid and gold tassels, and in the centre is embroidered 'The Border Terrier Club' in a semi-circle, with a red Border head with dark brown ears embroiderd either side in long-and-short stitch. On taking on such a task, Mrs Heslop said, 'I think we're mad!'

Mrs Heslop has the Corburn affix. Fifty years ago she 'went to buy a Dalmation and they were too expensive, so came home with a little Border Terrier'. She started at the bottom, knowing nothing about Borders, but eventually was exhibiting at shows and her Corburn Corn Dolly was Best Bitch at Crufts

President Mrs R A Sullivan owns the famous Dandyhow affix. Her Cleopatra was the top Challenge Certificate (CC) winner in 1994.

Hon Secretary Brian Staveley owns the Dykeside affix. He has been Secretary for over 18 years, and came into Borders when he married into a Border-owning family.

Annual Events:	February	Open Show
	March	Championship Show
	October	Open Show

The East Anglia Border Terrier Club

The President is Lionel Hamilton-Renwick, about whom I have written elsewhere for his family's Newminster Borders.

| Hon Secretary: | Mrs H Mitchell |

| Annual events: | April | Open Show |
| | October | Open Show |

The Midlands Border Terrier Club

Although only founded in 1984 this club already has over 300 members, with a strong overseas representation. It has a very good year book, and is usually present at Crufts as this show is held in its home patch.

I am indebted to Mrs Jena Tuck, the Hon Secretary, who gave me permission to copy the club's excellent Code of Conduct (see Chapter 3) and I advise you to read this before getting your first Border.

Annual events:	February	Open Show
	August	Championship Show
	October	Open Show

The Northern Border Terrier Club

| Hon Secretary: | Mrs O Tripcony |

Annual events:	April	Open Show
	July	Open Show
	November	Championship Show

The Scottish Border Terrier Club

| Hon Secretary: | Mr W Shorthose |

Annual events:	January	Limit Show
	June	Open Show
	November	Championship Show

They also have social events, including an annual rally with 'Going to Ground' in an artificial earth and terrier racing. This is usually held in the summer.

The Southern Border Terrier Club

With about 1000 members this is the largest club. Members come from the UK, Australia, Bermuda, Canada, Czech Republic, Denmark, Eire, Finland, France, Germany, Netherlands, New Zealand, Norway, Spain, Sweden, Switzerland, USA - is there anywhere else Borders are to be found? There is an excellent year book (£5, free to members) edited by Betty Rumsam, who breeds Wilderscot Borders.

This is 'my' club; I have belonged for over a decade, first with my husband and now on my own.

The Hon Secretary is Mrs F E Wagstaff and the current Patron is Mrs K Twist, who has done so much to gather together information about Borders and

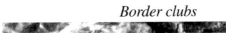

their breeding. She first exhibited Borders at Crufts when it was held in Islington and says they used the red Borders for otter hunting and the blues for fox.

Annual Events: March   AGM, followed by Limited Show
                 June   Championship Show
                 September   Open Show
                 November   Border Terrier Day, Devon
                 December   Teach-in and Christmas lunch (great fun!)

The Yorkshire, Lancashire and Cheshire Border Terrier Club
Secretary: Mrs C Knight

Annual events: January   Open Show
                 April   Open Show
                 September   Championship Show

The Fell and Moorland Working Terrier Club
This isn't specifically for Borders, but it is an extremely useful club to belong to once you own a Border as it has an excellent support scheme to help rescue any terrier that becomes trapped underground.

Barry Jones, the President, says the Club was formed in Cumberland in 1966 to help people who had a terrier stuck, perhaps when they were away from home or their friends were all out, and had no-one to help them. Since then it has grown to a nation-wide organisation with area representatives, every one of whom has authority, at their discretion, to hire machinery needed to rescue a terrier.

According to Barry, some machine owners are very generous, lending their equipment at little or no cost. Others charge full whack and these earth movers go through gallons of diesel every hour. Hiring equipment for one rescue in 1993 cost £1143. In some of the rockier areas it may be necessary to bring in equipment to blast out the dog. In one rescue it cost £900 to dynamite a terrier free bit by bit. It is heart-warming to talk to the Area Representatives, and hear that men have often risked their lives to rescue a dog. The Area Representative decides what is best for the dog in each case, knowing the terrain and whom to ask for help in an emergency.

In the past this has meant digging up trees (with permission), then putting down a shaft 13m deep and 90m long, and lowering men in the bucket of an earth-mover to dig out a terrier who was stuck fast. If greensand shifts any rescuer can be suffocated, as it is treacherous and unstable. However, on one rescue four men roped together went into a greensand excavation to dig out a terrier by the light of tractors. The fortunate terrier was eventually rescued in the middle of the night.

Area Representatives cover the country from Cornwall to Kent; Essex to Wales; the Pennines and Scotland. Barry, who is based in Kingswinford in the Midlands, has often helped in rescues, and has himself been trapped in a fall: 'Luckily a friend knew what to do and recovered me from a spoil heap.'

The club can also help by taking legal advice if your Border goes to ground in a badger sett, which, by law, you are not allowed to disturb. However, it does not condone the working of terriers in any illegal or unofficial manner.

Each area organises at least one show a year and funds from shows go into the central fund. This helps to keep down subscription (surely the bargain of all times at £3 per year). Each year at the AGM members discuss raising this, but the Treasurer says they have enough in the kitty - and he's a Scot!

The Hearing Dogs for the Deaf Christmas Card 1995, sent by 'Nick' (see Chapter 8). Nick is the Border Terrier pictured on the left of the card. He doesn't look guilty - yet...

Dear Verité

Happy Christmas! I'm on a diet! Vet says so. I sort of couldn't resist a whole box of Maltesers which someone had left for me (?) on the coffee table (I left the empty box, lid open, on the floor just to show my appreciation) and a whole

Front Cover: Photograph of Hearing Dogs "Nick" (left) and "Brendie" (right)

packet of liquorice whirls. It's all go go go! Since then I've pinched, or rather KILLED a haggis! That was DELICIOUS! All boss had on

With Best Wishes

for Christmas

and the New Year

Burns Night was neeps and tatties! Bet you darn't put this in your book!

Lots of licks from Nick (by name and nature!)

General Secretary is Ray Cutler, and he can tell you your nearest contact. If you are a member, and your dog is lost down a hole, you can phone your Area Representative immediately. He will decide what course of action to take (for instance, if it is better to wait and see if the dog will come out on its own, or if the diggers should go in straight away).

The Kennel Club

The primary object of the Kennel Club is to promote, in every way, the general improvement of dogs. There is a very helpful Secretariat who can give out names and addresses of secretaries of affiliated clubs and details of dog training classes near you.

The club developed out of the dog shows in Newcastle-upon-Tyne, which led to The Crystal Palace Show, first held in 1870. After the second show, Mr S E Shirley MP, of Ettington, called together a committee which resulted in 12 gentlemen meeting at 2 Albert Mansions, Victoria Street, London on 4 April 1873. This meeting marked the foundation of The Kennel Club.

The Committee formed a code of rules relating to dog shows. Societies which adopted this code of rules for their shows would be recognised and the winners at these shows would be eligible for the Stud Book which is published annually. The Kennel Gazette was first published in 1880 and has continued as a monthly publication since then.

By 1900 nearly 30 Championship Shows were held and the smaller informal shows were becoming popular. These shows are 'recognised', 'licensed' or 'sanctioned', provided that the executive of the show signs an undertaking to hold and conduct the show under and in accordance with Kennel Club Rules and Regulations.

In 1880, facing opposition at first, the club introduced registration; however, the advantages were soon seen when the different Gips, Jips, Rovers, Jets, and Bobs had to be identified. Last year over a quarter of a million named dogs were registered and over 3,000,000 dogs were recorded on their data base.

The Kennel Club Junior Organisation

This was formed to encourage young people between the ages of eight and eighteen to take an interest in the care and training of dogs and to enjoy all activities connected with dogs. It also promotes courtesy, sportsmanship, loyalty and self-discipline, and develops responsibility in canine activities. Members can take part in KCJO competitions and events, join organised visits to shows, dog training centres, local kennels and sanctuaries and other dog activities. You don't need to own a dog to join. For more information, contact The Kennel Club.

Belonging to a club

Even if you are not the sort who normally joins a club, the Border Terrier Clubs have something to interest everyone:

- Help in finding the right Border puppy or dog.
- Help and advice from others who have been down the puppy ownership path and can give you hints and tips. (For instance, Mrs Wilford of the Clystlands affix showed me the correct way to tear up paper for a puppy's bed - there is one!)
- A chance to meet other owners.
- Very good year books. Even if you belong to one club it is worth while buying the other clubs' year books, as they usually have fun stories and articles on subjects of interest.
- Insurance - and with a Border you may well need this!

But whatever you do, whether you already own a Border Terrier or have only just decided that this is the right dog for you, it has been fun thinking about you when writing about the best dogs in the world:

BORDER TERRIERS

Ch. Rubicon Reserve Owner: Mrs. Ruth Jordan

Bibliography

MORRIS, Desmond. **Dogwatching.**

ROSLIN-WILLIAMS, Anne. **The Border Terrier.**

HOBDAY, Ruth. **Agility is fun (2 vols).** Our Dogs Publishing Co Ltd, 5 Oxford Road, Station Approach, Manchester   M60 1SX
This publication takes you from the very beginning to competition level.

LEWIS, Peter. **The agility dog international.** Canine Publications, 21 Burridge Road, Burridge, Southampton   SO3 7BY
A useful book, giving training advice, good instructions for building obstacles to the correct specifications and general information on agility as a sport.

LEWIS, Peter and GILBERT, John. **Teaching agility.** Canine Publications.
Very useful for the advanced handler.

Useful addresses

KENNEL CLUBS:

The Kennel Club
1 Clarges Street
London W1Y 8AB   Tel: 0171-493 6651

The Scottish Kennel Club
3 Brunswick Place
Edinburgh   EH7 5HP   Tel: 0131-447 4784

BREED CLUBS

Great Britain

The Border Terrier Club
Hon Secretary: Mr Brian Staveley
'Parkside'
3 Dykes Terrace
Stanwix
Carlisle CA3 9AS   Tel: 01228-31263

The East Anglia Border Terrier Club
Hon Secretary: Mrs H Mitchell
5a Chalk Road
Walpole St Peter
Wisbech
Cambs   PE14 7PD   Tel: 01945-780466

The Midlands Border Terrier Club
Hon Secretary: Mrs Jena Tuck
2 Palmerston Road
Melton Mowbray
Leicester LE13 OSS   Tel: 01664-61752

The Northern Border Terrier Club
Hon Secretary: Mrs O Tripcony
25 The Crescent
Monkton
Jarrow-on-Tyne   NE32 5NG   Tel: 01914-891 053

The Scottish Border Terrier Club
Hon Secretary: Mr W Shorthose
2 Mid Hakett Cottages
Kalkett by Dunlop
Ayrs   KA3 4EW   Tel: 01505-850313

The Southern Border Terrier Club
Hon Secretary: Mrs F E Wagstaff
18 Pyke Road
Tewkesbury
Glos   GL20 8DX   Tel: 01684-294355

The Yorkshire, Lancashire and Cheshire Border Terrier Club
Hon Secretary: Mrs C Knight
51 Locksley Drive
Thurcroft
Rotherham
Yorks   Tel: 01709-544174

The Fell and Moorland Working Terrier Club
General Secretary: Ray Cutler   Tel: 01598 741 313)

Belgium

Club Royal de Terriers
Secretary: M André Demullier
Chaussée de Clorbus 107
7700 Mouscron   Tel: 00 32 56 33 36 39

Denmark

The Danish Terrier Club
v/ Kirsten Dunweber
Fuglesangsvej 21
26880 Solrod Strand   Tel: 56 14 87 87

Germany

Klub für Terrier
Schöne Aussicht 9
D-65451 Kelsterbach/Main

Netherlands

NBTC
Secretary: Mr G L M van Rijn
Zutphensestraatweg 55
NL-6953 Gj Dieren   Tel: 00 31 8330 13718

NBTC
Pup-Info: Mrs E Bons de Wever
Nr 3
NL-9453 VD Eldersloo   Tel: 00 31 5924 1227

International Dog Exhibition Maastricht,
Postbus 31,
6336 ZG Hulsberg   Tel: 00 31 4405 2263

USA

Border Terrier Club of America
Secretary: Laurale Stern
832, Lincoln Blvd.
Manitowoc, WI 54220   Tel: 414-683-3966

The Borderline
PO Box 545,
Silverhill, AL 36576   Tel: 205-928-2272

ASSOCIATIONS AND CHARITIES

The Agility Club
Hon Secretary: Kate Barratt
'Rufus Rest'
Bigfrith Lane
Cookham Dean
Berks   SL6 9PH   Tel: 01628-484961

Animal Health Trust
PO Box 5
Snailwell Road
Newmarket
Suffolk   CB8 7DW   Tel: 01638-661111

Assistance Dogs and People Together
2 Cyprus Road
London   N3 3RY   Tel: 0181-343 1775

Association of Pet Dog Trainers
Greengarth
Maddox Lane
Bookham
Surrey   KT23 3HT   Tel: 01372-457854

Association of Private Pet Cemeteries and Crematoria
200 Westerleigh Road
Pucklechurch
Bristol BS17 3PY   Tel: 01179-374554

Battersea Dogs' Home
4 Battersea Park Road
London   SW8 4AA   Tel: 0171-622 3628

Registered Charity No. 224392

Blue Cross
Field Centre
Shilton Road
Burford
Oxon   OX18 4PF   Tel: 01993-822651

Border Terrier Welfare
Co-ordinator: Mrs G Baldwin
Rose Cottage
Carshalton Road
Woodmansterne
Banstead
Surrey   Tel: 01737-358849

or

Hon Secretary: Miss S Wishart
8 Blake House
Porchester Mead
Beckenham
Kent   BR3 1TN   Tel: 0181-658 1845

British Field Sports Society
59 Kennington Road
London SE1 7PZ   Tel: 0171-928 4742

British Small Animal Veterinary Association
Kingsley House
Church Lane
Shurdington
Cheltenham   GL51 5TQ   Tel: 01242-862994

British Veterinary Association (BVA)
7 Mansfield Street
London W1M 0AT   Tel: 0171-636 6541

Canine Concern
Smocks
Monument Road
Wellington
Somerset   Tel: 01823-664300

The Cinnamon Trust
Director: Avril Jarvis
Poldarves Farm
Trescowe Common
Penzance   TR20 9RX   Tel: 01736 757900

Dogs for Disabled
Francis Hay House
Banbury Road
Bishops Tachbrook
Leamington Spa
Warcs   CV33 9UQ   Tel: 01926-651179

Feline Advisory Bureau
1 Church Close
Orcheston
Salisbury   SP3 4RP   Tel: 01747 871872

Hearing Dogs for the Deaf
London Road
Lewknor
Oxford   OX9 5RY   Tel: 01844-353898

National Canine Defence League postcard

National Canine Defence League (NCDL)
17 Wakley Street
London   EC1V 7LT

National Pet Week
PO Box 101
Northwood
Middlesex   HA6 3RH   Tel: 01923-836333

People's Dispensary for Sick Animals (PDSA)
Whitechapel Way
Priorslee
Telford
Salop   TF2 9PQ   Tel: 01952-290999

Pet Funeral Services
Brynford
Holywell
Chester   CH8 8AD   Tel: 01352-710500

Petsavers
Kingsley House
Church Lane
Shurdington
Cheltenham   GL51 5TQ   Tel: 01242-862994

PRO Dogs and Pets As Therapy (PAT)
4-6 New Road
Ditton
Kent   ME20 6AD   Tel: 01732-87222
                                     Help Line: 01334-420563

Royal Society for the Prevention of Cruelty to Animals (RSPCA)
Causeway
Horsham
West Sussex   RH12 1HG   Tel: 01403-264181

Scottish Society for the Prevention of Cruelty to Animals (SSPCA)
19 Melville Street
Edinburgh   EH3 7PL   Tel: 0131-225 6418

Society for Companion Animal Studies (SCAS)
1A Hilton Road
Milngavie
Glasgow   G62 7DN

Ulster Society for the Prevention of Cruelty to Animals
11 Drumvie Road
Lisburn
Co Antrim   BT27 6YF   Tel: 01232-813126

Index

u

v

w

xyz

Rubicon Remark   Photo; Robert Smith

Ch Rubicon Reserve   Photo: Robert Smith